WA 1302365 9

CROWN PROSECUTION SERVICE

D1586937

CROWN PROSECUTION SERVICE

Charging Standards

OXFORD
UNIVERSITY PRESS

OXFORD

UNIVERSITY PRESS

Great Clarendon Street, Oxford OX2 6DP

Oxford University Press is a department of the University of Oxford.
It furthers the University's objective of excellence in research, scholarship,
and education by publishing worldwide in

Oxford New York

Auckland Cape Town Dar es Salaam Hong Kong Karachi
Kuala Lumpur Madrid Melbourne Mexico City Nairobi
New Delhi Shanghai Taipei Toronto

With offices in

Argentina Austria Brazil Chile Czech Republic France Greece
Guatemala Hungary Italy Japan Poland Portugal Singapore
South Korea Switzerland Thailand Turkey Ukraine Vietnam

Oxford is a registered trademark of Oxford University Press
in the UK and in certain other countries

Published in the United States
by Oxford University Press Inc., New York

© Oxford University Press, 2005

The moral rights of the author have been asserted

Crown copyright material is reproduced under Class Licence
Number C01P0000148 with the permission of OPSI
and the Queen's Printer for Scotland

Database right Oxford University Press (maker)

First published 2005

British Library Cataloguing in Publication Data

Data available

Library of Congress Cataloging in Publication Data
Crown Prosecution Service charging Standards.
    p. cm.
Includes index.
ISBN 0-19-928513-6 (alk. paper)
1. Prosecution—England. 2. Great Britain. Crown Prosecution Service.
    I. Oxford University Press.
KD8348.C758 2005
345.42'05042—dc22

                                        2005018320

Typeset by Laserwords Private Limited, Chennai, India
Printed in Great Britain
on acid-free paper by
Ashford Colour Press Limited, Gosport, Hampshire

ISBN 0-19-928513-6   978-0-19-928513-6

10 9 8 7 6 5 4 3 2 1

Preface

This text collates the Crown Prosecution Service (CPS) Charging Standards, the Code for Crown Prosecutors, and the guidance documents on domestic violence, racist and religious aggravated crime, and the policy document on rape for the first time in a stand-alone volume.

Please note that the CPS does have specific policy guidance on prosecuting homophobic crime. However it is currently being reviewed and was not available at the time of going to press.

All CPS Charging Standards, the Code for Crown Prosecutors and the guidance and policy documents are available free on request from the CPS or can be downloaded from the CPS website: http://www.cps.gov.uk. All enquiries should be addressed to CPS Communications Branch, 50 Ludgate Hill, London, EC4M 7EX, tel: 020 7796 8442, fax: 020 7796 8030, e-mail: publicity.branch@cps.gsi.gov.uk.

There are references throughout the Charging Standards to *Blackstone's Criminal Practice 2005*, *Archbold: Criminal Pleading, Evidence and Practice* and *Wilkinson's Road Traffic Offences*. These are referenced as per the examples below:

- *Blackstone's Criminal Practice 2005*—**Blackstone's CP 2005**, A8.5 (etc.)
- *Archbold*—**Archbold**, 2-37 (etc.)
- *Wilkinson's Road Traffic Offences*—**Wilkinson**, 5.04 (etc.).

The CPS Charging Standards are published with permission of the CPS—all documents are published as a result of CPS permission—but the CPS does not endorse the book. All enquires related to this publication should be addressed to Oxford University Press: http://www.oup.co.uk.

All materials in this book are Crown copyright and reproduced with the permission of the Controller of Her Majesty's Stationery Office.

All the materials in this book are up to date as of 1 May 2005.

Contents

Table of Cases

Table of Cases

Tables of Legislation

Tables of Legislation

Tables of Legislation

Statutory Instruments

PART 1

The Decision to Prosecute and Charging

1

The Code for
Crown Prosecutors

1 INTRODUCTION

1.1 The decision to prosecute an individual is a serious step. Fair and effective prosecution is essential to the maintenance of law and order. Even in a small case a prosecution has serious implications for all involved—victims, witnesses, and defendants. The Crown Prosecution Service applies the Code for Crown Prosecutors so that it can make fair and consistent decisions about prosecutions.

1.2 The Code helps the Crown Prosecution Service to play its part in making sure that justice is done. It contains information that is important to police officers and others who work in the criminal justice system and to the general public. Police officers should apply the provisions of this Code whenever they are responsible for deciding whether to charge a person with an offence.

1.3 The Code is also designed to make sure that everyone knows the principles that the Crown Prosecution Service applies when carrying out its work. By applying the same principles, everyone involved in the system is helping to treat victims, witnesses, and defendants fairly, while prosecuting cases effectively.

2 GENERAL PRINCIPLES

2.1 Each case is unique and must be considered on its own facts and merits. However, there are general principles that apply to the way in which Crown Prosecutors must approach every case.

2.2 Crown Prosecutors must be fair, independent, and objective. They must not let any personal views about ethnic or national origin, disability, sex, religious beliefs, political views or the sexual orientation of the suspect, victim, or witness influence their decisions. They must not be affected by improper or undue pressure from any source.

2.3 It is the duty of Crown Prosecutors to make sure that the right person is prosecuted for the right offence. In doing so, Crown Prosecutors must always act in the interests of justice and not solely for the purpose of obtaining a conviction.

2.4 Crown Prosecutors should provide guidance and advice to investigators throughout the investigative and prosecuting process. This may include lines of inquiry, evidential requirements, and assistance in any pre-charge procedures. Crown Prosecutors will be proactive in identifying and, where possible, rectifying evidential deficiencies and in bringing to an early conclusion those cases that cannot be strengthened by further investigation.

2.5 It is the duty of Crown Prosecutors to review, advise on, and prosecute cases, ensuring that the law is properly applied, that all relevant evidence is put before the court, and that obligations of disclosure are complied with, in accordance with the principles set out in this Code.

2.6 The Crown Prosecution Service is a public authority for the purposes of the Human Rights Act 1998. Crown Prosecutors must apply the principles of the European Convention on Human Rights in accordance with the Act.

3　THE DECISION TO PROSECUTE

3.1　In most cases, Crown Prosecutors are responsible for deciding whether a person should be charged with a criminal offence, and if so, what that offence should be. Crown Prosecutors make these decisions in accordance with this Code and the Director's Guidance on Charging. In those cases where the police determine the charge, which are usually more minor and routine cases, they apply the same provisions.

3.2　Crown Prosecutors make charging decisions in accordance with the Full Code Test (see section 5 below), other than in those limited circumstances where the Threshold Test applies (see section 6 below).

3.3　The Threshold Test applies where the case is one in which it is proposed to keep the suspect in custody after charge, but the evidence required to apply the Full Code Test is not yet available.

3.4　Where a Crown Prosecutor makes a charging decision in accordance with the Threshold Test, the case must be reviewed in accordance with the Full Code Test as soon as reasonably practicable, taking into account the progress of the investigation.

4　REVIEW

4.1　Each case the Crown Prosecution Service receives from the police is reviewed to make sure that it is right to proceed with a prosecution. Unless the Threshold Test applies, the Crown Prosecution Service will only start or continue with a prosecution when the case has passed both stages of the Full Code Test.

4.2　Review is a continuing process and Crown Prosecutors must take account of any change in circumstances. Wherever possible, they should talk to the police first if they are thinking about changing the charges or stopping the case. Crown Prosecutors should also tell the police if they believe that some additional evidence may strengthen the case. This gives the police the chance to provide more information that may affect the decision.

4.3　The Crown Prosecution Service and the police work closely together, but the final responsibility for the decision whether or not a charge or a case should go ahead rests with the Crown Prosecution Service.

5　THE FULL CODE TEST

5.1　The Full Code Test has two stages. The first stage is consideration of the evidence. If the case does not pass the evidential stage it must not go ahead no matter how important or serious it may be. If the case does pass the evidential stage, Crown Prosecutors must proceed to the second stage and decide if a prosecution is needed in the public interest. The evidential and public interest stages are explained below.

The Evidential Stage

5.2 Crown Prosecutors must be satisfied that there is enough evidence to provide a 'realistic prospect of conviction' against each defendant on each charge. They must consider what the defence case may be, and how that is likely to affect the prosecution case.

5.3 A realistic prospect of conviction is an objective test. It means that a jury or bench of magistrates or judge hearing a case alone, properly directed in accordance with the law, is more likely than not to convict the defendant of the charge alleged. This is a separate test from the one that the criminal courts themselves must apply. A court should only convict if satisfied so that it is sure of a defendant's guilt.

5.4 When deciding whether there is enough evidence to prosecute, Crown Prosecutors must consider whether the evidence can be used and is reliable. There will be many cases in which the evidence does not give any cause for concern. But there will also be cases in which the evidence may not be as strong as it first appears. Crown Prosecutors must ask themselves the following questions:

Can the evidence be used in court?

a Is it likely that the evidence will be excluded by the court? There are certain legal rules which might mean that evidence which seems relevant cannot be given at a trial. For example, is it likely that the evidence will be excluded because of the way in which it was gathered? If so, is there enough other evidence for a realistic prospect of conviction?

Is the evidence reliable?

b Is there evidence which might support or detract from the reliability of a confession? Is the reliability affected by factors such as the defendant's age, intelligence, or level of understanding?

c What explanation has the defendant given? Is a court likely to find it credible in the light of the evidence as a whole? Does it support an innocent explanation?

d If the identity of the defendant is likely to be questioned, is the evidence about this strong enough?

e Is the witness's background likely to weaken the prosecution case? For example, does the witness have any motive that may affect his or her attitude to the case, or a relevant previous conviction?

f Are there concerns over the accuracy or credibility of a witness? Are these concerns based on evidence or simply information with nothing to support it? Is there further evidence which the police should be asked to seek out which may support or detract from the account of the witness?

5.5 Crown Prosecutors should not ignore evidence because they are not sure that it can be used or is reliable. But they should look closely at it when deciding if there is a realistic prospect of conviction.

The Public Interest Stage

5.6 In 1951, Lord Shawcross, who was Attorney General, made the classic statement on public interest, which has been supported by Attorneys General ever since: 'It has never been the rule in this country—I hope it never will be—that suspected criminal offences must automatically be the subject of prosecution.' (House of Commons Debates, volume 483, column 681, 29 January 1951.)

5.7 The public interest must be considered in each case where there is enough evidence to provide a realistic prospect of conviction. Although there may be public interest factors against prosecution in a particular case, often the prosecution should go ahead and those factors should be put to the court for consideration when sentence is being passed. A prosecution will usually take place unless there are public interest factors tending against prosecution which clearly outweigh those tending in favour, or it appears more appropriate in all the circumstances of the case to divert the person from prosecution (see section 8 below).

5.8 Crown Prosecutors must balance factors for and against prosecution carefully and fairly. Public interest factors that can affect the decision to prosecute usually depend on the seriousness of the offence or the circumstances of the suspect. Some factors may increase the need to prosecute but others may suggest that another course of action would be better.

The following lists of some common public interest factors, both for and against prosecution, are not exhaustive. The factors that apply will depend on the facts in each case.

Some common public interest factors in favour of prosecution

5.9 The more serious the offence, the more likely it is that a prosecution will be needed in the public interest. A prosecution is likely to be needed if:
   (a) a conviction is likely to result in a significant sentence;
   (b) a conviction is likely to result in a confiscation or any other order;
   (c) a weapon was used or violence was threatened during the commission of the offence;
   (d) the offence was committed against a person serving the public (for example, a police or prison officer, or a nurse);
   (e) the defendant was in a position of authority or trust;
   (f) the evidence shows that the defendant was a ringleader or an organizer of the offence;
   (g) there is evidence that the offence was premeditated;
   (h) there is evidence that the offence was carried out by a group;
   (i) the victim of the offence was vulnerable, has been put in considerable fear, or suffered personal attack, damage, or disturbance;
   (j) the offence was committed in the presence of, or in close proximity to, a child;

(k) the offence was motivated by any form of discrimination against the victim's ethnic or national origin, disability, sex, religious beliefs, political views or sexual orientation, or the suspect demonstrated hostility towards the victim based on any of those characteristics;

(l) there is a marked difference between the actual or mental ages of the defendant and the victim, or if there is any element of corruption;

(m) the defendant's previous convictions or cautions are relevant to the present offence;

(n) the defendant is alleged to have committed the offence while under an order of the court;

(o) there are grounds for believing that the offence is likely to be continued or repeated, for example, by a history of recurring conduct;

(p) the offence, although not serious in itself, is widespread in the area where it was committed; or

(q) a prosecution would have a significant positive impact on maintaining community confidence.

Some common public interest factors against prosecution

5.10 A prosecution is less likely to be needed if:

(a) the court is likely to impose a nominal penalty;

(b) the defendant has already been made the subject of a sentence and any further conviction would be unlikely to result in the imposition of an additional sentence or order, unless the nature of the particular offence requires a prosecution or the defendant withdraws consent to have an offence taken into consideration during sentencing;

(c) the offence was committed as a result of a genuine mistake or mis-understanding (these factors must be balanced against the seriousness of the offence);

(d) the loss or harm can be described as minor and was the result of a single incident, particularly if it was caused by a misjudgement;

(e) there has been a long delay between the offence taking place and the date of the trial, unless:
- the offence is serious;
- the delay has been caused in part by the defendant;
- the offence has only recently come to light; or
- the complexity of the offence has meant that there has been a long investigation;

(f) a prosecution is likely to have a bad effect on the victim's physical or mental health, always bearing in mind the seriousness of the offence;

(g) the defendant is elderly, or is, or was at the time of the offence, suffering from significant mental or physical ill health, unless the offence is serious or there is real possibility that it may be repeated. The Crown Prosecution Service, where necessary, applies Home Office guidelines about how to deal with mentally disordered offenders. Crown Prosecutors must balance the desirability of diverting a defendant who is suffering from significant mental or physical ill health with the need to safeguard the general public;

(h) the defendant has put right the loss or harm that was caused (but defendants must not avoid prosecution or diversion solely because they pay compensation); or

(i) details may be made public that could harm sources of information, international relations, or national security.

5.11 Deciding on the public interest is not simply a matter of adding up the number of factors on each side. Crown Prosecutors must decide how important each factor is in the circumstances of each case and go on to make an overall assessment.

The relationship between the victim and the public interest

5.12 The Crown Prosecution Service does not act for victims or the families of victims in the same way as solicitors act for their clients. Crown Prosecutors act on behalf of the public and not just in the interests of any particular individual. However, when considering the public interest, Crown Prosecutors should always take into account the consequences for the victim of whether or not to prosecute, and any views expressed by the victim or the victim's family.

5.13 It is important that a victim is told about a decision which makes a significant difference to the case in which they are involved. Crown Prosecutors should ensure that they follow any agreed procedures.

6   THE THRESHOLD TEST

6.1 The Threshold Test requires Crown Prosecutors to decide whether there is at least a reasonable suspicion that the suspect has committed an offence, and if there is, whether it is in the public interest to charge that suspect.

6.2 The Threshold Test is applied to those cases in which it would not be appropriate to release a suspect on bail after charge, but the evidence to apply the Full Code Test is not yet available.

6.3 There are statutory limits that restrict the time a suspect may remain in police custody before a decision has to be made whether to charge or release the suspect. There will be cases where the suspect in custody presents a substantial bail risk if released, but much of the evidence may not be available at the time the charging decision has to be made. Crown Prosecutors will apply the Threshold Test to such cases for a limited period.

6.4 The evidential decision in each case will require consideration of a number of factors including:

- the evidence available at the time;
- the likelihood and nature of further evidence being obtained;
- the reasonableness for believing that evidence will become available;
- the time it will take to gather that evidence and the steps being taken to do so;

- the impact the expected evidence will have on the case;
- the charges that the evidence will support.

6.5 The public interest means the same as under the Full Code Test, but will be based on the information available at the time of charge which will often be limited.

6.6 A decision to charge and withhold bail must be kept under review. The evidence gathered must be regularly assessed to ensure the charge is still appropriate and that continued objection to bail is justified. The Full Code Test must be applied as soon as reasonably practicable.

7 SELECTION OF CHARGES

7.1 Crown Prosecutors should select charges which:
   a reflect the seriousness and extent of the offending;
   b give the court adequate powers to sentence and impose appropriate post-conviction orders; and
   c enable the case to be presented in a clear and simple way.
   This means that Crown Prosecutors may not always choose or continue with the most serious charge where there is a choice.

7.2 Crown Prosecutors should never go ahead with more charges than are necessary just to encourage a defendant to plead guilty to a few. In the same way, they should never go ahead with a more serious charge just to encourage a defendant to plead guilty to a less serious one.

7.3 Crown Prosecutors should not change the charge simply because of the decision made by the court or the defendant about where the case will be heard.

8 DIVERSION FROM PROSECUTION

Adults

8.1 When deciding whether a case should be prosecuted in the courts, Crown Prosecutors should consider the alternatives to prosecution. Where appropriate, the availability of suitable rehabilitative, reparative, or restorative justice processes can be considered.

8.2 Alternatives to prosecution for adult suspects include a simple caution and a conditional caution.

Simple caution

8.3 A simple caution should only be given if the public interest justifies it and in accordance with Home Office guidelines. Where it is felt that such a caution is appropriate, Crown Prosecutors must inform the police so they can caution the suspect. If the caution is not administered, because the suspect refuses to accept it, a Crown Prosecutor may review the case again.

Conditional caution

8.4 A conditional caution may be appropriate where a Crown Prosecutor considers that while the public interest justifies a prosecution, the interests of the suspect, victim, and community may be better served by the suspect complying with suitable conditions aimed at rehabilitation or reparation. These may include restorative processes.

8.5 Crown Prosecutors must be satisfied that there is sufficient evidence for a realistic prospect of conviction and that the public interest would justify a prosecution should the offer of a conditional caution be refused or the offender fail to comply with the agreed conditions of the caution.

8.6 In reaching their decision, Crown Prosecutors should follow the Conditional Cautions Code of Practice and any guidance on conditional cautioning issued or approved by the Director of Public Prosecutions.

8.7 Where Crown Prosecutors consider a conditional caution to be appropriate, they must inform the police, or other authority responsible for administering the conditional caution, as well as providing an indication of the appropriate conditions so that the conditional caution can be administered.

Youths

8.8 Crown Prosecutors must consider the interests of a youth when deciding whether it is in the public interest to prosecute. However, Crown Prosecutors should not avoid prosecuting simply because of the defendant's age. The seriousness of the offence or the youth's past behaviour is very important.

8.9 Cases involving youths are usually only referred to the Crown Prosecution Service for prosecution if the youth has already received a reprimand and final warning, unless the offence is so serious that neither of these were appropriate or the youth does not admit committing the offence. Reprimands and final warnings are intended to prevent re-offending, and the fact that a further offence has occurred indicates that attempts to divert the youth from the court system have not been effective. So the public interest will usually require a prosecution in such cases, unless there are clear public interest factors against prosecution.

9 MODE OF TRIAL

9.1 The Crown Prosecution Service applies the current guidelines for magistrates who have to decide whether cases should be tried in the Crown Court when the offence gives the option and the defendant does not indicate a guilty plea. Crown Prosecutors should recommend Crown Court trial when they are satisfied that the guidelines require them to do so.

9.2 Speed must never be the only reason for asking for a case to stay in the magistrates' courts. But Crown Prosecutors should consider the effect of any likely delay if they send a case to the Crown Court, and any possible stress on victims and witnesses if the case is delayed.

10 ACCEPTING GUILTY PLEAS

10.1 Defendants may want to plead guilty to some, but not all, of the charges. Alternatively, they may want to plead guilty to a different, possibly less serious, charge because they are admitting only part of the crime. Crown Prosecutors should only accept the defendant's plea if they think the court is able to pass a sentence that matches the seriousness of the offending, particularly where there are aggravating features. Crown Prosecutors must never accept a guilty plea just because it is convenient.

10.2 In considering whether the pleas offered are acceptable, Crown Prosecutors should ensure that the interests of the victim and, where possible, any views expressed by the victim or victim's family, are taken into account when deciding whether it is in the public interest to accept the plea. However, the decision rests with the Crown Prosecutor.

10.3 It must be made clear to the court on what basis any plea is advanced and accepted. In cases where a defendant pleads guilty to the charges but on the basis of facts that are different from the prosecution case, and where this may significantly affect sentence, the court should be invited to hear evidence to determine what happened, and then sentence on that basis.

10.4 Where a defendant has previously indicated that he or she will ask the court to take an offence into consideration when sentencing, but then declines to admit that offence at court, Crown Prosecutors will consider whether a prosecution is required for that offence. Crown Prosecutors should explain to the defence advocate and the court that the prosecution of that offence may be subject to further review.

10.5 Particular care must be taken when considering pleas which would enable the defendant to avoid the imposition of a mandatory minimum sentence. When pleas are offered, Crown Prosecutors must bear in mind the fact that ancillary orders can be made with some offences but not with others.

11 PROSECUTORS' ROLE IN SENTENCING

11.1 Crown Prosecutors should draw the court's attention to:
- any aggravating or mitigating factors disclosed by the prosecution case;
- any victim personal statement;
- where appropriate, evidence of the impact of the offending on a community;
- any statutory provisions or sentencing guidelines which may assist;
- any relevant statutory provisions relating to ancillary orders (such as anti-social behaviour orders).

11.2 The Crown Prosecutor should challenge any assertion made by the defence in mitigation that is inaccurate, misleading, or derogatory. If the defence persist in the assertion, and it appears relevant to the sentence, the court should be invited to hear evidence to determine the facts and sentence accordingly.

12 RE-STARTING A PROSECUTION

12.1 People should be able to rely on decisions taken by the Crown Prosecution Service. Normally, if the Crown Prosecution Service tells a suspect or defendant that there will not be a prosecution, or that the prosecution has been stopped, that is the end of the matter and the case will not start again. But occasionally there are special reasons why the Crown Prosecution Service will re-start the prosecution, particularly if the case is serious.

12.2 These reasons include:

  a rare cases where a new look at the original decision shows that it was clearly wrong and should not be allowed to stand;

  b cases which are stopped so that more evidence which is likely to become available in the fairly near future can be collected and prepared. In these cases, the Crown Prosecutor will tell the defendant that the prosecution may well start again; and

  c cases which are stopped because of a lack of evidence but where more significant evidence is discovered later.

12.3 There may also be exceptional cases in which, following an acquittal of a serious offence, the Crown Prosecutor may, with the written consent of the Director of Public Prosecutions, apply to the Court of Appeal for an order quashing the acquittal and requiring the defendant to be retried, in accordance with Part 10 of the Criminal Justice Act 2003.

2

The Director's Guidance on Charging

[Guidance to Police Officers and Crown Prosecutors Issued by the Director of Public Prosecutions under s. 37A of the Police and Criminal Evidence Act 1984 (Second Edition: January 2005)]

The Director's Guidance on Charging

1   INTRODUCTION

What this Guidance is for, where it applies, and when it comes into effect

1.1   This Guidance[1] is to enable Custody Officers to decide how a person should be dealt with when:

- The Custody Officer determines there is sufficient evidence (in accordance with the Threshold Test) to charge a person with an offence,[2] or
- A person has been arrested for breach of bail who had previously been released on bail for a charging decision.[3]

1.2   This Guidance also specifies what information must be sent to a Crown Prosecutor to enable a charging or other decision to be made.[4]

1.3   This Guidance applies to those cases the Director of Public Prosecutions is required to take over in accordance with s. 3 of the Prosecution of Offences Act 1985.

1.4   This Guidance will come into effect in those Local Criminal Justice Board Areas and on the dates specified in the schedule hereto.

2   KEY PROVISIONS AND PRINCIPLES OF THIS GUIDANCE

Statutory provisions and key principles that underpin this Guidance

- Crown Prosecutors will determine whether a person is to be charged in all indictable only, either way, or summary offences subject to those cases specified in this Guidance which the police may continue to charge.
- Charging decisions by Crown Prosecutors will be made following a review of evidence in cases and will be in accordance with this Guidance.
- Custody Officers must comply with this Guidance in deciding how a person is to be dealt with in accordance with s. 37(7) of the Police and Criminal Evidence Act, as amended by Sch. 2 to the Criminal Justice Act 2003.
- Crown Prosecutors will seek to identify and resolve cases that are clearly not appropriate for prosecution at the earliest opportunity on consideration of whatever material is available.
- Crown Prosecutors will provide guidance and advice to investigators throughout the investigative and prosecuting process. This may include lines of enquiry, evidential requirements, and assistance in any pre-charge procedures. Crown Prosecutors will be pro-active in identifying and, where possible, rectifying evidential deficiencies, and in bringing to an early conclusion those cases that cannot be strengthened by further investigation.

---

[1] Issued by the Director of Public Prosecutions under s. 37A(1)(a) of the Police and Criminal Evidence Act 1984, as inserted by the Criminal Justice Act 2003.

[2] PACE, s. 37(7) as amended.

[3] PACE, s. 37C.

[4] PACE, s. 37A(1)(b).

- Crown Prosecutors will only require 'evidential reports' (see paragraph 7.2(i) below) where it is clear that the case will proceed to the Crown Court or is likely to be a contested summary trial, or where it appears to the Crown Prosecutor that the case is so complex or sensitive that a decision to charge cannot be made without an evidential report.
- Where it is necessary, pre-charge bail arrangements will be utilized to facilitate the gathering of evidence, including, in appropriate cases, all the key evidence on which the prosecution will rely, prior to the charging decision being taken (s. 37(7)(a) and s.47(1A) of the Police and Criminal Evidence Act).
- Crown Prosecutors will notify the officer involved in the investigation of any advice and charging or other decision in writing using the form MG3 (s. 37B(4) of the Police and Criminal Evidence Act).
- Persons may be charged whilst in police detention, or in accordance with s. 29 of the Criminal Justice Act 2003 (charging by post) when it is brought into force. [The summons procedure may be used until that change in the process arrangements.]
- Where a Crown Prosecutor notifies a Custody Officer that there is insufficient evidence to charge, or that though there is sufficient evidence to charge, a person should not be charged or given a caution, the Custody Officer shall give notice in writing to that person that he is not to be prosecuted (s. 37B(5) of the Police and Criminal Evidence Act).
- Where Crown Prosecutors decide that a person should be charged with an offence or given a caution, conditional caution, a reprimand, or final warning in respect of an offence, the person shall be charged or cautioned, or conditionally cautioned, or given a reprimand or final warning accordingly (s. 37B(6) of the Police and Criminal Evidence Act).
- Where Crown Prosecutors decide that a person should be cautioned but it proves not to be possible to give the person such a caution, the person shall instead be charged with the offence (s. 37B(7) of the Police and Criminal Evidence Act).
- In order to facilitate efficient and effective early consultations and make charging decisions, Crown Prosecutors will be deployed, as Duty Prosecutors, for such hours as shall be agreed locally to provide guidance and make charging decisions. This service will be complemented by a centrally managed out-of-hours duty prosecutor arrangement to ensure a continuous 24-hour service.

3 RESPONSIBILITY FOR DETERMINING CHARGES

3.1 Charging by Crown Prosecutors—the Principle

Duty of Crown Prosecutors to determine charge

(i) Crown Prosecutors will be responsible for the decision to charge and the specifying or drafting of the charges in all indictable only, either way, or summary offences where a Custody Officer determines that the Threshold Test is met in any case, except for those offences specified in this Guidance which may be charged or cautioned by the police without reference to a Crown Prosecutor.

3.2 Charging by Crown Prosecutors—Transitional Arrangements

(ii) Establishment of the principle set out in paragraph 3.1 above will be achieved incrementally and will be notified by further editions of this Guidance.

Transitional arrangements for charging some likely guilty plea cases

(iii) Until such notification, the police may determine the charge in any either way or summary offences where it appears to the Custody Officer that a guilty plea is likely and that the case is suitable for sentencing in the magistrates' court, but excluding those specified in Annex A to this Guidance.

(iv) Where the Custody Officer is uncertain whether a case falls under 3.2(iii) above, early consultation with a Duty Prosecutor should be undertaken to clarify whether the charging decision is one that should be made by a Crown Prosecutor.

3.3 Charging by the Police

Details, with exceptions, of cases the police may charge

The police may determine the charge in the following cases:

(i) Any offence under the Road Traffic Acts or any other offence arising from the presence of a motor vehicle, trailer, or pedal cycle on a road or other public place, except where (in respect of which the charge must be determined by a Crown Prosecutor):

- the circumstances have resulted in the death of any person; or
- there is an allegation of dangerous driving; or
- the allegation is one of driving whilst disqualified and there has been no admission in a PACE interview to both the driving and the disqualification; or
- the statutory defence to being in charge of a motor vehicle (unfit through drink or drugs or excess alcohol) may be raised under s. 4(3) or 5(2) of the Road Traffic Act 1988; or
- there is an allegation of the unlawful taking of a motor vehicle or the aggravated unlawful taking of a motor vehicle (unless the case is suitable for disposal as an early guilty plea in the magistrates' court).

(ii) Any offence of absconding under the Bail Act 1976 and any offence contrary to s. 5 of the Public Order Act 1986 and any offence under the Town Police Clauses Act 1847, the Metropolitan Police Act 1839, the Vagrancy Act 1824, the Street Offences Act 1959, s. 91 of the Criminal Justice Act 1967 or s. 12 of the Licensing Act 1872, any offence under any bylaw, and any summary offence punishable on conviction with a term of imprisonment of three months or less, except where (and the charge must therefore be determined by a Crown Prosecutor):

- the Director of Public Prosecutions publishes other arrangements for the charging and prosecution of these offences.

3.4 Review by Crown Prosecutors under s. 10 of the Prosecution of Offences Act 1985

Cases charged by the police to be reviewed by a Crown Prosecutor

Where by virtue of this Guidance the police determine the charge, that determination and the charge will be subject to a review by a Crown Prosecutor acting under s. 10 of the Prosecution of Offences Act 1985 and under s. 37B of the Police and Criminal Evidence Act 1984 (as amended).

3.5 Combinations of Persons and Offences

CPS to charge cases delegated to police in certain circumstances

Where the charges or joint charges to be preferred against one or more persons include a combination of offences, some of which may be determined by the police, and others that must be determined by a Crown Prosecutor, the Custody Officer shall refer all charges to a Crown Prosecutor for determination.

3.6 The Application of the Code for Crown Prosecutors

Application of Code for Crown Prosecutors to Custody Officers

When determining charges, Crown Prosecutors and Custody Officers will apply the principles contained in the latest edition of the Code for Crown Prosecutors.

3.7 Number and Seriousness of Charge(s)

Charge selection, range and number of charges

In determining the totality of charges to proceed, the selection of charges should seek to reflect the seriousness and the extent of the offending. It should also provide the court with adequate sentencing powers, and enable the case to be presented in a clear and simple way. Where appropriate, a schedule of other admitted offences may be listed on an MG18 for the charged person to ask the Court to take into consideration.

3.8 Application of the Full Code Test

General application of Full Code Test

In any case where the charging decision is to be made, and the information required to be considered under paragraph 7.2 (below) of this Guidance is available for review, the standard to be applied in reaching the charging decision will be the Full Test under the Code for Crown Prosecutors: namely (following a review of the evidential material provided), that there is enough evidence to provide a realistic prospect of conviction and that it is in the public interest to proceed.

3.9 Application of the Threshold Test to Charging Decisions

In cases where it is determined that it would not be appropriate for the person to be released on bail after charge and where the information referred to in paragraph 7.2 (below) of this Guidance is not available at the time the charging decision has to be taken, a staged approach will then apply:

The Threshold Test for charging in custody cases where an evidential file is unavailable

(i) Where the evidential material required under paragraph 7.2 (below) is not available, the Crown Prosecutor (or Custody Officer) will assess the case against the Threshold Test set out in paragraph 3.10. This should be noted on the MG3 and a review date for a Full Code Test agreed as part of the action plan.

When to apply a Full Code Test for Crown Prosecutors in custody cases

(ii) Subsequently, upon receipt of further evidence or a Report to Crown Prosecutor for a Charging Decision (MG3) accompanied by the information required in accordance with paragraph 7.2 of this Guidance, the Crown Prosecutor will review the case in accordance with the Full Code Test before deciding whether it is appropriate to continue with the offence(s) charged, or prefer additional or alternative charges.

A decision to charge and withhold bail must be kept under review. The evidence gathered must be regularly assessed to ensure the charge is still appropriate and that continued objection to bail is justified. Crown Prosecutors will only apply the Threshold Test for a limited period. The Full Code Test must be applied as soon as reasonably practicable, taking into account the progress of the investigation.

Where, however, the information specified in paragraph 7.2 is available at the time that the initial Report to Crown Prosecutor is made, the Full Code Test will be applied.

3.10 The Threshold Test

The Threshold Test

Application of the Threshold Test will require an overall assessment of whether in all the circumstances of the case there is at least a reasonable suspicion against the person of having committed an offence (in accordance with Article 5 of the European Convention on Human Rights) and that at that stage it is in the public interest to proceed.

The evidential decision in each case will require consideration of a number of factors including: the evidence available at the time and the likelihood and nature of further evidence being obtained; the reasonableness for believing that evidence will become available; the time that will take and the steps being taken to gather it; the impact of the expected evidence on the case, and the charges the totality of the evidence will support.

The public interest means the same as under the Full Code Test, but will be based on the information available at the time of charge, which will often be limited.

Application of the above Tests to police charged cases

3.11 Where, in accordance with this Guidance, Custody Officers make the charging decision without referral to Crown Prosecutors, they will apply the Full Code Test. Where the case is one in which it is not proposed to release the person on bail after charge and the evidential material required to apply the Full Code Test is not available, the Custody Officer will proceed to apply the Threshold Test in accordance with paragraph 3.10 above.

3.12 **Emergency Cases—Expiry of PACE Time Limits**

Emergency charging by the police of CPS cases

In cases where the charging responsibility lies with a Crown Prosecutor in accordance with this Guidance and it is proposed to withhold bail for the purposes of making an application to a court for a remand in custody (or for bail conditions that may only be imposed by a court), but it proves not to be possible to consult with a Crown Prosecutor in person or by telephone before the expiry of any PACE custody time limit applicable before charge, a Custody Officer may proceed to charge, but only on the authority of a Duty Inspector. The Duty Inspector shall note the custody record and MG3 to confirm that it is appropriate to charge under this emergency provision. The case must be referred to a Crown Prosecutor as soon as is practicable for authority to proceed with the prosecution.

4 DECISIONS ANCILLARY TO THE CHARGING DECISION

4.1 **Consultations where it is Proposed to Withhold Bail or Impose Conditions**

Consultations prior to applications to withhold bail at court and short remands to police custody

Whilst decisions to detain or bail persons are exclusively matters for a Custody Officer, where it appears that a person in police detention should not be released and should be detained for the purposes of an application being made to a court for a remand in custody, including short periods in police custody for the purpose of enquiries into other offences, the Custody Officer may wish to consult a Duty Prosecutor to confirm that any proposed application for a remand in custody or the imposition of bail conditions which can only be imposed by a court is justified in accordance with the Bail Act 1976, is proportionate and is likely to be ordered by the court, and that sufficient detail to support any such application is recorded on the MG7.

4.2 Determination of the Court for First Appearance

Court selection

When Crown Prosecutors make charging decisions concerning cases that are to be bailed directly to an initial hearing, the Crown Prosecutor will determine whether the case is appropriate for an Early First Hearing Court or an Early Administrative Hearing Court. This will be indicated on the form MG3 with the charge decision.

4.3 Special Procedure for Persistent Young Offenders

Special provisions for PYO cases

Crown Prosecutors will be responsible for the decision to charge in all cases involving Persistent Young Offenders unless the charge is one specified in paragraph 3.3 of this Guidance.

Whenever a person who is, or appears to be, under 18 years of age is taken into custody, the Custody Officer will undertake an immediate check to ascertain whether the person is a Persistent Young Offender.

Where it appears to an Investigating Officer or Custody Officer that the person under investigation may be a Persistent Young Offender, early consultation will be undertaken with the Duty Prosecutor to confirm the likely charges and the evidential requirements in the case. Early consultation will be utilized to proactively manage all Persistent Young Offender cases to secure consistent performance in progressing these cases.

Where it appears that the case will be contested, the Duty Prosecutor and Investigating Officer will agree, as soon as practicable and in any case within three days of the arrest, on the evidential requirements to progress the case and on a date for the completion of the agreed work, including any pre-charge bail period, taking into account the 71-day target from arrest to sentence for concluding such cases.

5   DEPLOYMENT OF AND ROLE OF DUTY PROSECUTOR

5.1 Deployment

Deployment and duty of Crown Prosecutors

Chief Crown Prosecutors will make arrangements for the deployment of Crown Prosecutors to act as Duty Prosecutor in locally agreed locations having regard to the area business and wherever possible on a face-to-face basis, or to be otherwise available for the purposes of fulfilling the CPS's statutory duty. Duty Prosecutors will be available for consultation and will render such early legal advice and guidance, including where appropriate the making of such charging decisions as will facilitate the efficient and effective preparation and disposal of criminal prosecutions.

5.2 Early Consultations

When early advice may be sought by the police

Early consultation and advice may be sought and given in any case (including those in which the police may themselves determine the charge) and may include lines of enquiry, evidential requirements, and any pre-charge procedures. In exercising this function, Crown Prosecutors will be pro-active in identifying and, where possible, rectifying evidential deficiencies, and will identify those cases that can proceed to court for an early guilty plea as an expedited report.

Stopping weak cases early

5.3 Early consultation should also seek to identify evidentially weak cases, which cannot be rectified by further investigation, either at that stage or at all, so that these investigations may, where appropriate, be brought to an early conclusion.

5.4 Reviewing the Report to Crown Prosecutor for a Charging Decision (MG3) and Evidence

Duty Prosecutor's action on receipt of a case

Where Crown Prosecutors receive a 'Report to Crown Prosecutor for a Charging Decision' (MG3) accompanied by the information specified in paragraph 7.2 below, it is the duty of the Crown Prosecutor to review the evidence as soon as is practicable, having regard to any bail return dates, and decide whether it is appropriate or not, at that stage, to charge the person with an offence or divert them from the criminal justice system.

Written notice of charging or other decision

5.5 Once a charging (or other) decision has been made, Crown Prosecutors will give written notice of the decision by completing the second part of the Report to Crown Prosecutor for a Charging Decision (MG3) which will be provided to an officer involved in the investigation of the offence. A copy will be retained by the Crown Prosecutor.

Agreeing an action plan to build a case file

5.6 Where during the course of a consultation or following receipt of the Report to Crown Prosecutor for a Charging Decision (MG3) it is clear that a charging decision in the case cannot be reached at that stage, the Crown Prosecutor consulted will advise on the further steps to be taken, including the evidence to be gathered or the statements to be obtained before the decision can be reached, and will agree with the investigating officer the action to be taken and the time in which that is to be achieved. This agreement will be recorded on the MG3 and a copy will be provided to an officer involved in the investigation. A copy will be retained by the Crown Prosecutor. In providing such advice, Crown Prosecutors should avoid simply requiring full files to be produced but will specify the precise evidence required or to be sought in accordance with paragraph 7.2 below. Persons will not be charged until all agreed actions have been completed.

Referrals of cases in special circumstances

5.7 Where it appears at an early consultation that the case is of such complexity or sensitivity that it is more appropriate for referral to a specialist unit or prosecutor, or for an individual prosecutor to be allocated to the case from the outset, the Duty Prosecutor, or any Crown Prosecutor consulted, will contact the appropriate Area Unit Head forthwith to make the necessary arrangements.

Building evidential files: use of police pre-charge bail

5.8 In cases identified as likely to be contested or to be sent to the Crown Court, Crown Prosecutors will detail the requirements for preparation of an evidential report where that information is not immediately available before a full charging decision can be taken. Where the person is suitable for release on bail, the Custody Officer will then bail the person for such a period as is sufficient to allow any agreed action to be completed and the case to be reported to a Crown Prosecutor for a charging decision.

6 DECISIONS NOT TO PROSECUTE

6.1 Insufficient Evidence or not in the Public Interest to Charge

Written notice by Custody Officer of no prosecution

Where the Crown Prosecutor notifies a Custody Officer that there is not sufficient evidence to charge the person with an offence, or that there is sufficient evidence but the public interest does not require the person to be charged or given a caution in respect of an offence, the Custody Officer will notify the person in writing to that effect.

Written notice by Custody Officer of no prosecution, but possible further action

6.2 Where, however, it appears to the Crown Prosecutor that should further evidence or information come to light in the future the case may be reconsidered under the Code for Crown Prosecutors, the Crown Prosecutor will notify the Custody Officer to that effect who will notify the person in writing accordingly.

7 INFORMATION TO BE SENT TO CROWN PROSECUTORS FOR CHARGING DECISIONS

Evidence needed to make a charging decision

7.1 In making charging decisions, Crown Prosecutors will examine and assess the evidence available before reaching a decision. Wherever possible, Crown Prosecutors will seek to make the decision on the evidence presented to them by the investigator. Where, however, this is not possible, Custody Officers will arrange for persons to be released on bail, if it is necessary and appropriate to do so, to permit the required information to be provided as soon as is practicable.

Form of reports

7.2 The information to be provided by an officer involved in the investigation to a Crown Prosecutor to determine charges will be in the form of the 'Report to Crown Prosecutor for a Charging Decision' (MG3) and must be accompanied by the following:

Crown Court and likely not guilty cases

(i) All cases proceeding to the Crown Court or expected to be contested: Evidential Report. Where it is clear that the case is likely to or will proceed to the Crown Court or is likely to be contested, the Report to Crown Prosecutor for a Charging Decision (MG3) must be accompanied by an Evidential Report containing the key evidence upon which the prosecution will rely together with any unused material which may undermine the prosecution case or assist the defence (including crime reports, initial descriptions, and any previous convictions of key witnesses).

The Evidential Report must also be accompanied by suggested charge(s), a record of convictions and cautions of the person, and any observations of the reporting or supervising officer.

All other cases

(ii) Other cases referred to a Crown Prosecutor for a charging decision: Expedited Report

In any other case to be referred to a Crown Prosecutor for a charging decision, the Report to Crown Prosecutor must be accompanied by an Expedited Report containing key witness statements, any other compelling evidence,[5] and a summary of an interview. Where the offence has been witnessed by no more than four police officers, a key witness statement and a summary of the other evidence may suffice. Whether the summary of the interview or of other police witnesses is to be oral or written will be at the discretion of the Duty Prosecutor concerned.

The Expedited Report must be accompanied by any other information that may have a bearing on the evidential or public interest test, a record of convictions and cautions, and any observations of the reporting or supervising officer.

7.3 **Custody Cases—Threshold Test—Expedited Report**

File information in custody cases

Where in accordance with this Guidance and in order to facilitate the making of an application to a court for a remand in custody, a charging decision is to be taken in accordance with paragraph 3.9(i) above, the Report to Crown Prosecutor (MG3) must be accompanied by an Expedited Report containing sufficient material then available and brief details of any previous convictions or cautions of the person to allow the Threshold Test to be applied. The Manual

---

[5] For example, visually recorded evidence of the crime taking place from which it is possible to clearly identify the offender

of Guidance remand file will be provided for the first and subsequent interim hearings, until the completed Report to Crown Prosecutor, or further evidence referred to in paragraph 3.9(ii) above, is submitted.

7.4 Requirement for Early Consultation in Evidential Report Cases

Early consultation in evidential report cases

Early consultation with a Duty Prosecutor should be undertaken to identify those cases in which an evidential file will be required, and to agree the time-scales for the completion and submission of the Report to Crown Prosecutor for a Charging Decision (MG3). An officer involved in the investigation must submit the completed Report to Crown Prosecutor for a Charging Decision (MG3) within the agreed timescale together with the evidential material referred to in paragraphs 5.6 and 7.2(i) above.

7.5 Complex or Sensitive Cases—Evidential Report

Complex or sensitive cases

In any case where it appears to a Duty Prosecutor that the case is so complex or sensitive that a decision to charge, or not as the case may be, cannot be made without fuller information, the Report to Crown Prosecutor for a Charging Decision (MG3) must be accompanied by an evidential file and the material mentioned in paragraphs 5.6 and 7.2(i) above.

7.6 Case Requirements Unclear—Consult with a Duty Prosecutor

When police uncertain about the information required

Where an Investigating Officer considers that a defence may have been raised by a person in interview, or is uncertain whether a person has fully admitted an offence and requires clarification of the information required to accompany the Report to Crown Prosecution for a Charging Decision, early consultation with a Duty Prosecutor should occur to determine whether the case is likely to proceed and to establish the report requirements to facilitate the making of the charging decision.

8 ROLES AND RESPONSIBILITIES OF CUSTODY OFFICERS UNDER S. 37(7)(a) TO (d) OF THE POLICE AND CRIMINAL EVIDENCE ACT, AS AMENDED BY SCH. 2 TO THE CRIMINAL JUSTICE ACT 2003

8.1 Requirement for Early Consultations

Early consultation where offence to be charged by CPS

Where it appears likely that a charge will be determined by a Crown Prosecutor, a Custody Officer must direct Investigating Officers to consult a Duty Prosecutor as soon as is practicable after a person is taken into custody. This will enable early agreement to be reached as to the Report and evidential requirements and, where appropriate, for any period of bail to be determined to permit submission of the Report to the Crown Prosecutor for a Charging Decision (MG3).

Early decisions

8.2 Early consultation with a Duty Prosecutor will allow the early identification of weak cases and those where the charging decision may be made upon consideration of limited information.

8.3 **Referrals where the Police do not Wish to Proceed**

Referrals where police do not wish to prosecute where evidence sufficient to charge on Threshold Test

In any indictable-only case in which the Threshold Test is met and in which an investigating or supervisory officer decides that he does not wish to proceed with a prosecution, the case must be referred to a Crown Prosecutor to confirm whether or not the case is to proceed. Early consultation in such a case may allow the investigation and preparation of case papers to be curtailed unless the complexity or sensitivity of the case determines otherwise.

8.4 **The Standard to be Applied in Determining Whether the Case is to be Referred to a Crown Prosecutor or the Person Released on Bail**

Stage at which cases must be referred to a Crown Prosecutor

In determining whether there is sufficient evidence to charge in accordance with s. 37(7) of the Police and Criminal Evidence Act, Custody Officers will apply the Threshold Test set out in paragraph 3.10 above. Where, in any case, it appears that there is manifestly no evidence and the Threshold Test is not met in respect of a detained person, the Custody Officer need not refer the case to a Crown Prosecutor before releasing that person, whether on bail or otherwise. In any case where this Guidance requires charges to be determined by Crown Prosecutors and a Custody Officer concludes that the Threshold Test is met, the Custody Officer will ensure that the case is referred to a Crown Prosecutor as soon as is practicable, or, where the person is suitable for bail, release the person detained on pre-charge bail, with or without conditions, in accordance with s. 37(7)(a).

8.5 **Delaying Charging and Releasing Persons Suitable on Bail**

Application of police pre-charge bail

In any case where this Guidance requires charging decisions to be made by Crown Prosecutors and the required information is not then available, Custody Officers will release those persons suitable for bail (with or without conditions as appropriate) to allow for consultation with a Crown Prosecutor and the submission of an evidential Report to a Crown Prosecutor for a Charging Decision (MG3) in accordance with this Guidance.

Early disclosure to defence

8.6 The period of bail should be such as to allow the completion of the investigation, submission of a Report to a Crown Prosecutor for a Charging Decision (MG3), for the person to be charged, and for early disclosure of the evidence and any unused material referred to in paragraph 7.2 to be provided to the defence prior to the first appearance.

Delayed charges—other reasons

8.7 Where a Custody Officer determines that there is sufficient evidence to charge a person but concludes that it is not appropriate at that stage to charge the person with an offence or to seek a charging decision from a Crown Prosecutor, and proposes to release the person from police custody in accordance with s. 37(7)(b) of the Police and Criminal Evidence Act, the person may only be released on unconditional bail. The Custody Officer should record the reasons for so acting.

9 CAUTIONS, REPRIMANDS, AND FINAL WARNINGS

Diversion from prosecution, police to caution, reprimand, etc

9.1 Where the police consider that the Threshold Test is met in a case, other than an indictable only offence, and determine that it is in the public interest instead to administer a simple caution, or to administer a reprimand or final warning in the case of a youth, the police may issue that caution, reprimand, or final warning as appropriate, without referring the case to a Crown Prosecutor.

Consultation on decision to caution

9.2 Notwithstanding the above, an investigating officer may wish to consult with a Crown Prosecutor in respect of any case in which it is proposed to deal with a person by way of a caution, reprimand, or final warning.

Actions on conditional caution cases

9.3 Where a conditional cautioning scheme is in force locally and the police wish to conditionally caution any person for an offence, the Custody Officer must refer the case to a Crown Prosecutor for decision.

Review by Crown Prosecutors

9.4 Where in accordance with this Guidance, the police have determined to initiate proceedings against a person by way of a charge, and a Crown Prosecutor, acting under s. 10 of the Prosecution of Offences Act 1985 and s. 37B of the Police and Criminal Evidence Act 1984 (as amended) notifies a Custody Officer that it is more appropriate to proceed by way of a conditional caution (if a scheme is in force locally), simple caution, reprimand, or final warning, the Custody Officer will ensure that the person is given a conditional caution, simple caution, reprimand, or final warning as appropriate.

Decisions to charge or caution by Crown Prosecutors

9.5 Crown Prosecutors, when undertaking a charging review in accordance with this Guidance, may determine that a charge, conditional caution (if a scheme is in force locally), simple caution, reprimand, or final warning is appropriate. Written notice of the decision will be given to the Custody Officer on an MG3.

Where it subsequently proves not to be possible to give the person a conditional caution (if this scheme is enforced locally), simple caution, reprimand, or final warning, the matter will be referred back to the Crown Prosecutor to determine whether the person is instead to be charged with the offence.

10   BREACH OF PRE-CHARGE BAIL CONDITIONS

Action on breach of bail conditions pending CPS charging decision

10.1   Where a person is released on bail pending a CPS decision on charge, or re-released following arrest for breach of a condition of bail for that purpose [under s. 37(7)(a) or 37C(2)(b) of the Police and Criminal Evidence Act], and that person is subsequently arrested under s. 46A(1A) of the Police and Criminal Evidence Act on reasonable grounds of having broken any of the conditions of bail, or for failing to surrender to bail at the police station, and a Custody Officer concludes that the person should be detained in custody for the purpose of an application to the court for a remand in custody, the Custody Officer will consult a Crown Prosecutor for a decision as to whether to charge with the offence for which the person had previously been released on bail or with any other offence, or be released without charge either on bail or without bail.

Charging breach of bail — emergency situations

10.2   In any such case where it has proved not to be possible to consult with a Crown Prosecutor in person or by telephone before the expiry of any PACE custody time limit and it is proposed to withhold bail for the purposes of an application for a remand into custody (or for bail conditions that may only be imposed by the court), a Custody Officer may proceed to charge, but only on the authority of a Duty Inspector. The Duty Inspector shall note the custody record and MG3 to confirm that it is appropriate to charge under the emergency provisions. The case must be referred to a Crown Prosecutor as soon as is practicable for authority to proceed with the prosecution.

11   POLICE ACTION POST-REFERRAL AND ESCALATION PROCEDURE

Police action post referral

11.1   In any case where the Threshold Test is met and the case has been referred to a Crown Prosecutor for a charging decision, and the decision of the Crown Prosecutor is to charge, caution, obtain additional evidence, or take no action, the police will not proceed in any other way without first referring the matter back to a Crown Prosecutor.

Dispute resolution

11.2 Where in any case an Investigating or Custody Officer is not in agreement with the charging decision, the Report requirements, or any diversion proposal of a Crown Prosecutor and wishes to have the case referred for further review, the case must be referred to the BCU Crime Manager (normally Detective Chief Inspector), or appointed Deputy, for consultation with a CPS Unit Head, or appointed Deputy for resolution. If further escalation is required, the involvement of the Divisional Commander and the Level E Unit Head or Chief Crown Prosecutor should be obtained. Procedures should be in place for this review to be conducted speedily.

12 FORM OF REPORT TO CROWN PROSECUTOR FOR A CHARGING DECISION (MG3)

Form of MG3

12.1 The Report to Crown Prosecutor for a Charging Decision to be used will be the form MG3, a copy of which is attached at Annex B to this Guidance. The Manual of Guidance Editorial Board may vary this form from time to time.

13 REQUIREMENTS TO COMPLY WITH THE MANUAL OF GUIDANCE PROVISIONS

Compliance with Manual of Guidance

13.1 All consultation arrangements and procedures for the preparation, processing, and submission of prosecution files and the disclosure of unused material will be carried out in accordance with the provisions of the latest edition of the Manual of Guidance as agreed between the Home Office, the Association of Chief Police Officers, and the Crown Prosecution Service.

SCHEDULE

This Guidance is to come into operation in the following areas with effect from 4 January 2005: Avon & Somerset, Cleveland, Greater Manchester, Humberside, Kent, Lancashire, London, Merseyside, Northumbria, Nottinghamshire, South Yorkshire, Thames Valley, West Midlands, and West Yorkshire.

This Guidance is to come into effect in the following areas on the dates specified below:

Local Criminal Justice Board Area	Date of coming into effect	Authorization of Director of Public Prosecutions
Bedfordshire		
Cambridgeshire		
Cheshire		
Cumbria		
Derbyshire		
Dorset		
Devon & Cornwall		
Durham		
Dyfed Powys		
Essex		
Gloucestershire		
Gwent		
Hampshire	18 April 2005	
Hertfordshire		
Leicestershire		
Lincoln		
Norfolk		
North Wales		
North Yorkshire		
Northamptonshire		
South Wales		
Staffordshire		
Suffolk		
Surrey		
Sussex		
Warwickshire		
West Mercia		
Wiltshire		

ANNEX A

Offences or Circumstances, which must always be Referred to a Crown Prosecutor for Early Consultation and Charging Decision—Whether Admitted or not

- Offences requiring the Attorney General's or Director of Public Prosecution's consent.
- Any indictable-only offence.
- Any either-way offence triable only on indictment due to the surrounding circumstances of the commission of the offence or the previous convictions of the person.

In so far as not covered by the above:

- Offences under the Terrorism Act 2000 or any other offence linked with terrorist activity.
- Offences under the Anti-Terrorism, Crime and Security Act 2001.
- Offences under the Explosive Substances Act 1883.
- Offences under any of the Official Secrets Acts.
- Offences involving any racial, religious, or homophobic aggravation.
- Offences classified as domestic violence.
- Offences under the Sexual Offences Act 2003 committed by or upon persons under the age of 18 years.
- Offences involving Persistent Young Offenders, unless chargeable by the police under paragraph 3.3.
- Offences arising directly or indirectly out of activities associated with hunting wild mammals with dogs under the Hunting Act 2004.
- The following specific offences:[6]
  - Wounding or inflicting grievous bodily harm, contrary to s. 20 of the Offences Against the Person Act 1861
  - Assault occasioning actual bodily harm, contrary to s. 47 of the Offences Against the Person Act 1861
  - Violent disorder, contrary to s. 2 of the Public Order Act 1986
  - Affray, contrary to s. 3 of the Public Order Act 1986
  - Offences involving deception, contrary to the Theft Acts 1968 and 1978
  - Handling stolen goods, contrary to s. 22 of the Theft Act 1968.

---

[6] File requirements for these cases will be in accordance with the Manual of Guidance expedited file, to include key witness statements or other compelling evidence and a short descriptive note of any interview conducted.

ANNEX B

REPORT TO CROWN PROSECUTOR FOR CHARGING DECISION

DECISION LOG & ACTION PLAN   Page ..... of .....

Not Disclosable

URN ☐☐☐☐

REPORT TO CROWN PROSECUTOR (FOR POLICE COMPLETION)

Suspect 1: PO/PYO/YO* M/F*	**Proposed charge(s):**
Surname:	....
Forename(s):	....
D.O.B: .... Custody Ref:	....
Ethnicity code (self-defined):	....
Suspect 2: PO/PYO/YO* M/F*	**Proposed charge(s):**
Surname:	....
Forename(s):	....
D.O.B: .... Custody Ref:	....
Ethnicity code (self-defined):	....

Officer seeking advice: .... Supervisor's name: .... Consulted Y/N*

Material provided to CPS (*indicate if attached*)

	Date of item		Date of item
Statement of:		Pocket note book/Incident report book:	
Statement of:		Pocket incident log:	
Statement of:		Video/photographs:	
Interview record:		Previous convictions/disposals:	
Forensic/expert evidence:		Other:	

<hr>

Outline of circumstances and decision/advice sought (*unless verbal report given*)

(Consider: time limit on proceedings (if applicable); strengths and weaknesses of case; possible lines of defence; witness assessment; public safety/bail issues; disclosure; any financial or asset recovery issues; orders on conviction; public interest.)

Continue on separate sheet if necessary

Officer completing: .... Rank & No./Job title: .... Date: ....

Contact details (station, tel, mobile, e-mail): .... Signature: ....

<hr>

Page ..... of ....

CHARGING DECISION/ADVICE & CASE ACTION PLAN (FOR CPS COMPLETION)　 URN: ....

Charging decision and advice, specifying or attaching charges (*refer to documents/evidence seen, decision on offences*)

Continue on separate sheet if necessary

Code	Advice	Suspect 1	Suspect 2	Code	Advice	Suspect 1	Suspect 2
Prosecutor to indicate general nature of decision and advice (*Tick one box only*)							
A	Charge + request Full File			H	Request Evidential File		
B	Charge + request Expedited File			I	Request Expedited File		
C	Simple caution			J	Further investigation—resubmit		
D	Conditional caution			K	NFA–Evidential		
E	Reprimand			L	NFA–Public Interest		
F	Final warning			M	Other (please specify)		
G	TIC			N	Refer for financial investigation		
If 'K', enter Evidential code:				If 'C, D, E, F or L', enter Public Interest code:			

Further action agreed: **Action date by:**

1.   1.

2.   2.

3.   3.

4.   4.

Asset recovery case: Yes/No*.. Charging review/action date: ....

Return bail date: .... PYO Provisional trial date: ....

Further consultation needed pre-charge: Y /N*
(If further consultation necessary, use continuation sheet MG3 A)

Prosecutor name (*print*): .... Contact details: .... Date: ....

Investigation stage at which advice sought:

Pre arrest ☐   Post Arrest ☐   Post Interview ☐   Post bail for further enqs ☐   Bail for charging decision ☐

How advice delivered:

Face to Face ☐   Video Conferencing ☐   Telephone ☐   CPS Direct ☐   Written ☐

PART 2

Crown Prosecution Service Charging Standards

3

Offences Against the Person, incorporating the Charging Standard

INTRODUCTION

Code for Crown Prosecutors — Considerations

For general guidance concerning charging, refer to Charging Standard below in this section.

Think carefully about the interests of the victim when deciding whether or not it is in the public interest to proceed. Where the victim was in the process of committing an offence at the time of the assault, also refer to Self Defence and the Prevention of Crime on the CPS website when reviewing the case.

CPS Policy on domestic violence and race-related issues will often be relevant: see Domestic Violence and Racially and Religiously Aggravated Crime on the CPS website.

Paragraph 5.9d of the Code for Crown Prosecutors states that a prosecution is likely to be in the public interest if the offence was committed against a person serving the public. (Examples may include police and prison officers, doctors, nurses, and bus or train drivers.)

Harassment

For guidance on harassment, refer to Protection from Harassment Act 1997 section on the CPS website.

CHARGING STANDARD — PURPOSE

There is no longer a separate and free-standing charging standard for Offences Against the Person. Instead, the Charging Standard, having been revised, is now contained within this chapter.

This standard covers the following offences:

- Common assault, contrary to s. 39 of the Criminal Justice Act 1988;
- Assault upon a constable in the execution of his duty, contrary to s. 89 of the Police Act 1996;
- Assault with intent to resist arrest, contrary to s. 38 of the Offences Against the Person Act 1861 ('the Act');
- Assault occasioning actual bodily harm, contrary to s. 47 of the Act;
- Unlawfully wounding/inflicting grievous bodily harm, contrary to s. 20 of the Act;
- Unlawful wounding/inflicting grievous bodily harm with intent, contrary to s. 18 of the Act; and
- Attempted murder, contrary to s. 1(1) of the Criminal Attempts Act 1981.

GENERAL PRINCIPLES: CHARGING STANDARD

The standard contained in this chapter is designed to assist prosecutors in selecting the most appropriate charge, in the light of the facts that can be proved, at the earliest possible opportunity.

The standard set out below:

- Should not be used in the final determination of any investigatory decision, such as the decision to arrest;
- Does not override any guidance issued on the use of appropriate alternative forms of disposal short of charge, such as cautioning;
- Does not override the principles set out in the Code for Crown Prosecutors and in particular paragraph 7.1 of the Code by which prosecutors are to select charges which reflect the seriousness and extent of the offending and provide the Court with adequate sentencing powers;
- Does not override the need for consideration to be given in every case as to whether a charge/prosecution is in the public interest;
- Does not override the need for each case to be considered on its individual merits, nor fetter the discretion to charge and to prosecute the most appropriate offence depending on the particular facts of the case.

1   Common Assault, Contrary to s. 39 of the Criminal Justice Act 1988

(i)   An offence of common assault is committed when a person either assaults another person or commits a battery.

(ii)   An assault is committed when a person intentionally or recklessly causes another to apprehend the immediate infliction of unlawful force (*Archbold*, **19-166 and 19-172;** *Blackstone's CP 2005*, **B2.1 and B2.5**).

(iii)   A battery is committed when a person intentionally and recklessly applies unlawful force to another (*Archbold*, **19-166a and 19-174 to 19-175;** *Blackstone's CP 2005*, **B2.1 and B2.6 to B2.10**).

(iv)   It is a summary offence, which carries a maximum penalty of six months' imprisonment and/or a fine not exceeding the statutory maximum. However, if the requirements of s. 40 of the Criminal Justice Act 1988 are met, then common assault can be included as a count on an indictment (refer to Criminal Justice Act 1988, ss. 40 and 41; Crime and Disorder Act 1998, s. 51 and Sch. 3, para. 6).

(v)   Where there is a battery the defendant should be charged with 'assault by beating' (*DPP v Little* [1992] 1 All ER 299).

(vi)   In law, the only factors that distinguish common assault from assault occasioning actual bodily harm, contrary to s. 47 of the Offences Against the Person Act 1861, are the degree of injury that results and the sentence available to the sentencing court.

(vii) Where battery results in injury, a choice of charge is available. The Code for Crown Prosecutors recognizes that there will be factors, which may properly lead to a decision not to prefer or continue with the gravest possible charge. Thus, although any injury that is more than transient or trifling can be classified as actual bodily harm, the appropriate charge (subject to paragraph (viii) below) will be contrary to s. 39 where injuries amount to no more than the following:

- grazes;
- scratches;
- abrasions;
- minor bruising;
- swellings;
- reddening of the skin;
- superficial cuts;
- a 'black eye'.

(viii) You should always consider the injuries first, and in most cases the degree of injury will determine whether the appropriate charge is s. 39 or s. 47. There will be borderline cases, such as where an undisplaced broken nose has resulted. Generally, when the injuries amount to no more than those described at sub-paragraph (vii) above, common assault will be the appropriate charge.

However, there may be cases where the injuries suffered by a victim would usually amount to common assault but, due to the presence of serious aggravating features, they could more appropriately be charged as actual bodily harm contrary to s. 47 of the Offences Against the Person Act 1861.

Such serious aggravating features would include:

(a) the nature of the assault, such as the use of a weapon, biting, gouging, or kicking of a victim whilst on the ground, or strangulation which is more than fleeting and which caused real fear to the victim; or

(b) the vulnerability of the victim, such as when the victim is elderly, disabled, or a child assaulted by an adult (so that where an assault causes any of the injuries referred to in sub-paragraph (vii) above, other than reddening of the skin, the charge will normally be assault occasioning actual bodily harm, although prosecutors must bear in mind that the definition of assault occasioning actual bodily harm requires the injury to be more than transient and trifling); or

(c) other circumstances when though the injuries are relatively minor the existence of aggravating features means that the sentencing powers of the court may not be adequate (refer to lawful correction in paragraph 9(i) of this section).

(ix) Currently, as common assault is not an alternative verdict to more serious offences of assault, a jury may only convict of common assault if the count has been preferred in the circumstances set out in s. 40 of the Criminal Justice Act 1988. However, this changed when s. 11 of the Domestic Violence, Crime and Victims Act 2004 came into force on 31 March 2005. Section 11 makes common assault an alternative verdict to more serious offences of assault even if the count has not been preferred in the indictment.

(x) Where a charge contrary to s. 47 has been preferred, the acceptance of a plea of guilty to an added count for common assault will rarely be justified in the absence of a significant change in circumstances that could not have been foreseen at the time of review.

(xi) Common assault is capable of being racially/religiously aggravated under the Crime and Disorder Act 1998. The racially/religiously aggravated version of s. 39 is an either way offence (refer to Racially and Religiously Aggravated Crime, on the CPS website).

2 Assault on Constable in the Execution of his/her Duty, Contrary to s. 89(1) of the Police Act 1996

Refer to *Archbold*, 19-265; *Blackstone's CP 2005*, B2.23 to B2.26 for the law.

The offence is committed when a person assaults either:

- a constable acting in the execution of his or her duty; or
- a person assisting a constable in the execution of his or her duty.

(i) It is a summary only offence, which carries a maximum penalty of six months' imprisonment and/or a fine not exceeding the statutory maximum.

(ii) If an assault on a constable results in an injury as described in paragraph 1(vii), a prosecution under s. 89(1) of the Police Act 1996 will be appropriate, provided that the officer is acting in the execution of his or her duty.

(iii) Where the evidence that the officer was acting in execution of his or her duty is insufficient, but proceedings for an assault are nevertheless warranted, the appropriate charge will be under s. 39 of the Criminal Justice Act 1988.

(iv) The fact that the victim is a police officer is not, in itself, an exceptional reason for charging an offence contrary to s. 47 of the Offences Against the Person Act 1861 when the injuries are minor. When the injuries are such that an offence contrary to s. 47 would be charged in relation to an assault on a member of the public, s. 47 will be the appropriate charge for an assault on a constable.

3 Assault with Intent to Resist Arrest, Contrary to s. 38 of the Offences Against the Person Act 1861

Refer to *Archbold*, 19-255; *Blackstone's CP 2005*, B2.11 to B2.15 for the law.

(i) The offence is committed when a person assaults another person with the intent to resist arrest or prevent the lawful apprehension/detention of himself/herself or another, for any offence.

(ii) It is an either way offence, which carries a maximum penalty on indictment of two years' imprisonment and/or an unlimited fine. Summarily, the maximum penalty is six months' imprisonment and/or a fine not exceeding the statutory maximum.

(iii) A charge contrary to s. 38 may properly be used for assaults on persons other than police officers, for example store detectives, who may be trying to apprehend or detain an offender.

(iv) When a police officer is assaulted, a charge under s. 89(1) will be more appropriate unless there is clear evidence of an intent to resist apprehension or prevent detention and the sentencing powers available under s. 89(1) or for common assault are inadequate. This will rarely be the case when injuries are minor and inflicted in the context of a struggle.

(v) It is not bad for duplicity to charge, 'resist or prevent the lawful apprehension or detainer' etc. in the one count: Rule 7 of the Indictments Rules 1971 (*Archbold*, 1-228; *Blackstone's CP 2005*, D10.21).

4 Assault Occasioning Actual Bodily Harm, Contrary to s. 47 of the Offences Against the Person Act 1861

Refer to *Archbold*, 19-190; *Blackstone's CP 2005*, B2.16 to B2.22 for the law.

(i) The offence is committed when a person assaults another, thereby causing actual bodily harm. Bodily harm has its ordinary meaning and includes any hurt calculated to interfere with the health or comfort of the victim: such hurt need not be permanent, but must be more than transient and trifling (*R v Donovan* (1934) 25 Cr App Rep 1, CCA). It is an either way offence, which carries a maximum penalty on indictment of five years' imprisonment and/or an unlimited fine not exceeding the statutory maximum.

(ii) As stated in paragraph 1(vi) above, the factors in law that distinguish a charge under s. 39 from a charge under s. 47 are the degree of injury resulting and the sentencing powers available to the sentencing court. Refer to paragraphs 1(vii) and (viii) for instances where common assault will be the appropriate charge. Where the injuries exceed those that can suitably be reflected by a common assault, a charge of assault occasioning actual bodily harm should normally be preferred. By way of example, the following injuries should normally be prosecuted under s. 47:

- loss or breaking of tooth or teeth;
- temporary loss of sensory functions, which may include loss of consciousness (*T v Director of Public Prosecutions* [2003] Crim LR 62).
- extensive or multiple bruising;
- displaced broken nose;
- minor fractures;
- minor, but not merely superficial, cuts of a sort probably requiring medical treatment (e.g. stitches);
- psychiatric injury that is more than mere emotions such as fear, distress, or panic. In any case where psychiatric injury is relied upon, as the basis for an allegation of assault occasioning actual bodily harm, and the matter is

(iii)   not admitted by the defence, then expert evidence must be called by the prosecution (*R v Chan-Fook* (1994) 99 Cr App R 147, CA).

(iii)   A verdict of assault occasioning actual bodily harm may be returned on proof of an assault together with proof of the fact that actual bodily harm was occasioned by the assault.

(iv)   The test of recklessness is as per *R v Cunningham* (*Archbold*, 19-167; *Blackstone's CP 2005*, B2.22).

(v)   This offence is capable of being racially aggravated under the Crime and Disorder Act 1998 (refer to Racially and Religiously Aggravated Crime on the CPS website).

5   Unlawful Wounding/Inflicting Grievous Bodily Harm, Contrary to s. 20 of the Act

Refer to *Archbold*, 19-200; *Blackstone's CP 2005*, B2.31 to B2.37 for the law.

(i)   The offence is committed when a person unlawfully and maliciously, either:

- wounds another person; or
- inflicts grievous bodily harm upon another person.

(ii)   It is an either way offence, which carries a maximum penalty on indictment of five years' imprisonment and/or an unlimited fine. Summarily, the maximum penalty is six months' imprisonment and/or a fine not exceeding the statutory maximum.

(iii)   Wounding means the breaking of the continuity of the whole of the outer skin, or the inner skin within the cheek or lip. It does not include the rupturing of internal blood vessels (*Archbold*, 19-212; *Blackstone's CP 2005*, B2.37).

(iv)   The definition of wounding may encompass injuries that are relatively minor in nature, for example a small cut or laceration. An assault resulting in such minor injuries should more appropriately be charged contrary to s. 47. An offence contrary to s. 20 should be reserved for those wounds considered to be serious (thus equating the offence with the infliction of grievous, or serious, bodily harm under the other part of the section).

(v)   Grievous bodily harm means serious bodily harm (*Archbold*, 19-206; *Blackstone's CP 2005*, B2.37). It is for the jury to decide whether the harm is serious. However, examples of what would usually amount to serious harm include:

- injury resulting in permanent disability or permanent loss of sensory function;
- injury which results in more than minor permanent, visible disfigurement; broken or displaced limbs or bones, including fractured skull;
- compound fractures, broken cheekbone, jaw, ribs, etc.;
- injuries which cause substantial loss of blood, usually necessitating a transfusion;
- injuries resulting in lengthy treatment or incapacity;

- psychiatric injury. As with assault occasioning actual bodily harm, appropriate expert evidence is essential to prove the injury.

(vi) In accordance with the recommendation in *R v McCready* [1978] 1 WLR 1376, if there is any reliable evidence that a sufficiently serious wound has been inflicted, then the charge under s. 20 should be of unlawful wounding, rather than of inflicting grievous bodily harm. Where both a wound and grievous bodily harm have been inflicted, discretion should be used in choosing which part of s. 20 more appropriately reflects the true nature of the offence.

(vii) The prosecution must prove under s. 20 that either the defendant intended, or actually foresaw, that the act might cause some harm. It is not necessary to prove that the defendant either intended or foresaw that the unlawful act might cause physical harm of the gravity described in s. 20. It is enough that the defendant foresaw some physical harm to some person, albeit of a minor character, might result (*R v Savage, DPP v Parmenter* [1992] 1 AC 699).

(viii) This offence is capable of being racially/religiously aggravated under the Crime and Disorder Act 1998 (refer to Racist and Religious Crime in Chapter 11 of this book).

6 Wounding/Causing Grievous Bodily Harm with Intent, Contrary to s. 18 of the Offences Against the Person Act 1861

Refer to *Archbold*, 19-199; *Blackstone's CP 2005*, B2.38 to B2.43 for the law.

(i) The offence is committed when a person unlawfully and maliciously, with intent to do some grievous bodily harm, or with intent to resist or prevent the lawful apprehension or detainer of any other person, either:

- wounds another person; or
- causes grievous bodily harm to another person.

(ii) It is an indictable only offence, which carries a maximum penalty of imprisonment for life.

(iii) For the definition of wounding and grievous bodily harm, see paragraphs 5(iii) to 5(v) above.

(iv) The distinction between charges under s. 18 and s. 20 is one of intent.

(v) The gravity of the injury resulting is not the determining factor, although it may provide some evidence of intent.

(vi) When charging an offence involving grievous bodily harm, consideration should be given to the fact that a s. 20 offence requires the infliction of harm, whereas a s. 18 offence requires the causing of harm. This may be of some significance when considering alternative verdicts (refer to section 8 below). However, this distinction has been greatly reduced by the decision of the House of Lords in *R v Ireland, R v Burstow* [1998] AC 147 (***Archbold*, 19-208; *Blackstone's CP 2005*, B2.43**).

(vii) Factors that may indicate the specific intent include:

- a repeated or planned attack;

- deliberate selection of a weapon or adaptation of an article to cause injury, such as breaking a glass before an attack;
- making prior threats;
- using an offensive weapon against, or kicking the victim's head.

(viii) The evidence of intent required is different if the offence alleged is a wounding, or the causing of grievous bodily harm with intent to resist or prevent the lawful apprehension or detainer of any person. This part of s. 18 is of assistance in more serious assaults upon police officers, where the evidence of an intention to prevent arrest is clear, but the evidence of an intent to cause grievous bodily harm is in doubt (*Archbold*, 19-213 to 19-214; *Blackstone's CP 2005*, **B2.43**).

(ix) It is not bad for duplicity to indict for wounding with intent to cause grievous bodily harm or to resist lawful apprehension in one count, although it is best practice to include the allegations in separate counts. This will enable a jury to consider the different intents and the court to sentence on a clear basis of the jury's finding.

7 Attempted Murder, Contrary to s. 1(1) of the Criminal Attempts Act 1981

Refer to *Archbold*, **19-191**; *Blackstone's CP 2005*, **A6.31 and B1.1** for the law. For guidance on the substantive offence of murder, refer to Homicide on the CPS website.

(i) The offence is committed when a person does an act that is more than merely preparatory to the commission of an offence of murder, and at the time the person has the intention to kill.

(ii) It is an indictable only offence, which carries a maximum penalty of imprisonment for life.

(iii) Unlike murder, which requires an intention to kill or cause grievous bodily harm, attempted murder requires evidence of an intention to kill alone. This makes it a difficult allegation to sustain and careful consideration must be given to whether on the facts a more appropriate charge would be s. 18. Another possible charge may be s. 16 making threats to kill (see Guidance on other relevant offences, below).

(iv) The courts will pay particular attention to counts of attempted murder and justifiably will be highly critical of any such count unless there is clear evidence of an intention to kill.

(v) When considering the choice of charge, prosecutors should consider what alternative verdicts may be open to a jury on an allegation of attempted murder. Section 6(3) of the Criminal Law Act 1967 applies. Prosecutors should note the judgment in *R v Morrison* [2003] 1 WLR 1859, in which, on a single count of attempted murder, the Court of Appeal held that the trial judge had been right to leave to the jury an alternative count of attempting to cause grievous bodily harm with intent, because a defendant could not intend to kill without also intending to cause grievous bodily harm. If an alternative count can be left to the jury, prosecutors should not normally add it to the indictment, but should draw to the attention of counsel that the alternative count may be available (see paragraph 8(vii) below).

(vi) It should be borne in mind that the actions of the defendant must be more than merely preparatory and although words and threats may provide prima facie evidence of an intention to kill, there may be doubt as to whether they were uttered seriously or were mere bravado.

(vii) Evidence of the following factors may assist in proving the intention to kill:

- calculated planning;
- selection and use of a deadly weapon;
- threats (subject to paragraph (vi) above);
- severity or duration of attack;
- relevant admissions in interview.

8 Alternative Verdicts

(i) In certain circumstances, it is possible for a jury to find the accused not guilty of the offence charged, but guilty of some other alternative offence. The general provisions are contained in s. 6(3) of the Criminal Law Act 1967, and are supplemented by other provisions that relate to specific offences (*Archbold*, **4-455 to 4-456; *Blackstone's CP 2005*, D17.19 to D17.25**).

(ii) For offences against the person, the following alternatives may be found by a jury:

Causing grievous bodily harm with intent, contrary to s. 18 of the Act:

- Attempting to cause grievous bodily harm with intent.
- Inflicting grievous bodily harm, contrary to s. 20 of the Act.
- Unlawful wounding, contrary to s. 20 of the Act.

Wounding with intent, contrary to s. 18 of the Act:

- Attempting to wound with intent.
- Unlawful wounding, contrary to s. 20 of the Act.
- Assault occasioning actual bodily harm, contrary to s. 47 of the Act.

Inflicting grievous bodily harm, contrary to s. 20 of the Act:

- Assault occasioning actual bodily harm, contrary to s. 47 of the Act.

Unlawful wounding, contrary to s. 20 of the Act:

- Assault occasioning actual bodily harm, contrary to s. 47 of the Act.

(iii) In the case of racially/religiously aggravated s. 20 and racially/religiously aggravated s. 47, a jury can return an alternative verdict of the unaggravated offence.

(iv) Previously it was not open for a jury to find common assault as an alternative to any offence contrary to s. 18, 20, or 47 of the Act. Therefore, where it is judged appropriate, a specific alternative count alleging common assault had to be included on the indictment pursuant to the provisions of s. 40 of the Criminal Justice Act 1988. Neither was it open to a jury to find common assault as an alternative verdict to a charge of racially/religiously aggravated common assault. However, this changed when s. 11 of the Domestic Violence, Crime and Victims Act 2004 came into force on 31 March 2005. Section 11 makes common assault an alternative verdict to more serious offences of assault even if the count has not been preferred in the indictment.

(v) It is essential, however, that the charge that most suits the circumstances of the case is always preferred. It will never be appropriate to charge a more serious offence in order to obtain a conviction (whether by plea or verdict) to a lesser offence.

(vi) There is authority to support the proposition that a jury may convict of wounding, contrary to s. 20 of the Act, as an alternative to a count of causing grievous bodily harm with intent, contrary to s. 18 of the Act (*R v Wilson, R v Jenkins & Jenkins* (1983) 77 Cr App R 319, HL; *R v Mandair* [1994] 2 WLR 1376, HL).

(vii) Notwithstanding that authority, prosecutors should nevertheless consider including a separate count on the indictment alleging wounding, contrary to s. 20, where there is a possibility that the jury might not convict the defendant of the s. 18 offence (***Blackstone's CP 2005**, B2.41*).

9 Defences to Assaults

(i) Consent (***Archbold**, 19-180; **Blackstone's CP 2005**, B2.9*).

Lawful correction (***Archbold**, 19-185; **Blackstone's CP 2005**, B2.10*) (refer to paragraph 1(viii) above).

It should be noted that s. 58 of the Children Act 2004, which came into force on 15 January 2005, limits the availability of the lawful correction defence to common assault, contrary to s. 39 of the Criminal Justice Act 1988.

Self-defence (***Archbold**, 19-41 to 19-45; **Blackstone's CP 2005**, A3.30*) (refer to Self-defence and Prevention of Crime on the CPS website).

Defence of property (***Archbold**, 19-47; **Blackstone's CP 2005**, A3.33*) (refer to Self-defence and Prevention of Crime on the CPS website).

Prevention of crime (***Archbold**, 19-188; **Blackstone's CP 2005**, A3.30*) (refer to Self-defence and Prevention of Crime on the CPS website).

Execution of process (***Archbold**, 19-189*).

(ii) Prosecutors must consider all assaults in the context in which they were allegedly committed. There will be cases in which the surrounding circumstances will be of help in deciding whether to bring criminal proceedings.

(iii) Particular care must be taken in dealing with cases of assault where the allegation is made by a 'victim' who was, at the time, engaged in criminal activity himself. For instance, a burglar who claims to have been assaulted by the occupier of the premises concerned.

(iv) It is lawful for an individual to use reasonable force in any of, or combination of, the following circumstances:

- self-defence;
- to defend another;
- to defend property;
- to prevent crime;
- to lawfully arrest.

(v) Where the use of force in any of these circumstances is reasonable, the 'assailant' has an absolute defence and charges relating to the assault should not be brought.

(vi) In assessing the reasonableness of the force used, two questions should be asked:

- was the force used justified in the circumstances? (i.e. was there a need for any force at all?); and
- was the force used excessive in the circumstances?

(vii) The courts have indicated that both questions are to be answered on the basis of the facts as the accused honestly believed them to be. To that extent it is a subjective test. There is, however, an objective element to the test, as the court must then go on to ask whether, on the basis of the facts as the accused believed them to be, a reasonable person would regard the force used as reasonable or excessive (*Archbold*, 19-42; *Blackstone's CP 2005*, A3.35).

(viii) There can be a fine line, however, between what constitutes reasonable and unreasonable force. When considering whether the force used was reasonable or excessive, it is important to consider the words of Lord Morris in *Palmer v R* [1971] AC 814, which emphasize the difficulties often facing someone confronted by an intruder or defending himself against attack:

> If there has been an attack so that defence is reasonably necessary, it will be recognised that a person defending himself cannot weigh to a nicety the exact measure of his defensive action. If the jury thought that in a moment of unexpected anguish a person attacked had only done what he honestly and instinctively thought necessary, that would be the most potent evidence that only reasonable defensive action had been taken . . .

OTHER RELEVANT OFFENCES

Whilst the charging standard provides guidance on a range of frequently experienced offences against the person, there are also other offences that may be relevant, including the following:

- Attempting to choke, suffocate, or strangle with intent to enable the commission of an indictable offence, contrary to s. 21 of the Offences Against the Person Act 1861 (*Archbold*, **19-215 to 19-218;** *Blackstone's CP 2005*, **B2.42**).
- Causing to be taken or administering a drug with intent to enable the commission of an indictable offence, contrary to s. 22 of the Offences Against the Person Act 1861 (*Archbold*, **19-219 to 19-222**).
- Administering poison or noxious thing thereby endangering life or inflicting grievous bodily harm, contrary to s. 23 of the Offences Against the Person Act 1861 (*Archbold*, **19-223 to 19-231;** *Blackstone's CP 2005*, **B2.44 to B2.50**).
- Administering poison or noxious thing with intent to injure, aggrieve, or annoy, contrary to s. 24 of the Offences Against the Person Act 1861 (*Archbold*, **19-223 to 19-231;** *Blackstone's CP 2005*, **B2.51 to B2.56**).
- Causing bodily injury by explosives, contrary to s. 28 of the Offences Against the Person Act 1861 (*Archbold*, **19-232 to 19-240;** *Blackstone's CP 2005*, **B12.134 to B12.137**).

    Unlike offences under the Explosive Substances Act 1883, charging causing bodily injury contrary to s. 28 of the Offences Against the Person Act 1861 does not require the consent of the Attorney General. However, prosecutors should not charge the s. 28 offence simply to avoid obtaining the Attorney General's consent. Prosecutors should consider whether on the facts of the case there is an appropriate alternative offence before seeking the Attorney General's fiat. For guidance as to the Explosive Substances Act, refer to Explosives on the CPS website.
- Sending, throwing, or using explosive or corrosive substance or noxious thing with intent to do grievous bodily harm, contrary to s. 29 of the Offences Against the Person Act 1861 (*Archbold*, **19-232 to 19-240;** *Blackstone's CP 2005*, **B12.138 to B12.141**).
- Threats to kill, contrary to s. 16 of the Offences Against the Person Act 1861 (*Archbold*, **19-124 to 19-129;** *Blackstone's CP 2005*, **B1.94 to B1.98**).

    Threats can be calculated and premeditated, or said in the heat of the moment. The defendant does not have to have the intention to kill but there has to be an intent that the person to whom the threat has been issued would fear it would be carried out. Where it is doubtful whether the threat carried the necessary intent, a charge under s. 4 of the Public Order Act 1986 may be appropriate. Refer also to Public Order Offences, incorporating the Charging Standard, above.

    If the threat accompanies an assault, adding a charge under s. 16 will normally be unnecessary. There may be an exception where the severity of the threat is not matched by the physical injury sustained in the assault. The offence will be particularly appropriate if there has been no assault or if an assault has been prevented, yet the person to whom the threat was made was given real cause to believe it would be carried out.
- Kidnapping (*Archbold*, **19-331 to 19-348;** *Blackstone's CP 2005*, **B2.63 and B2.68**).

    There are four elements to this common law offence:
    - the taking or carrying away of one person by another;

- by force or fraud;
- without the consent of the person so taken or carried away; and
- without lawful excuse.

Often the kidnapping will be followed by the commission of further offences of sexual or aggravated assault. For kidnapping of children, see *Archbold*, 19-334; *Blackstone's CP 2005*, B2.67. For the offence of child abduction *Archbold*, 19-308; *Blackstone's CP 2005*, B2.69 to B2.81. Regardless of the severity of any act that follows (with the possible exception of murder), kidnapping is such a grave offence that it will be usual to reflect it with a count in the indictment.

- False imprisonment (*Archbold*, 19-331 to 19-348; *Blackstone's CP 2005*, B2.57 to B2.62).

False imprisonment is a common law offence involving the unlawful and intentional or reckless detention of the victim. An act of false imprisonment may amount in itself to an assault. If a separate assault accompanies the detention, this should be reflected in the particulars of the indictment.

If the detention was for the purpose of committing another indictable offence, and such an offence was committed, a count for the substantive offence will usually be enough. Where the detention was for a period of several hours, or days, then it will be proper to reflect the unlawful detention with a count for false imprisonment.

GENERAL POINTS

These offences contain a variety of alternative allegations. Check them carefully before making the appropriate selection.

- The above offences, except threats to kill, kidnapping, and false imprisonment, all carry a maximum sentence of life imprisonment except s. 23 (ten years) and s. 24 (five years). With s. 24 the sentencing approach is to equate it with either a s. 20 or a fairly serious s. 47, as they all carry the same penalty. Threats to kill is an either way offence which carries a maximum penalty on indictment of ten years' imprisonment. Kidnapping and false imprisonment are common law offences, punishable by fine or imprisonment, or both.
- Where serious injury has resulted there is little to be gained from charging one of these more unusual offences instead of an offence contrary to s. 18 provided the necessary intention to do grievous bodily harm can be proved. Do not charge just because a poison or corrosive fluid has been used to cause injury. They should be confined to situations where the evidence does not support the more usual charges of aggravated assault set out in the Guidance.
- These offences are relevant in circumstances where the injury does not amount to grievous bodily harm, or where the acts of the defendant are not sufficiently proximate to the indictable offences to allow a charge of attempting to commit that indictable offence.

Acceptability of Pleas

(i)   All decisions concerning the acceptability of pleas should be made in accordance with the principles set out in the Code for Crown Prosecutors.

(ii) Where the aggravated offence has been charged, prosecutors should not accept a guilty plea to the basic offence alone unless there are sound reasons for doing so. An example would be that the evidence needed to prove the aggravated element of the offence was no longer available, or the court refused to allow the evidence to be given (refer to Guidance on Prosecuting Cases of Racist and Religious Crime, in part 3 of this book).

4

Theft Acts, incorporating the Charging Standard

CHARGING STANDARD — PURPOSE

This charging standard gives guidance concerning the charge which should be preferred if the criteria set out in the Code for Crown Prosecutors are met. The purpose of charging standards is to make sure that the most appropriate charge is selected, in the light of the facts, which can be proved, at the earliest possible opportunity.

Adoption of this standard should lead to a reduction in the number of times charges have to be amended, which in turn should lead to an increase in efficiency and a reduction in avoidable extra work for the police, CPS, and the courts.

The guidance set out in this charging standard:

- should not be used in the determination of any investigatory decision, such as the decision to arrest;
- does not override any guidance issued on the use of appropriate alternative forms of disposal short of charge, such as cautioning, or conditional cautioning;
- does not override the principles set out in the Code for Crown Prosecutors;
- does not override particular policy guidance involving hate crimes, such as Homophobic, Racially or Religiously Aggravated, or Domestic Violence offences;
- does not override the need for consideration to be given in every case to whether a charge/prosecution is in the public interest;
- does not remove the need for each case to be considered on its individual merits, nor fetter the discretion to charge and to prosecute the most appropriate offence depending on the particular facts of the case.

GENERAL CHARGING PRACTICE

You should always have in mind the following general principles when selecting the appropriate charge(s):

(i) the charge(s) should accurately reflect the extent of the accused's alleged involvement and responsibility, thereby allowing the courts the discretion to sentence appropriately;

(ii) the choice of charges should ensure the clear and simple presentation of the case, particularly when there is more than one accused;

(iii) there should be no overloading of charges by selecting more charges than are necessary just to encourage the accused to plead guilty to a few;

(iv) there should be no overcharging by selecting a charge that is not supported by the evidence in order to encourage a plea of guilty to a lesser allegation.

JURISDICTION

We can prosecute for certain offences if a 'relevant event' occurred in England or Wales—Criminal Justice Act 1993, Part 1 (**Archbold, 2-37; Blackstone's CP 2005,** A8.4) and Home Office Circular 19/1999. This applies whether or not the defendant was in England or Wales at any material time, and whether or not he was a British citizen at any such time (***Archbold*, 2-44; *Blackstone's CP 2005*, A8.5**).

POLICING PRIORITIES FOR FRAUD CASES

Prosecutors should be aware of the 'Policing Priorities for Fraud Cases' document. This is a joint document, drawn up by representatives from the SFO, CPS, DTI, and police, and it lists the priorities that the police should take into account when deciding whether to accept a fraud case or not. A copy is attached at Annex A.

SPECIMEN CHARGES/COUNTS

Refer to Drafting the Indictment on the CPS website.

CHARGING PRACTICE: SPECIFIC OFFENCES

Theft, contrary to s. 1 of the 1968 Act

(***Archbold*, 21-6; *Blackstone's CP 2005*, B4.1**)
   The offence consists of dishonest appropriation of property belonging to another with the intention of permanently depriving the other of it.
   Theft is an either way offence, which carries a penalty on conviction on indictment of up to seven years' imprisonment. On summary conviction it carries a penalty of imprisonment for up to six months and/or a fine of up to the statutory maximum.
   There are five elements of the offence:

- Dishonesty.
  In assessing whether dishonesty can be proved, you should apply the twofold test set out in the case of *R v Ghosh* (1982) 75 Cr App R 154 (***Archbold*, 21-24; *Blackstone's CP 2005*, B4.37**). Remember that a jury will have to consider the same two tests before they are entitled to conclude that an accused was dishonest:
     First, according to the ordinary standards of reasonable and honest people, was what was done dishonest?
     Secondly, if it was dishonest by those standards, did the accused realize that reasonable and honest people would regard his conduct as dishonest?
  If the answer to either of these two questions is no, a prosecution will fail. You should also consider the provisions of s. 2 of the 1968 Act, which set out the circumstances when an appropriation is not to be regarded as dishonest (***Archbold*, 21-23; *Blackstone's CP 2005*, B4.35**).
- Appropriation.
  Section 3 of the 1968 Act (***Archbold*, 21-31; *Blackstone's CP 2005*, B4.25**) provides that any assumption by a person of the rights of an owner amounts to an

appropriation. The Prosecution do not have to prove that the appropriation was without the owner's consent. An appropriation will take place as an objective fact irrespective of whether the owner authorized or consented to the appropriation. The mental state of the accused is also irrelevant to the question of appropriation. The accused's state of mind is only relevant to issues of dishonesty and intention to permanently deprive (*Lawrence v Metropolitan Police Commissioner* (1971) 55 Cr App R 471 (***Archbold*, 21-33; *Blackstone's CP 2005*, B4.29**) and *R v Gomez* [1993] AC 442, HL (***Archbold*, 21-34; *Blackstone's CP 2005*, B4.26**)).

- Property.

The 1968 Act describes property as including money and all other property, real or personal, including things in action and other intangible property.

When a case involves cheques or funds in bank accounts, it is important to identify and analyse exactly what has taken place. You should examine bank account details, and it may be necessary to ask the police to obtain further evidence or information before deciding on the appropriate charge.

In normal circumstances, the holder of the bank account has a right to sue the bank for the amount of any credit balance and any agreed overdraft. The right to sue is a 'chose in action' and is 'property' under s. 4 of the 1968 Act (***Archbold*, 21-48; *Blackstone's CP 2005*, B4.10**).

When it can be proved that the dishonest actions of an accused had the effect of extinguishing a chose in action in a bank account belonging to another person, it would be appropriate to charge the theft of a credit balance belonging to the account holder.

In some cases, when an accused has dishonestly appropriated a credit balance and created a credit balance in an account, which he controls, the subsequent withdrawal of cash from that account may constitute the theft of money. To prove the theft of cash, it will be necessary to prove that cash was withdrawn, and that the cash withdrawn could not have represented funds which were legitimately in the account in addition to the dishonestly obtained funds. This will involve examining the state of the account both before and after the dishonest funds were paid into the account.

If the account was overdrawn and the agreed overdraft limit was exceeded, there is no chose in action to steal because the debt is not enforceable against the bank (***Archbold*, 21-50; *Blackstone's CP 2005*, B4.14**). Consider attempt theft.

Where it is alleged that funds have been appropriated by means of a banker's draft, before charging the theft of a credit balance, it is necessary to identify a debit in a bank account, which corresponds to the amount of the draft. Where a banker's draft has been forged, there will probably be no corresponding debit and it may be appropriate to consider charges under the Forgery and Counterfeiting Act 1981 (***Archbold*, 22-5; *Blackstone's CP 2005*, B6.28**).

Sometimes it is not possible to say from the evidence whether it was theft of a chose in action, or the proceeds of it. This can arise when the defendant has cashed a cheque from someone who intended the proceeds to be dealt with in a certain way, but the evidence does not reveal whether the proceeds were paid to the defendant in cash or he received credit for the amount in some other way (*R v Hallam* [1993] Crim LR 323 and *Blackstone's CP 2005*, **B4.3**).

- Belonging to another.

  The 1968 Act provides that property shall be regarded as belonging to any person having possession or control of it, or having in it any propriety right or interest. If a person receives property from or on account of another and he is obliged to retain and deal with it in a particular way, the property still belongs to that other person. Property that has been abandoned cannot be stolen.

  Property can be owned by more than one legal or human person. A company is a separate legal person from its directors. A director can be guilty of theft from a company (*Regina (A) v Snaresbrook Crown Court*, The Times, 12.07.01).

  A defendant, with a proprietary interest in property, who acts so as to interfere with the interest of a co-owner, can be guilty of theft.

- With the intention of permanently depriving the other of it.

  When a person gets property by another's mistake and is obliged to make restoration in whole or part of that property, an intention not to make restoration shall be regarded as an intention to permanently deprive that person of the property—s. 5 of the 1968 Act (*Archbold*, **21-58**; *Blackstone's CP 2005*, **B4.17**).

  See s. 6 of the 1968 Act (*Archbold*, **21-76**) for the statutory definition of appropriating property.

Examples when a charge of theft would be appropriate

- Switching price labels on goods so that a lower price is paid for the property.
- When the accused has collected money on behalf of a charity or other organization, opens the collection box or envelopes and uses the money for his or her own purposes.
- When a shop assistant dishonestly sells items at an under-value to a friend.
- Theft should be charged if there is difficulty in proving that force was used in order to steal property from a victim, or in circumstances when the theft was complete before there was any use of force by the accused.

Examples when it would not generally be appropriate to charge theft

- When a handbag or a mobile phone is snatched from a person's grasp following a struggle you should normally charge robbery (refer to Robbery, below).
- When a person learns that goods which he has bought in good faith at a reasonable price were in fact stolen, and he then sells the property without disclosing his lack of title. You should consider whether a charge contrary to s. 15 of the 1968 Act (*Archbold*, **21-172**; *Blackstone's CP 2005*, **B5.23**) is appropriate.
- When a motor vehicle has been taken and later abandoned, and there is insufficient evidence to prove that the taker intended the owner to be permanently deprived of it, you should charge taking the vehicle without the owner's consent, contrary to s. 12 of the 1968 Act (*Archbold*, **21-141**; *Blackstone's CP 2005*, **B4.90**).

- When a person puts petrol into a vehicle's tank at a self-service petrol station and then drives off without paying, there may not be sufficient evidence to prove a dishonest intention prior to putting the petrol in the tank; in which case, you should consider charging the offence of making off without paying, contrary to s. 3 of the 1978 Act (*Archbold*, 21-349; *Blackstone's CP 2005*, B5.68).
- When an electricity supply is tampered with—since electricity is not property—you should charge the offence of abstracting electricity, contrary to s. 13 of the 1968 Act (*Archbold*, 21-165; *Blackstone's CP 2005*, B4.111).

Charging considerations

- General deficiency cases.
  Each appropriation of property should be separately charged. Sometimes, however, it is not possible to prove when such appropriations took place. In those circumstances, a single general deficiency charge should be preferred, for example, when, over a period of time, a milkman steals money, which has been given to him by his customers. In contrast, when an insurance broker has stolen premiums received by him for clients, he should normally be charged with separate offences of theft relating to each identifiable premium on the basis of his documentary records (refer to Specimen Counts on the CPS website) (*Archbold*, 1-144; *Blackstone's CP 2005*, B4.3).
- Theft/handling stolen goods in the alternative.
  (*Archbold*, 21-280 to 21-293; *Blackstone's CP 2005*, B4.139)
  It is sometimes difficult to show whether a person in possession of stolen goods is a thief, or a handler of goods that have already been stolen. Theft and handling stolen goods may be charged in the alternative. If the evidence clearly points to theft by the accused, it would not be appropriate to add a further charge of handling. Charging in the alternative should only be used when there is a real possibility of doubt. This occurs when the evidence is ambiguous, for example when property taken during the course of a burglary is discovered within a very short time in the accused's possession. It may be inferred, in the absence of any alternative explanation, that the accused was either a thief/burglar, or had dishonestly handled stolen property.

Attempts

The appropriation may be complete even if the criminal's purpose is not fulfilled, for example thief puts shopping into his bag dishonestly intending not to pay, but is caught before leaving the shop. Charge theft, not attempt theft.

The Prosecution does not have to prove that there is in existence property capable of being stolen. For example, the would-be pickpocket who put a hand into someone else's empty pocket searching for something to steal will be guilty of an attempt theft. In this example, the charge should be drafted as an attempt to steal property belonging to the victim.

If you cannot charge attempt because there is no act which is more than merely preparatory, consider s. 25 of the Theft Act—going equipped to steal, cheat, or burgle (*Archbold*, 21-324; *Blackstone's CP 2005*, B4.118).

Theft: Gas and Water

These are property that can be stolen (*Archbold*, 21-52).

Abstracting Electricity, Contrary to s. 13 of the 1968 Act

(*Archbold*, 21-164; *Blackstone's CP 2005*, B4.111 to B4.116)

Abstracting electricity is committed when a person dishonestly uses without due authority, or dishonestly causes to be wasted or diverted, any electricity.

Abstracting electricity is an either way offence, which carries a penalty of conviction on indictment of a maximum term of five years' imprisonment. On summary conviction, the offence carries a maximum term of six months' imprisonment and/or a fine not exceeding the statutory maximum.

The elements of the offence are:

- Dishonesty.
  The test of dishonesty is the same as that for theft (*R v Ghosh* (1982) 75 Cr App R 154; refer to Theft, above). (**Also** *Archbold*, 21-24; *Blackstone's CP 2005*, B4.37.)
- Uses without due authority or causes to be wasted or diverted.
  It is not necessary to prove that an electricity meter had been tampered with in order for this offence to be made out. 'Use' simply means that some consumption of electricity had occurred which would not have occurred but for an act of the accused.
- Any electricity.
  Electricity is not property for the purpose of the 1968 Act.

Examples when a charge of abstracting electricity would be appropriate

- When a device is fitted to an electricity meter so that the meter gives a false reading.
- When the electricity supply to a house is reconnected without the consent of the electricity company.
- When the electricity supply to a house by-passes the meter.

Example when it would be inappropriate to charge abstracting electricity

- When an unauthorized telephone call has been made from a telephone belonging to another person. A charge contrary to ss. 125 or 126 of the Communications Act 2003 is usually more appropriate (refer to Telecommunications, below).

Charging considerations

- Since electricity is not property, it is not possible to charge an offence of theft of electricity.

- You must prove that the accused was responsible for the dishonest use of electricity. When there is more than one occupant of the premises, you must prove that the accused either tampered with the meter or used electricity knowing that the meter had been tampered with.

Telecommunications—ss. 125 or 126 of the Communications Act 2003

- Dishonestly obtaining a telecommunications service with intent to avoid payment of the charge—use ss. 125 or 126 of the Communications Act 2003 (*Archbold*, 25-363; *Blackstone's CP 2005*, B4.117).
- A telephone call cannot be 'appropriated' or stolen.

Handling Stolen Goods—s. 22 of the Theft Act 1968

(*Archbold*, 21-271; *Blackstone's CP 2005*, B4.126)

A person handles stolen goods if (otherwise than in the course of stealing), knowing or believing them to be stolen goods, he dishonestly receives the goods, or dishonestly undertakes or assists in their retention, removal, disposal, or realization by or for the benefit of another person, or if he arranges to do so.

Handling stolen goods is an either way offence, which carries a penalty on conviction on indictment of imprisonment for a term not exceeding fourteen years. On summary conviction it carries a penalty of a term of imprisonment up to six months and/or a fine not exceeding the statutory maximum.

The offence of handling stolen goods is a single offence. However, there are two limbs to the offence:

- Dishonestly receiving stolen goods.
- Dishonestly undertaking or assisting in the retention, removal, disposal, or realization of stolen goods by or for the benefit of another person, or arranging to do so.

    Whichever limb of s. 22 is to be charged, the elements of the offence are:

- Dishonesty.
  The test of dishonesty is the same as that for theft (*R v Ghosh* (1982) 75 Cr App R 154; refer to Theft, above (*Archbold*, 21-24; *Blackstone's CP 2005*, B4.37).
- Stolen goods.
  Evidence may be from the loser of the property or by proof of the conviction of the thief under s. 75 of the Police and Criminal Evidence Act 1984 (*Archbold*, 9-83; *Blackstone's CP 2005*, F11.2). Consider identification of the goods and continuity evidence between the goods identified by the loser and those recovered from the defendant.

    Circumstantial evidence may also be sufficient. Evidence may be given of the circumstances in which the accused came into possession of the goods, such as the time when the goods were received (see the doctrine of recent possession, *Archbold*, 21-319; *Blackstone's CP 2005*, F3.29), the price paid (if any), the state of the property, the identity of the seller, and the circumstance in which the goods were offered.

An admission by the accused that he knew or believed the goods to be stolen is not sufficient to prove that the goods were in fact stolen, but his admissions as to how he came by the property may provide the necessary proof that they were stolen (*Archbold*, 21-295; *Blackstone's CP 2005*, B4.133, B4.147, and F15.12).

- Knowledge or belief that goods were stolen.
  You must prove that the accused knew or believed that the goods were stolen. The accused may be said to know that goods are stolen when someone with first-hand knowledge—such as the thief—tells him. Belief is something short of knowledge. Thus an accused will believe that the goods are stolen if his state of mind is such that, with the knowledge he has, there can be no other reasonable conclusion except that the property is stolen. If, despite the circumstances, the accused still refuses to believe what should be obvious, this still amounts to a belief that the goods are stolen. Suspicion that goods are stolen is not enough, even when coupled with the fact that an accused shut his eyes to the circumstances—although those matters may be taken into account by a court when deciding whether or not an accused had the necessary knowledge or belief. Mere suspicion is not sufficient.

Undertaking or assisting in the retention, removal, disposal, or realization of stolen goods by or for the benefit of another person, or arranging to do so

For this limb of the offence you must also prove that the accused's conduct was by or for the benefit of another.

Charging considerations

- When it is not clear whether the offence committed was by way of receiving stolen goods, or by way of undertaking or assisting in the retention, etc., of the property, it is permissible to charge both forms of handling in one charge. If, on the other hand, it is clear that the accused could only have handled the stolen goods in one form, then only that particular limb of s. 22 should be charged.
- When the evidence is such that the accused could be either a thief or a handler of stolen goods, it is permissible to charge both offences. Both charges, however, should only be preferred when there is a real and not a fanciful possibility that the evidence might support one rather than the other.
- A theft charge is more appropriate if the defendant did not know or believe the goods to be stolen when he received them, but later discovered they were stolen and then dishonestly kept, or otherwise appropriated, them.
- When the accused is in possession of property that has been stolen over a period of time and there is insufficient evidence to show that the accused was the thief, you should consider charging both theft and handling.
- Use one charge if the property came from several thefts (or burglaries, robberies, etc.) but was all received on one occasion.

- If a number of items of property have been received by the accused on different occasions, you should have a separate charge for each occasion, unless:
  - (i) there is a continuous series of closely linked offences, and it is not possible to show the dates or amounts of individual receipts (*Archbold*, 21-276; *Blackstone's CP 2005*, B4.128);
  - (ii) the evidence of receiving the goods on separate occasions comes from the defendant, and this is not accepted by the prosecution.
- When an accused is found in possession of stolen property some time after the theft has been committed, in circumstances when it is not clear whether the accused is the thief or the handler, applying the decision in *R v Gomez* [1993] AC 442, HL, you may consider charging the accused with stealing the item on a date between the theft and the item being found in the possession of the accused.
- Consider whether the defendant's intention was to launder the proceeds of crime. A money laundering offence may be appropriate when a person has possessed criminal proceeds in large amounts, or repeatedly in lesser amounts where assets are laundered for profit. A person may be guilty of a money laundering offence, even if it is the benefit of his own criminal conduct that he is laundering. The Prosecution need to prove that the defendant knew or suspected that the assets, which he has concealed, acquired, used, possessed, or in respect of which he has entered into an arrangement which he knows or suspects facilitates the acquisition, retention, use or control of criminal property by or on behalf of another person, are the proceeds of criminal conduct, rather than from a specific offence or class of offences. The criminal conduct may have been committed anywhere in the world, provided that the original conduct would be illegal if it had been committed in the United Kingdom. For money laundering offences committed after 23 February 2003, please refer to ss. 327, 328, 329, and 340(3)(b) of the Proceeds of Crime Act 2002 (*Archbold*, 33-11, 33-12, 33-13, and 33-29; *Blackstone's CP 2005*, B22.8, B22.9, B22.12, and B22.14, respectively) and refer to Money Laundering on the CPS website. Money laundering committed after 23 February 2003 is a lifestyle offence, and the police financial investigator will need to prepare a report on a defendant's assets and expenses over the previous six years to determine whether an application for a confiscation order is appropriate.

Examples when a charge of handling stolen goods would be appropriate

- When the accused buys goods in a public house at an absurdly low price and the origin of the property has been disguised by obscuring or removing any identification mark or serial number.
- When the accused takes possession of stolen goods late at night, which have been delivered covertly to his premises.
- When the accused stores or arranges to store stolen goods on behalf of the thief or burglar.
- When an accused disposes of stolen goods on behalf of the thief.

Example when it would not be appropriate to charge handling goods

- When an accused purchases goods innocently and later realizes the goods are stolen. If he subsequently sells them, he may commit an offence of obtaining money by deception from the purchaser.

Attempts

A person may dishonestly handle goods which he believes to be stolen but which are either not stolen, or cannot be proved to be stolen. See s. 1 of the Criminal Attempts Act 1981 (*Archbold*, 34-84; *Blackstone's CP 2005*, A6.40) and *R v Shivpuri* [1987] AC 1 (*Archbold*, 25-463).

In these circumstances, a charge of attempted handling may be appropriate. This should be considered where the property is mass-produced goods, such as a car radio or a mobile phone, for which there is an illicit trade and no recognizable owner.

Section 27(3) of the Theft Act 1968—Citing of Previous Convictions

This section allows for admittance of previous convictions of theft and handling, five years preceding the date of the current offence, in order to prove guilty knowledge.

It can only be used when handling is the only charge that a defendant is facing, and notice must be served seven days prior to trial of the intention to prove the previous conviction (*Archbold*, 21-313 to 21-318; *Blackstone's CP 2005*, F12.32).

Robbery, Contrary to s. 8(1) of the 1968 Act

(*Archbold*, 21-85; *Blackstone's CP 2005*, B4.46)

The offence is committed when a person steals and, immediately before or at the time of doing so and in order to do so, he uses force on any person, or puts or seeks to put any person in fear of being then and there subject to force.

Robbery is an offence triable only on indictment. The maximum penalty on conviction is imprisonment for life.

The elements of the offence are:

- Steals.
  This means theft in accordance with the provisions of s. 1 of the 1968 Act.
- The use of force against the person.
  The force must be immediately before or at the time of the stealing and for the purposes of stealing. Force used after a theft is complete will not amount to a robbery, although that force may constitute a separate criminal act. The force must also be used against the person. Whether force has been used against a person is a matter of fact to be determined according to the circumstances of each case.
- Puts or seeks to put anyone in fear.
  The threat of use of force against the person must also be made immediately before or at the time of the stealing and for the purpose of stealing. Where threats of force are used they must amount to threats of then and there subjecting the victim, or some other person, to force.

Examples when a charge of robbery would be appropriate

- When a handbag or mobile phone is forcibly snatched from a person's grasp, you should normally charge robbery.
- When an 11 year old hands over a small amount of money following threats of significant violence made by an older and physically larger youth, you should normally charge robbery.
- When no force is used or threatened but a weapon is produced or made visible to the victim (on the basis of an implied threat).
- When a car is taken using force or the threat of force and the evidence supports the inference that the offender did not intend the victim to recover the car intact (e.g. the car is not recovered, or is recovered but seriously damaged or burnt out).

Examples when it would not be appropriate to charge robbery

- When a bag has been taken from off the shoulder of a victim without any force being used or threatened on the victim.
- When a shoulder strap is cut and the victim is unaware of this until after the handbag has been stolen.

Charging consideration

When there is no theft, or difficulty in proving an essential element of theft, but there is evidence of the use of force against the victim, a charge of threatening behaviour, assault, or assault with intent to rob may be more appropriate.

Alternative charges

A charge of theft should be considered instead of a charge of robbery in the following circumstances:

- When there is difficulty in proving that force has been used against the victim.
- When the use or threat of force was against property alone.
- When the property was stolen before there was a use of force on the victim. You should also consider separate charges to reflect the use of force against the victim, for example, assault or threatening behaviour.
- When the threats made against the victim amount to threats to use force at some time in the future. You should also consider the possibility of a charge of blackmail.
- When the threats made are to use force against property.

Charges of blackmail, assault, TWOC, or aggravated TWOC should be considered instead of a charge of robbery when a motor vehicle has been taken by the use of force or the threat of force, but there is insufficient evidence of an intention to permanently deprive the owner of the vehicle (e.g. when the vehicle is later abandoned intact).

Additional charges

- When a firearm, or imitation firearm is carried or used during the course of a robbery, appropriate charges under the Firearms Act 1968 should always be preferred in addition to a charge of robbery. See *R v Guy* (1991) 93 Cr App R 108; *Archbold*, 24-49; *Blackstone's CP 2005*, B4.48). This also applies to offensive weapons. It is important that such charges are included on an indictment due to the possible implications for the sentencing of an offender charged with robbery, either on this or some future occasion. See s. 109 of the Powers of Criminal Courts (Sentencing) Act 2000 (*Archbold*, 5-214; *Blackstone's CP 2005*, E1.22).

Attempts

- A charge of attempted robbery will be appropriate when the conduct of the accused is more than merely preparatory to the commission of an offence of robbery. When there is a significant time lapse between the assault and the theft, you should charge assault with intent to rob.
- When force is used against a victim causing the victim to drop property, for example a handbag, and the accused runs off without taking the property, you should normally charge attempted robbery.

Assault with intent to rob contrary to s. 8(2) of the 1968 Act

(*Archbold*, 21-103; *Blackstone's CP 2005*, B4.46)

Section 8(2) of the 1968 Act provides for the offence of assault with intent to rob. The offence is triable only on indictment and carries a maximum penalty on conviction of life imprisonment.

Elements of the offence are:

- An assault.

  An assault is any act which intentionally or recklessly causes another person to apprehend immediate and unlawful personal violence. When the assault is more than merely preparatory to the commission of an offence of robbery, a charge of attempted robbery should be preferred.
- An intention to rob.

  The intention to rob will be a matter to be inferred from the circumstances of the case, including any admission made by the accused.

Charging consideration

- When there is an unsuccessful attempt to rob (i.e. when no property is stolen) following or involving actual violence such as blows being inflicted or the victim is knocked to the ground, you should normally charge assault with intent to rob.

Burglary, Contrary to s. 9 of the Theft Act 1968

(*Archbold*, 21-108; *Blackstone's CP 2005*, B4.54)

Section 9 of the 1968 Act creates two offences:

- Entry as a trespasser in any building or part of a building with the intention of stealing, inflicting GBH, or committing unlawful damage therein (s. 9(1)(a) of the 1968 Act (*Archbold*, 21-109; *Blackstone's CP 2005*, B4.63)).
- Having entered as a trespasser any building or part of a building, stealing, attempting to steal, or inflicting or attempting to inflict GBH on any person therein (s. 9(1)(b) of the 1968 Act (*Archbold*, 21-110; *Blackstone's CP 2005*, B4.69)).

Burglary is an offence which carries a maximum penalty on conviction on indictment of imprisonment for fourteen years and/or an unlimited fine, if the offence is committed in relation to a building, or part of a building, which is a dwelling. Otherwise the maximum penalty is ten years and/or an unlimited fine. On summary conviction, the maximum penalty is imprisonment for six months and/or a fine up to the statutory maximum.

Burglary is an either way offence, except in the following circumstances when it is an indictable only offence:

- it comprises the commission of, or an intention to commit, an offence which is triable only on indictment;
- the offence is committed in a dwelling and any person in the dwelling was subjected to violence or the threat of violence—s. 17(1) of and para. 28 of Sch. 1 to the Magistrates' Court Act 1980 (*Archbold*, 1-28; *Blackstone's CP 2005*, B4.55);
- the accused, if convicted, is liable to a minimum term of imprisonment for a period of three years under the provisions of s. 111 of the Powers of Criminal Courts (Sentencing) Act 2000 (*Archbold*, 5-216; *Blackstone's CP 2005*, E1.30). This applies when the accused is alleged to have committed a domestic burglary after 30 November 1999 and he has two convictions on separate occasions for domestic burglaries, both of which were committed after 30 November 1999, and she/he was 18 or over at the date of commission of the third burglary.

The elements of both offences of burglary are:

- Entry as a trespasser.
  Trespass means entry or presence on the premises without authority, and can include a partial entry, for example by a hand or an instrument through a letter box or an open window.
- Building or part of a building.
  Building includes outhouses or sheds and inhabited vehicles or vessels.

The offence of burglary contrary to s. 9(1)(a) involves the further element of an intention to commit one of the offences referred to in s. 9(2).

The offence contrary to s. 9(1)(b) involves the accused having committed one of the offences referred to in that sub-section.

Examples when a charge of burglary would be appropriate

- When an accused breaks a shop window, reaches through and takes a radio.
- When a thief enters office premises and steals from handbags or clothing.

Example when a charge of theft would be more appropriate than a charge of burglary

- When an accused, who is a customer in a shop, reaches over the counter and steals money from the till or an assistant's handbag.

Charging considerations

- When there are any factual difficulties with the degree of entry, consideration should be given to charging another offence, for example theft.
- Complications may arise when a spouse or partner who has been excluded from the former matrimonial home returns there and takes property. When the issue of trespass is or may be difficult to prove, you should consider charging theft or attempted theft. Remember that the DPP's consent is required for such cases (refer to Consents to Prosecute on the CPS website).
- When an accused has been formally barred from shop premises, the circumstances, which have resulted in the accused being excluded, may not be admissible in evidence on the basis that they result from alleged previous misconduct by the accused. If you form the view that the facts, which led to the accused being excluded, are unlikely to be admitted in evidence, or that it cannot be proved that the defendant knew about the notice, you should consider charging theft or attempted theft. The sentence for such a burglary would be unlikely to be more than for theft. The exclusion notice could be drawn to the court's attention when sentencing for theft.
- A person acting as lookout for a burglar should be charged as a principal with the full offence.
- Offences contrary to s. 9(1)(a) require proof of the specific intent at the time of entry to the premises. In the case of 'intent to steal', this may be readily inferred from the possession of housebreaking equipment. The specific intent to commit GBH or criminal damage may be more difficult to infer in the absence of admissions. In such circumstances, it may be appropriate to charge an offence of GBH or criminal damage assuming there is sufficient evidence. The unauthorized entry would be an aggravating feature.
- When an accused enters premises and removes a motor vehicle it is necessary, in order to charge an offence of burglary, to prove an intention to permanently deprive the owner of the vehicle or of the vehicle keys. If the evidence in relation to the vehicle is consistent only with an offence of taking without consent, burglary should not be charged in relation to the entry to the premises unless other property such as the vehicle keys are taken and not recovered.

Alternative charges

- Being found on enclosed premises—s. 4 of the Vagrancy Act 1824 (*Archbold*, 31-123)—is a summary only offence and carries a maximum sentence of three months' imprisonment and/or a level 3 fine. This charge will be appropriate for an accused against whom there is insufficient evidence of burglary or attempt burglary, but who is found within an enclosed area for an unlawful purpose.

- Theft, GBH, or criminal damage—if the element of trespass required for a charge under s. 9(1)(a) cannot be proved.
- Trespass with intent to commit a sexual offence, contrary to s. 63 of the Sexual Offences Act 2003.
- Going equipped to steal—if the accused is in possession of housebreaking implements.
- Taking without consent, or aggravated taking without consent if the entry to the premises was solely to take a motor vehicle for the purpose of joy-riding.
- Attempted burglary—this may be appropriate if the degree of entry is in dispute, but the circumstances clearly demonstrate that an unauthorized entry to the premises was intended.

Aggravated burglary, contrary to s. 10 of the 1968 Act

(*Archbold*, 21-130; *Blackstone's CP 2005*, B4.70)

Aggravated burglary is committed when an accused commits any burglary and at the time has with him any firearm, imitation firearm, weapon of offence, or any explosive.

Aggravated burglary is an indictable only offence, which carries a maximum sentence on conviction of life imprisonment.

This offence should be charged only when it is clear that the accused had the firearm, weapon, or explosive at the time of the burglary. The relevant time is as follows:

- under s. 9(1)(a)—the time of entry;
- under s. 9(1)(b)—the time of the commission of the theft or attempted theft to the infliction or attempt to inflict GBH.

Charging consideration

- If it is not clear that the accused had the firearm, imitation firearm, weapon of offence, or the explosive at the time of the burglary, you should charge the accused with burglary and consider additional charges of assault and possession of a firearm, offensive weapon, or explosives, as appropriate.

Attempt burglary

Only charge this if there is clear evidence that he attempted entry with the necessary intent.

Alternative charges

- Criminal damage (*Archbold*, 23-1; *Blackstone's CP 2005*, B8.1).
- Going equipped (*Archbold*, 21-324; *Blackstone's CP 2005*, B4.118)

Obtaining Property by Deception—s. 15 of the Theft Act 1968

Specimen Indictment: *Indictment Precedent Manual*.

Definition: *Archbold*, 21-172; *Blackstone's CP 2005*, B5.23.

Use one charge for each obtaining, but there can be more than one representation in each charge.

You should generally have direct evidence from the person deceived to prove that the deception operated on their mind. This can be inferred however (*Archbold*, 21-198; *Blackstone's CP 2005*, B5.10).

It is generally not possible to deceive a machine. Where a computer is involved, an offence under the Computer Misuse Act 1990 may be appropriate if it is not possible to show a conspiracy to (defraud); s. 1 of the Theft Act may also apply (*Blackstone's CP 2005*, B5.4).

Attempt deception

Consider attempt if the deception is not operative because the victim knows it is false, or does not rely on it.

Deception: existing, not future facts

The deception must relate to an existing fact, not a future one. However, a deception can relate to a present intention as to future events. For example,

- 'by falsely representing that A then intended to give B £100 within 28 days' is acceptable but;
- 'by falsely representing that A would give B £100 within 28 days' is not (*Archbold*, 21-183; *Blackstone's CP 2005*, B5.11).

Obtaining Property by Deception: Overlap with Theft

In many cases obtaining property by deception will also be theft (*R v Gomez* [1993] AC 442, HL and *Archbold*, 21-179; *Blackstone's CP 2005*, B5.16).

Consider:

- Theft carries a lower minimum sentence.
- A charge should describe what actually happened and reflect the true criminality.
- The indictment or charges should be as simple as reasonably possible.

Generally, charge an obtaining of property by deception under s. 15, not as theft.

Charge theft when a defendant has swapped price labels on an item to buy it cheaper. This avoids the argument that where the ticket is a bar code read by a machine, there was no deception operating on the mind of the till operator.

Obtaining Property by Deception: Use of Cheques and Cheque Cards

A person using a cheque implies two representations:

- he/she has an account with the bank;
- the existing state of the account is such that in ordinary course the cheque will be met (*Archbold*, 21-187; *Blackstone's CP 2005*, B5.11).

Where the cheque is backed with a cheque card, there is also an implied representation that he/she has authority to bind the bank to honour the cheque.

If a cheque is not met on presentation, the implied representation that it will be met is not necessarily false just because there are no funds in the account. Consider:

- Was there an overdraft facility?
- Can the defendant say he intended to put sufficient funds in before the cheque was presented? (Especially if the cheque is post-dated.)
- Can we prove dishonesty, as opposed to commercial misjudgement?

If a stolen cheque or card is used, but the property in goods has passed or services have been performed before the cheque or credit card is tendered, consider a charge of evading liability by deception under s. 2(1)(b) of the Theft Act 1978 (*Archbold*, 21-343; *Blackstone's CP 2005*, B5.58).

If the cheque is stolen, and the recipient knows it is, consider:

- Theft or handling of the cheque.
- Conspiracy.
- Making or using a forged instrument.

Obtaining Property by Deception: use of Credit Cards

Similar principles apply as to the use of cheques (*Archbold*, 21-194; *Blackstone's CP 2005*, B5.9).

Obtaining Property by Deception: Credit Sale and Hire Purchase Agreements

If the defendant has obtained property by giving false details in a credit agreement, it is simplest to charge under s. 15.

You should:

- examine the agreement; and
- set out all the false particulars in the charge.

Obtaining a Money Transfer by Deception—s. 15A of the Theft Act 1968 (as Amended by the Theft (Amendment) Act 1996, s. 1)

Specimen Indictment: *Indictment Precedent Manual*.

Definition: *Archbold*, 21-213; *Blackstone's CP 2005*, B5.30.

Unlike obtaining property by deception and theft, you do not have to prove intent permanently to deprive. (It is likely that such an intent will be involved, however.)

The transfer is usually done by:

- cheque; or
- telegraphic transfer; or
- clearing House Automated Payment System ('CHAPS') order.

In some cases, e.g. a mortgage loan, the advance may be paid into the account of a third party (e.g. a solicitor acting for the building society) for onward payment to the vendor of the property. This does not affect the wording of the charge.

Obtaining Services by Deception—s. 1 of the Theft Act 1978

Specimen Indictment: *Indictment Precedent Manual*.
 Definition: *Archbold*, 21-341; *Blackstone's CP 2005*, B5.51.

Evasion of Liability by Deception—s. 2 of the Theft Act 1978

Specimen Indictment: *Indictment Precedent Manual*.
 Definition: *Archbold*, 21-343; *Blackstone's CP 2005*, B5.58.
 Section 2 of the Theft Act 1978 creates three offences.
 You need evidence to prove an intent permanently to evade liability for all of them (*Archbold*, 21-346; *Blackstone's CP 2005*, B5.64).
 Examples:

- s. 2(1)(a)—Smith borrows £1,000 from Jones and then dishonestly tells him that he has been made redundant and cannot repay. Jones tells him he need not repay.
- s. 2(1)(b)—Smith borrows £1,000 from Jones to be repaid in a month. He never intends to repay and dishonestly gives Jones a cheque, which he knows will not be met.
- s. 2(1)(c)—a man waves a library card at a ticket inspector at a railway station. The inspector lets him through, believing he has a valid ticket.

Obtaining a Pecuniary Advantage by Deception—s. 16 of the Theft Act 1968

Specimen Indictment: *Indictment Precedent Manual*.
 Definition: *Archbold*, 21-215; *Blackstone's CP 2005*, B5.35.
 Sometimes this offence will overlap with s. 15 or s. 15A. When it does, charge one of those sections. They are much simpler.

Making off without Payment—s. 3 of the Theft Act 1978

Specimen Indictment: *Indictment Precedent Manual*.
 Definition: *Archbold*, 21-349; *Blackstone's CP 2005*, B5.68.
 For theft, the dishonesty and the appropriation must coincide in time. Sometimes it is not possible to prove this.
 Consider a charge of making off without payment if, e.g.:

- defendant fills up his car with petrol and drives off without paying;
- defendant has a meal in a restaurant and walks out without paying.

False Accounting—s. 17 of the Theft Act 1968

Specimen Indictment: *Indictment Precedent Manual*.

Definition: *Archbold*, 21-226; *Blackstone's CP 2005*, B6.3.

False accounting: no intent permanently to deprive needed

You need to prove defendant had a view to gain for himself or another, or intent to cause loss to another.

This gain or loss can be temporary or permanent, so you do not need to prove an intent permanently to deprive, as you do with theft or s. 15 obtaining property by deception (*Archbold*, 21-234; *Blackstone's CP 2005*, B6.13).

For example, a solicitor with a cash flow problem dishonestly 'borrows' money by transferring it from his client account, where it is held in trust, to his office account to pay staff salaries. He creates false bills to conceal the fraud from his staff and the auditors. After six months he is able to repay the money and does so. False accounting, not theft, would be the proper charge.

False accounting: evidence of accounting purpose

You need to prove that the item was required for an accounting purpose. You should request evidence of the actual use of the document if possible, as only a little evidence of this may make the difference between conviction and acquittal (*R v Sundhers* [1998] Crim LR 497 and *Archbold*, 21-232; *Blackstone's CP 2005*, B6.9); though it may be open to the court to find this without such evidence (*R v Manning* [1998] 2 Cr App R 461, CA).

False Accounting: Overlap with Theft

Generally you should decide whether false accounting or theft is more suitable, and only charge one offence for each transaction.

Occasionally it may be best to charge both if a temporary gain could be the intent (*R v Eden* (1971) 55 Cr App R 193 and *Archbold*, 21-238; *Blackstone's CP 2005*, B6.8), but consider:

- the need to keep matters simple;
- both false accounting and theft carry seven years' imprisonment maximum.

Procuring the Execution of a Valuable Security by Deception

Specimen Indictment: *Indictment Precedent Manual*.

Definition: *Archbold*, 21-243; *Blackstone's CP 2005*, B5.43.

'Execution' means doing something to the face of the document, e.g. signing it, or carrying out formalities to make it valid. It does not mean an act which merely carries out the instructions on the document, e.g. delivering goods or paying money (*R v Kassim* [1992] 1 AC 9, HL and *Archbold*, 21-252; *Blackstone's CP 2005*, B5.48).

If a s. 15 offence can be proved, charge that, as it is simpler.

Obtaining advances from banks and building societies (including mortgage advances) should generally be charged under s. 15A.

Taking a Vehicle without the Owner's Consent/Aggravated Vehicle Taking

Refer to Driving Offences, incorporating the Charging Standard in Chapter 8 of this book.

CODE FOR CROWN PROSECUTORS—PUBLIC INTEREST CONSIDERATIONS

Offences Triable only on Indictment

The Theft Acts create serious offences of dishonesty, including robbery, aggravated burglary, and blackmail, as well as less serious offences such as theft of items of small value. Only in exceptional circumstances will it not be in the public interest to prosecute offences, which are triable only on indictment.

Arguments over Ownership of Property Including Arguments between Spouses or other Domestic Relationships

The criminal law may be an unsuitable method to regulate such disputes. However, situations will arise where the issues are clear and the offences are serious. If so, do not exclude the possibility of prosecution simply because the offence arose out of a dispute over ownership of the property.

Check before the trial whether the parties have reconciled their disputes. This may affect both the evidential and the public interest test. In such cases prosecutors should also ensure familiarity with the Domestic Violence Guidance for Prosecutors.

Section 80 of the Police and Criminal Evidence Act 1984 governs the compellability of spouses in criminal proceedings. The Prosecution cannot currently compel a spouse to give evidence for Theft Act offences (*Archbold*, **8-46**; *Blackstone's CP 2005*, F4.11).

The Director's consent is required for a prosecution of a husband or wife for stealing the property of his or her spouse (and the inchoate offences) unless:

1. the husband and wife are jointly charged with committing the offence; or
2. by virtue of any judicial decree the offender and spouse are under no obligation to cohabit at the time of the offence.

The consent can be given locally and the case does not need referring to Headquarters (refer to Consents to Prosecute on the CPS website and *Archbold*, **21-334**; *Blackstone's CP 2005*, D1.73).

Loss to a Third Party

Where there is a domestic relationship between the victim and the offender, there may also be a loss to a third party, e.g. where a son steals his father's credit card and uses it to obtain goods from a store. There may be a public interest in a prosecution for obtaining the goods, even in circumstances where there is no prosecution for theft of the card.

Borderline Cases between Civil and Criminal Liability

These sometimes amount to little more than non-payment of a civil liability, or a dispute over ownership of property. Consider these public interest factors:

- Are there civil law concepts which will be difficult for the jury, such as contractual obligations or constructive trusts?
- Does the complainant have a clear and adequate remedy in civil law?
- Is it best left to the civil courts to establish liability or ownership?

(See also *Archbold*, 21-336; *Blackstone's CP 2005*, F9.14.)

Breach of Trust

This is a factor in favour of prosecution. It most commonly arises when the offender is an employee of the victim (although it may arise in other contexts, such as theft by a carer from someone in their care). Consider:

- The seniority of the defendant within any relevant organization.
- The degree of trust placed in him or her.
- The period of time during which the trust has been abused.
- The degree of suspicion cast on fellow employees or partners.
- The extent of the loss or gain.
- The extent to which the offender has sought to hide their activities.
- The impact of the offence on the public and public confidence.

An employer may have an ulterior motive in making a complaint. Consider:

- Has the conduct been tacitly condoned over a period of time?
- Is there an ongoing dispute between the employer and employee?

Reparation

Consider:

- Whether the payment was a spontaneous and genuine act of remorse.
- The gravity of the offence.
- The extent of the loss.
- Whether the loss can be adequately compensated for in money.

Offenders must not avoid prosecution simply because they can pay compensation.

ANNEX A

1st September 2004

Dear Chief Officer

POLICING PRIORITIES FOR FRAUD CASES

A working group on which the Serious Fraud Office, Home Office, Crown Prosecution Service, Department of Trade and Industry, and police were represented has drawn up the following list of priorities to be taken into account by the police when deciding whether to accept a fraud case for investigation. These priorities are not specific rules governing which cases the police will accept, nor are they intended to be exhaustive, or ranked in any particular order. Nothing in these guidelines should be taken as preventing the police from investigating any case that they consider it appropriate to investigate.

Fraud encompasses a wide variety of offences. For the purposes of these priorities, 'fraud' is being taken as including:

- theft;
- all offences of deception under the Theft Acts;
- forgery and counterfeiting offences;
- other documentary frauds, such as false accounting;
- fraudulent trading;
- insider dealing;
- offences under the Financial Services and Markets Act relating to misleading market practices;
- conspiracy to defraud.

We recognize that police fraud squads usually also investigate allegations of corruption. The priorities set out here have been identified as relevant when considering how to pursue an allegation of one of the types of offences set out above. Further consideration is being given to appropriate priorities for corruption cases.

The decision on whether to investigate an allegation of fraud, and on the resources to be devoted to any investigation, rests solely with the police. The police will only investigate in circumstances where there are good grounds to believe that a criminal offence has been committed. In some cases, some form of preliminary inquiry may assist the police in determining whether the case is suitable for a full investigation. In making this decision, the police will have regard to the resources available, government and local policing priorities, and the competing priorities of other fraud and criminal cases already under investigation as well as the priorities set out below.

The police will need cooperation and support from victims at all stages of investigation and prosecution. Victims will need to identify and preserve original documents and provide them to the police if necessary.

Priorities

- Frauds involving substantial sums of money. (NB: Cases meeting the acceptance criteria of the SFO may be referred directly to the SFO, either by the victim or the police.)
- Frauds having a significant impact on the victim(s). A negligible loss to a large company, for example, could be catastrophic for a private individual or small business.
- Frauds affecting particularly vulnerable victims (e.g. the elderly, people with disabilities, businesses providing key services in difficult circumstances) or in distinct communities.
- Frauds giving rise to significant public concern (possibly highlighted by a high degree of press interest).
- Frauds committed by, or knowingly facilitated by, professional advisers (e.g. lawyers, accountants, merchant bankers).
- Frauds likely to undermine confidence in leading UK institutions or otherwise undermine the economy.
- Frauds committed by members of Boards or other senior managers.
- Frauds where law enforcement action could have a material deterrent effect.
- Frauds which indicate a risk of more substantial/extensive fraud occurring.
- Cases where the victim has devoted significant resources to fraud prevention, or has been willing to participate in appropriate crime prevention partnerships or otherwise assist the police.
- Frauds which it has been agreed should be a current law enforcement priority.

Cases Where a More Cautious Approach Might be Appropriate

- Cases where the victim's motive for making the complaint appears to be malicious, primarily focused on recovering monies owed, or designed to distract attention from the complainant's own involvement in the fraud. (Such cases might nevertheless merit investigation, particularly where there are other victims involved.)
- Cases where victims are not prepared to cooperate fully with investigation and prosecution, although the police will always consider carefully how to assist victims and witnesses who have concerns about safety.
- Frauds more suitable for investigation by another enforcement or regulatory agency.
- Cases where another police force has decided not to investigate other than for geographical reasons.
- Frauds that have already been investigated by the police or other enforcement agency, or that have been the subject of regulatory proceedings, unless significant new evidence has come to light or the previous investigation had a narrow remit that did not address all the relevant issues.
- Cases where the existence of other proceedings might have a detrimental effect on a criminal investigation and subsequent prosecution.

- Frauds where the victim's conduct has contributed to the loss, in particular where the police have previously given guidance or warnings to victims about fraud risks that have not been acted upon.
- Frauds which took place a long time ago (probably more than 2 years) unless there are exceptional circumstances.
- Frauds where the likely eventual outcome, in terms of length of sentence and/or financial penalty, is not sufficient to justify the likely cost and effort of the investigation.

Note: Police forces have a responsibility to provide support to the investigation of cases occurring in their respective police areas and accepted by the SFO. In London, the City of London Police will provide additional investigative resources for Metropolitan Police cases and to other forces in the South East under the terms of its regional 'Lead Force' role for SFO cases.

5

Public Order Offences, incorporating the Charging Standard

Public Order Offences, incorporating the Charging Standard

INTRODUCTION

The criminal law in respect of public order offences is intended to penalize the use of violence and/or intimidation by individuals or groups. The principal public order offences are contained in Part I of the Public Order Act 1986 ('the Act'). Reference is also made to the offence of drunk and disorderly behaviour. This document provides guidance about the charge which should be preferred if the criteria set out in the Code for Crown Prosecutors are met.

CHARGING STANDARD—PURPOSE

This charging standard gives guidance concerning the charge which should be preferred if the criteria set out in the Code for Crown Prosecutors are met. The purpose of charging standards is to make sure that the most appropriate charge is selected, in the light of the facts, which can be proved, at the earliest possible opportunity.

Adoption of this standard should lead to a reduction in the number of times charges have to be amended, which in turn should lead to an increase in efficiency and a reduction in avoidable extra work for the police, CPS, and the courts. The guidance set out in this charging standard:

- should not be used in the determination of any investigatory decision, such as the decision to arrest;
- does not override any guidance issued on the use of appropriate alternative forms of disposal short of charge, such as cautioning or conditional cautions;
- does not override the principles set out in the Code for Crown Prosecutors;
- does not override the need for consideration to be given in every case as to whether a charge/prosecution is in the public interest;
- does not remove the need for each case to be considered on its individual merits, or fetter the discretion to charge and to prosecute the most appropriate offence depending on the particular facts of the case.

This standard covers the following offences:

- riot—s. 1 of the Act;
- violent disorder—s. 2 of the Act;
- affray—s. 3 of the Act;
- using threatening, abusive, or insulting words or behaviour causing fear of or provoking violence—s. 4 of the Act;
- using threatening, abusive, or insulting words or behaviour, or disorderly behaviour intending to and causing harassment, alarm, or distress—s. 4A of the Act;
- using threatening, abusive, or insulting words or behaviour, or disorderly behaviour likely to cause harassment, alarm, or distress—s. 5 of the Act;
- drunk and disorderly behaviour—s. 91 of the Criminal Justice Act 1967;
- bind overs.

Offences involving public disorder are often a precursor to, or part of, the commission of other offences. An offence under the Act may, for example, also lead to or involve an assault, unlawful possession of a weapon, or the causing of criminal damage. See Additional Charges and Charge Selection below for guidance on the selection of the appropriate number and type of charges in such cases.

GENERAL CHARGING PRACTICE

You should always have in mind the following general principles when selecting the appropriate charge(s):

(i)   the charge(s) should accurately reflect the extent of the accused's alleged involvement and responsibility, thereby allowing the courts the discretion to sentence appropriately;

(ii)   the choice of charges should ensure the clear and simple presentation of the case, particularly when there is more than one accused;

(iii)   there should be no overloading of charges by selecting more charges than are necessary just to encourage the accused to plead guilty to a few;

(iv)   there should be no overcharging by selecting a charge which is not supported by the evidence in order to encourage a plea of guilty to a lesser allegation.

GENERAL PRINCIPLE: PUBLIC ORDER OFFENCES

The purpose of public order law is to ensure that individual rights to freedom of speech and freedom of assembly are balanced against the rights of others to go about their daily lives unhindered.

RIOT

(*Archbold*, 29-4 to 29-9; *Blackstone's CP 2005*, B11.17 to B11.28)
Under s. 1 of the Act, it must be proved that:

- twelve or more persons;
- present together;
- used or threatened unlawful violence (all charged must use);
- for a common purpose; and that
- the conduct of them (taken together);
- was such as to cause;
- a person of reasonable firmness;
- present at the scene;
- to fear for his personal safety.

For a definition of unlawful violence—s. 8 of the Act (*Archbold*, 29-38; *Blackstone's CP 2005*, B11.24).

For the requisite standard of mens rea—s. 6 of the Act (*Archbold*, 29-35; *Blackstone's CP 2005*, B11.27 and B11.28).

Provided the above conditions are met, each of the persons using unlawful violence for a common purpose is guilty of riot. Others can commit this offence by aiding, abetting, counselling, or procuring the use of violence, e.g. encouraging, planning, directing, or coordinating the activities of those involved in violent action. These should be charged as joint principals.

For additional assistance on drafting the indictment, see *Tyler and Others* (1992) 96 Cr App R 332, CA.

Charges under s. 1 should only be used for the most serious cases, usually linked to planned or spontaneous serious outbreaks of sustained violence.

Conduct which falls within the scope of this offence might have one or more of the following characteristics:

- the normal forces of law and order have broken down;
- due to the intensity of the attacks on police and other civilian authorities, normal access by emergency services is impeded by mob activity;
- due to the scale and ferocity of the disorder, severe disruption and fear is caused to members of the public;
- the violence carries with it the potential for a significant impact upon a significant number of non-participants for a significant length of time;
- organized or spontaneous large-scale acts of violence on people and/or property.

An offence under s. 1 is triable on indictment only. The maximum penalty on conviction is ten years' imprisonment and/or a fine of unlimited amount.

A prosecution for riot or incitement to riot may be commenced only by, or with the consent of, the Director of Public Prosecutions (refer to Consents to Prosecute on the CPS website).

The decision to charge riot should be discussed with the Chief Crown Prosecutor (ACCP in London). CCPs (ACCPs in London) should notify the Director where any charge of riot is being pursued.

VIOLENT DISORDER

(*Archbold*, 29-10 to 29-16; *Blackstone's CP 2005*, B11.29 to B11.35)

An offence under s. 2 is triable either way. It is difficult to see circumstances in which it would be appropriate to represent that charges brought under s. 2 would be suitable for summary disposition. The maximum penalty on conviction on indictment is five years' imprisonment and/or a fine of unlimited amount. On summary conviction the maximum penalty is six months' imprisonment and/or a fine not exceeding level 5.

Under s. 2 of the Act, it must be proved that:

- three or more persons;
- present together;
- used or threatened;

- unlawful violence;
- so that the conduct of them (taken together) would cause;
- a person of reasonable firmness;
- present at the scene;
- to fear for his or her personal safety.

For the requisite standard of mens rea—s. 6 of the Act (**Archbold, 29-35; Blackstone's CP 2005, B11.36**).

This offence should only be charged in relation to instances of serious disorder falling short of those elements required to establish an offence under s. 1. Planning may be an important ingredient in a case of violent disorder, but regard should be had for the potential of minor incidents to flare up into serious disorder sufficient to meet the requirements of this section.

The offence may be committed in a public or private place. The relevant conduct may be directed against a person or persons, or against property.

Examples of the type of conduct which may be appropriate for a s. 2 offence include:

- fighting between three or more people involving the use of weapons, between rival groups in a place to which members of the public have access (for example a town centre or a crowded bar), causing severe disruption and/or fear to members of the public;
- an outbreak of violence which carries with it the potential for significant impact on a moderate scale on non-participants;
- serious disorder at a public event, where missiles are thrown and other violence is used against and directed towards the police and other civil authorities.

Whilst three or more persons must have been present and used or threatened unlawful violence, it is not necessary that three or more persons should actually be charged and prosecuted: *R v Mahroof* (1988) 88 Cr App R 317; *R v Fleming & Robinson* (1989) 153 JP 517. The charge must make clear, however, that the defendant was one of the three or more involved in the commission of the offence.

AFFRAY

(*Archbold, 29-18 to 29-24; Blackstone's CP 2005, B11.37 to B11.44*)

An offence under s. 3 is triable either way. The maximum penalty on conviction on indictment is three years' imprisonment and/or a fine of unlimited amount. On summary conviction the maximum penalty is six months' imprisonment and/or a fine not exceeding level 5.

Under s. 3 of the Act, it must be proved that a person has used or threatened:

- unlawful violence;
- towards another;
- and his conduct is such as would cause;
- a person of reasonable firmness;

- present at the scene;
- to fear for his personal safety.

The seriousness of the offence lies in the effect that the behaviour of the accused has on members of the public who may have been put in fear. There must be some conduct, beyond the use of words, which is threatening and directed towards a person or persons. Mere words are not enough. Violent conduct towards property alone is not sufficient for the purposes of an offence under s. 3. For a definition of 'violence' in affray—s. 8 of the Act (*Archbold, 29-38; Blackstone's CP 2005, B11.42*).

The offence may be committed in a public or private place.

The notional bystander test is explained in the case of *R v Sanchez* [1996] Crim LR 572, CA, and asserts that the hypothetical bystander, rather than the victim, must be put in fear for his or her personal safety. Apart from the hypothetical bystander, there must be present a 'victim' against whom the violence is to be directed (*I & Others v DPP* [2002] 1 AC 285, HL).

The level of conduct appropriate for charges under s. 3 will often fall comfortably within the ambit of that anticipated within s. 4 of the Public Order Act. Affray should be considered in circumstances of serious and indiscriminate violence. Examples of the type of conduct appropriate for a s. 3 offence include:

- a fight between two or more people in a place where members of the general public are present (for example in a public house, discotheque, restaurant, or street), with a level of violence such as would put them in substantial fear (as opposed to passing concern) for their safety (even though the fighting is not directed towards them);
- indiscriminate throwing of objects directed towards a group of people in circumstances where serious injury is, or is likely to be, caused;
- the wielding of a weapon of a type or in a manner likely to cause people substantial fear for their safety, or a person armed with a weapon who, when approached by police officers, brandishes the weapon and threatens to use it against them;
- incidents within a dwelling should not be charged as affray merely because a lesser public order charge is not available. Offences of assault are likely to be more appropriate. Affray should be considered in circumstances analogous to those listed above where serious violence is used or threatened, and with due regard to the principles set out in *R v Sanchez*.

The accused must have intended to use or threaten violence, or have been aware that his conduct may be violent or may threaten violence.

The Crown Court is likely to be the more appropriate venue if a charge of affray is preferred.

OFFENCES CONTRARY TO SS. 4, 4A, AND 5 OF THE ACT AND S. 91 OF THE CRIMINAL JUSTICE ACT 1967

There is an overlap in the conduct required to commit any one of these offences. To use this section of the Charging Guidance you should:

- consider which category the behaviour complained of falls into; and
- refer to the relevant paragraphs to identify which offence may be appropriate to charge and prosecute.

Table 1 Elements Required to Prove Offences Contrary to s. 91 of the CJA 1967, and ss. 4, 4A, and 5 of the Public Order Act— Disorderly Behaviour

Drunk and Disorderly contrary to s. 91, CJA 1967	Section 5 of the Act	Section 4A of the Act	Section 4
disorderly behaviour	threatening, abusive, or insulting words or behaviour, or disorderly behaviour	threatening, abusive, or insulting words or behaviour, or disorderly behaviour	threatening, abusive, or insulting words or behaviour towards another person
In any public place	in a public or private place (but not when confined to a dwelling house—see footnote)	in a public or private place (but not when confined to a dwelling house—see footnote)	in a public or private place (but not when confined to a dwelling house—see footnote)
while drunk	with intention or awareness that behaviour may be disorderly; or with intention or awareness that such behaviour may be threatening, abusive, or insulting	with intent to cause and thereby causing	*Either*: with intent to cause that person to believe that immediate unlawful violence will be used against him or another by any person *or*: with intent to provoke the immediate use of unlawful violence by that person or another *or*: whereby that person is likely to believe that such violence will be used *or*: it is likely that such violence will be provoked
	within the hearing or sight of a person likely to be caused harassment, alarm, or distress	harassment, alarm, or distress	

Sections 4, 4A, and 5 may take place in a public or private place. No offence under these sections is committed, however, if such conduct takes place inside a dwelling and the person to whom it is directed is inside that or another dwelling.
   The definition of a dwelling is set out in s. 8 of the Act and discussed at **Archbold, 29-38; Blackstone's CP 2005, B11.53.**

Section 4

(*Archbold*, 29-25 to 29-33; *Blackstone's CP 2005*, B11.45 to B11.54)
   By virtue of s. 4(2), s. 4 can occur in a public and private place but not a dwelling.

The definition of 'dwelling' is contained in s. 8 of the Act (**Archbold**, 29-38; **Blackstone's CP 2005**, **B11.53**). Where common parts (a communal landing) were the means of access to living accommodation, they were not part of a dwelling, even though access was via an entry phone system, and were not part of the living area or home (*Rukwira v DPP* [1993] Crim LR 882).

The following types of conduct are examples which may at least be capable of amounting to threatening, abusive, or insulting words or behaviour:

- threats made towards innocent bystanders or individuals carrying out public service duties;
- the throwing of missiles by a person taking part in a demonstration or other public gathering where no injury is caused;
- scuffles or incidents of violence, or threats of violence committed in the context of a brawl (such as in or in the vicinity of a public house);
- incidents which do not justify a charge of assault where an individual is picked on by a gang.

Conduct which may be capable of amounting to threatening, abusive, or insulting words or behaviour for the purposes of an offence under s. 4 will be more serious than that required under s. 5 or s. 4A.

By virtue of s. 31 of the Crime and Disorder Act 1998, s. 4 is capable of being racially aggravated (refer to Racially Aggravated Offences on the CPS website).

Racially aggravated s. 4 is an either way offence, with the maximum penalty on indictment being two years' imprisonment, or a fine, or both. The maximum penalty on summary conviction being six months' imprisonment, or a fine not exceeding the statutory maximum, or both.

Section 4A

(**Archbold**, 29-34 to 29-34a; **Blackstone's CP 2005**, **B11.55 to B11.63**)

Section 4A carries a greater penalty than s. 5 and is intended for the more directed and persistent type of behaviour required to prove the elements of intent and causation. The evidence of intention may be inferred from the targeting of a vulnerable victim.

Because it carries an equal penalty to s. 4, it may also be considered appropriate for violent conduct beyond the scope of that normally considered appropriate to s. 5.

Where the conduct is directed towards an individual and is so persistent that a restraining order should be sought, then proceedings under s. 2 or s. 4 of the Protection from Harassment Act 1997 should be considered preferable to available offences under the Public Order Act 1986.

By virtue of s. 4(2), s. 4A can occur in a public and private place but not a dwelling.

The definition of 'dwelling' is contained in s. 8 of the Act (**Archbold**, 29-38; **Blackstone's CP 2005**, **B11.53**). Where common parts (a communal landing) were the means of access to living accommodation, they were not part of a dwelling, even though access was via an entry phone system, and were not part of the living area or home (*Rukwira v DPP* [1993] Crim LR 882).

By virtue of s. 31 of the Crime and Disorder Act 1998, s. 4A is capable of being racially aggravated (refer to Racially Aggravated Offences on the CPS website).

Racially aggravated s. 4A is an either way offence, with the maximum penalty on indictment being two years' imprisonment, or a fine, or both. The maximum penalty on summary conviction being six months' imprisonment, or a fine not exceeding the statutory maximum, or both.

Section 5

(Stone's Justices' Manual, 8-27724; Blackstone's CP 2005, B11.64 to B11.77)

Whether behaviour can be properly categorized as disorderly is a question of fact. Disorderly behaviour does not require any element of violence, actual or threatened; and it includes conduct that is not necessarily threatening, abusive, or insulting. It is not necessary to prove any feeling of insecurity, in an apprehensive sense, on the part of a member of the public: see *Chambers and Edwards v DPP* [1995] Crim LR 896. The following types of conduct are examples, which may at least be capable of amounting to disorderly behaviour:

- causing a disturbance in a residential area or common part of a block of flats;
- persistently shouting abuse or obscenities at passers-by;
- pestering people waiting to catch public transport or otherwise waiting in a queue;
- rowdy behaviour in a street late at night which might alarm residents or passers-by, especially those who may be vulnerable, such as the elderly or members of an ethnic minority group;
- causing a disturbance in a shopping precinct or other area to which the public have access or might otherwise gather;
- bullying.

Section 5 should be used in cases which amount to less serious incidents of anti-social behaviour. Where violence has been used, it is not normally appropriate to charge an offence under s. 5 unless the physical behaviour amounts merely to pushing or undirected lashing out of a type likely to cause no more than a glancing blow, minor bruising, or grazing. Such conduct may also be classified as disorderly and suitable for a charge under s. 91 of the Criminal Justice Act 1967 in appropriate circumstances.

There must be a person within the sight or hearing of the suspect who is likely to be caused harassment, alarm, or distress by the conduct in question. A police officer may be such a person, but remember that this is a question of fact to be decided in each case by the magistrates. In determining this, the magistrates may take into account the familiarity which police officers have with the words and conduct typically seen in incidents of disorderly conduct (*DPP v Orum* [1988] Crim LR 848).

Although the existence of a person who is caused harassment, alarm, or distress must be proved, there is no requirement that they actually give evidence. In appropriate cases, the offence may be proved on a police officer's evidence alone.

Police officers are aware of the difficult balance to be struck in dealing with those whose behaviour may be perceived by some as exuberant high spirits but by others as disorderly. In such cases informal methods of disposal may be appropriate and effective; but if this approach fails and the disorderly conduct continues then criminal proceedings may be necessary.

In deciding whether a charge under s. 5 is appropriate, the nature of the conduct must be considered in light of the penalty that the suspect is likely to receive on conviction.

Where there is reliable evidence that the accused was drunk in a public place at the time of the alleged offence to the extent that the accused had lost the power of self-control, a charge of drunk and disorderly behaviour should be preferred where otherwise a s. 5 charge would be appropriate.

By virtue of s. 31 of the Crime and Disorder Act 1998, s. 5 is capable of being racially aggravated (refer to Racially Aggravated Offences on the CPS website).

Racially aggravated s. 5 is a summary only offence, with the maximum penalty being a fine not exceeding level 4 on the standard scale.

RELIGIOUSLY AGGRAVATED PUBLIC ORDER OFFENCES

Part 5 of the Anti-Terrorism, Crime and Security Act 2001 came into force on 14 December 2001. It created new offences of 'religiously' aggravated assault, criminal damage, public order, and harassment. The Act amended Part 2 of the Crime and Disorder Act 1998 so that the existing offences under ss. 29–32 of the 1988 Act described as 'racially aggravated' are committed if they are aggravated by either racial or religious hostility (refer to Racist and Religious Crime in Chapter 11 of this book).

Racial Hatred

Refer to Racially Aggravated Offences on the CPS website.

Harassment

Refer to Harassment on the CPS website.

ALTERNATIVE VERDICTS

The Act recognizes that there may be some overlap between some public disorder offences by providing for the return of an alternative verdict where the offences of affray or violent disorder have been tried on indictment. In these circumstances, the jury may, in finding the defendant not guilty as charged, find him guilty of an offence under s. 4. It is important to emphasize, however, that the offence that is most appropriate to the circumstances of the case should always be charged. An offence of affray or violent disorder should never be charged with a view to obtaining a guilty verdict under s. 4.

The operation of s. 6(3) of the Criminal Law Act 1967 is not affected by the Act. Hence, a jury may on an indictment for riot, return an alternative verdict of guilty of violent disorder or guilty of affray (*R v Fleming* (1989) 153 JP 517). Section 6(3) may also be used where a defendant faced with an indictment charging either violent disorder or affray wishes to plead not guilty as charged, but guilty to an offence contrary to s. 4 (*R v O'Brian* (1992) 156 JP 925).

Similar provisions do not exist for the return of alternative verdicts in the magistrates' courts.

ADDITIONAL CHARGES AND CHARGE SELECTION

At most public order incidents there will often be evidence of other offences.

Each course of conduct should be considered in the light of the facts of the particular case. The following should be considered in deciding which combination of offences should be charged where more than one is possible:

- Where the offence is basically one of public disorder in which other, less serious offences are made out, it may be appropriate to charge the public order offences alone.
- Where there are aggravating features to an assault, such as the use of a weapon, it is likely that an assault charge should be preferred.
- Where a proper reflection of the defendant's conduct would involve charging an assault, that charge should be preferred.
- If loss, damage, or personal injury arose from group activity in which the defendant took part, and there is sufficient connection between his participation and the offence, a compensation order can be made regardless of the nature of the offence charged (s. 130 of the Powers of the Criminal Court (Sentencing) Act 2000).
- If the public order offence is needed as well as other charges to reflect the defendant's conduct then both or all should be charged.

The section below outlines combinations of public order offences and other offences, which may be charged together, and those which are probably best to avoid charging together.

The purpose behind the careful selection of charges is to ensure that wherever possible there is one trial of the issues, and to avoid the risk of witnesses having to give the same evidence twice in different venues.

Charges Relating to Violence Against the Person

Charges of assault that are appropriate to link to those of public order are set out in the chart below.

If there is sufficient evidence to justify a charge under s. 1 of the Public Order Act and an assault contrary to:

- s. 18 of the Offences Against the Person Act 1861; or
- s. 20 of the Offences Against the Person Act 1861;

It will usually be appropriate to charge both. It will not normally be appropriate to charge s. 47 of the Offences Against the Person Act 1861 or common assault contrary to s. 39 of the Criminal Justice Act 1988 together with an offence contrary to s. 1 of the Act.

If there is sufficient evidence to justify a charge under ss. 2 or 3 of the Public Order Act and an assault contrary to:

- s. 18 of the Offences Against the Person Act 1861; or
- s. 20 of the 1861 Act; or
- s. 47 of the 1861 Act.

It will usually be appropriate to charge both. It will not normally be appropriate to charge common assault (s. 39 of the Criminal Justice Act 1988) together with an offence contrary to ss. 2 or 3 of the Act.

If there is sufficient evidence to justify a charge under ss. 4, 4A, or 5 of the Act and an assault contrary to:

- s. 18 of the Offences Against the Person Act 1861; or
- s. 20 of the 1861 Act; or
- s. 47 of the 1861 Act.

It will usually be appropriate to charge the assault alone. In cases of s. 4 conduct, if other victims have not been assaulted, it will usually be appropriate to charge s. 4 in addition to the assault.

Where you have evidence to prove conduct contrary to ss. 4, 4A, or 5, together with a common assault (s. 39 of the Criminal Justice Act 1988), it will usually be appropriate to proceed on the common assault alone. But if the conduct contrary to ss. 4, 4A, or 5 was directed at others who were not victims of common assault, consider charging both.

For guidance on charging for assaults, refer to Offences against the Person, incorporating the Charging Standard in Chapter 3 of this book.

Firearms and Offensive Weapons

If firearms offences can be proved against individuals they should be charged.

Where any type of weapon is carried by those involved in public disorder, this is an aggravating factor to be taken into account in the presentation of the case. The approach to be taken will depend on the following factors:

- the type of weapon concerned;
- whether the weapon was used or its use threatened;
- how the weapon was used;
- the potential for serious injury;
- the time when the weapon was discovered or produced (i.e. was it produced during the incident, or found on arrest).

Where a summary only public order offence is appropriate, but where the defendant is in unlawful possession of an offensive weapon or bladed article, prosecutors should consider carefully whether it might be more appropriate to focus on the possession of the offensive weapon or bladed article (which are offences triable either way) and recount the circumstances of the disorder in presenting the case to the relevant tribunal. If, however, the summary public order offence is itself serious, consider charging both offences.

Where an indictable public order offence is made out you should reflect the unlawful possession of an offensive weapon or bladed article in a separate charge where the evidence is sufficient.

For guidance on weapons' charges, refer to Offensive Weapons and Firearms Offences on the CPS website.

Criminal Damage

Offences of criminal damage are frequently committed during public disorder. Where there is sufficient evidence to support both offences, consider charging both. If, however, the public disorder is serious and the criminal damage is minor, charge the public disorder offence alone. If the criminal damage is serious and the public order minor then consider charging the criminal damage alone. Charge the offence which most accurately reflects the facts

For guidance on criminal damage charges refer to Criminal Damage on the CPS website.

ALTERNATIVE DISPOSAL—BIND OVER

(*Archbold*, 5-323 to 5-324; *Blackstone's CP 2005*, E15.1 to E15.5)

When an incident of public disorder is reviewed, the decision of whether or not it is in the public interest to proceed with a charge will generally include consideration of a bind over as an alternative means of disposal.

Both the Crown Court and magistrates' courts may make an order binding over an individual to keep the peace. An application for a bind over should never be made as a matter of convenience and should not be made in the Crown Court except in exceptional circumstances. A court may be asked to exercise its power to bind over where:

- there has been an outbreak of bad behaviour which is not sufficiently serious to prefer a charge under the Act but which amounts to a breach of the peace;
- there is a danger that the conduct complained of will be repeated; and
- the accused consents to the proposed course of action.

The court may be asked to exercise its power in one of three ways:

(a) by way of compromising proceedings already commenced. Where a decision to prosecute an offence has been made in accordance with the Code for Crown Prosecutors, the circumstances in which it will be appropriate to dispose of the case by way of a bind over will be rare. This should only be done if circumstances have changed since the decision to prosecute a particular charge was made, such as where a witness has not attended but there remains evidence that the defendant was involved in a disturbance. If there has been no change in circumstances then continuation of the original charge is appropriate. Even where there has been a change in circumstances, a prosecutor should be aware of the argument that a dismissal may be a more appropriate disposal. A bind over order is neither a conviction nor properly speaking an acquittal. Victims of offences often feel cheated if an order is accepted for convenience; or

(b) by complaint on summons. There may be a difficulty with this, particularly if there has to be a trial, in that by the time the case has finished there may no longer be a continued danger of a breach of the peace; or

(c) by complaint when a defendant has been detained for court by the police. This will result in bail being imposed in the pre-Bail Act form of 'in his own recognizance of £x' without conditions if the case is not resolved at the first hearing.

Either (a) or (b) should be used if no charge is appropriate. Bind over orders are not convictions and experience has shown that they may be difficult to enforce. These procedures can be useful but should be treated with care.

A suitable case for a complaint might be in a domestic argument where a s. 4 Public Order Act offence could have been charged against one party if it were not for the fact that the incident took place inside a house.

For conduct to constitute a breach of the peace, the conduct must involve violence or the threat of violence. The violence need not be perpetrated by the defendant, provided that the natural consequence of his conduct was that others would be provoked to violence (*Percy v DPP* [1995] Crim LR 714). However, lawful behaviour, even if provocative, may not be sufficient to constitute a breach of the peace (*Redmond-Bate v DPP* (1999) 163 JP 789).

It maybe appropriate to seek a bind over where conduct falling short of that required for a substantive offence under the Act has been committed. If you have identified the case as one which should proceed by way of bind over, then you should pursue the case on the basis of a complaint rather than charge for an offence even though no Bail Act conditions may apply if the case is adjourned.

SELF-DEFENCE

A public order offence may not be used as an alternative to an assault where self-defence is in issue. The law of self-defence is equally applicable to public order offences. If it be proved that the defendant was not entitled to use or threaten violence in defence of himself or another, or of property, a public order offence reliant on that element will fail, as would an assault.

See *R v Rothwell and Barton* [1993] Crim LR 626 and s. 5(3) of the Public Order Act.

(*Archbold*, 29-16; *Blackstone's CP 2005*, B11.42, self-defence and violent disorder)

(*Archbold*, 29-23; *Blackstone's CP 2005*, B11.42, self-defence and affray)

(*Archbold*, 29-32; *Blackstone's CP 2005*, B11.42, self-defence and s. 4 of the Act)

PROCEDURE—PRE-TRIAL

Casework Location

Cases of large-scale disorder of particular local concern, which either involve complex legal issues or have a significant political, or racial, or religious ingredient, should be considered by the CCP (ACCP in London), who will determine where the case should be dealt with. If necessary the CCP (ACCP in London) will liaise with Casework Directorate.

Referral to Headquarters

Major outbreaks of disorder suitable for a riot charge will be referred to the CCP. Where appropriate the CCP will report the matter to Casework Directorate in order that a decision can be reached on whether:

- the Area will deal with the incident out of existing resources; or
- staff from other Areas or Casework Directorate should be seconded; or
- the whole incident should be handled by Casework Directorate.

Refer to Criteria for Referral to Casework Directorate on the CPS website.

6

Public Justice Offences, incorporating the Charging Standard

INTRODUCTION

A large number of offences cover conduct which hinders or frustrates the administration of justice, the work of the police, prosecutors, and courts.

CHARGING STANDARD—PURPOSE

This charging standard gives guidance concerning the charge which should be preferred if the criteria set out in the Code for Crown Prosecutors are met. The purpose of charging standards is to make sure that the most appropriate charge is selected, in the light of the facts, which can be proved, at the earliest possible opportunity.

This will help the police and Crown Prosecutors in preparing the case. Adoption of this standard should lead to a reduction in the number of times charges have to be amended, which in turn should lead to an increase in efficiency and a reduction in avoidable extra work for the police and the Crown Prosecution Service.

The guidance set out in this charging standard:

- should not be used in the determination of any investigatory decision, such as the decision to arrest;
- does not override any guidance issued on the use of appropriate alternative forms of disposal short of charge, such as cautioning or conditional cautioning;
- does not override the principles set out in the Code for Crown Prosecutors;
- does not override the need for consideration to be given in every case as to whether a charge/prosecution is in the public interest;
- does not remove the need for each case to be considered on its individual merits, or fetter the discretion to charge and to prosecute the most appropriate offence depending on the particular facts of the case.

This standard covers the following offences:

- perverting the course of justice;
- perjury:
  - offences akin to perjury;
- offences concerning witnesses and jurors:
  - intimidation—criminal proceedings,
  - intimidation—civil proceedings,
  - offences committed by jurors;
- offences concerning the police:
  - obstructing a police officer,
  - wasting police time,
  - impersonating a police officer,
  - refusing to assist a constable;
- offences concerning prisoners and offenders:
  - escape,
  - harbouring,

- assisting an offender,
- prison mutiny;
- offences concerning the coroner:
  - obstruction,
  - preventing burial of a body.

GENERAL CHARGING PRACTICE

You should always have in mind the following general principles when selecting the appropriate charge(s):

(i)   the charge(s) should accurately reflect the extent of the accused's alleged involvement and responsibility, thereby allowing the courts the discretion to sentence appropriately;

(ii) the choice of charges should ensure the clear and simple presentation of the case, particularly when there is more than one accused;

(iii) there should be no overloading of charges by selecting more charges than are necessary just to encourage the accused to plead guilty to a few;

(iv) there should be no overcharging by selecting a charge which is not supported by the evidence in order to encourage a plea of guilty to a lesser allegation.

CHARGING PRACTICE FOR PUBLIC JUSTICE OFFENCES

The following factors will be relevant to all public justice offences when assessing the relative seriousness of the conduct and which offence, when there is an option, should be charged. Consider whether the conduct:

- was spontaneous and unplanned, or deliberate and elaborately planned;
- was momentary and irresolute, or prolonged and determined;
- was motivated by misplaced loyalty to a relative/friend, or was part of a concerted effort to avoid, pervert, or defeat justice;
- whether the activities of the defendant drew in others;
- was intended to result in trivial or 'serious harm' to the administration of justice;
- actually resulted in trivial or 'serious harm' to the administration of justice.

Examples of 'serious harm' include conduct which:

- enables a potential defendant in a serious case to evade arrest or commit further offences;
- causes an accused to be granted bail when he might otherwise not have been;
- avoids a police investigation for disqualified driving or other serious offences;
- misleads a court;
- puts another person in real jeopardy of arrest/prosecution, or results in the arrest/prosecution of another person;
- avoids a mandatory penalty such as disqualification;
- results in the police losing the opportunity to obtain important evidence in a case.

In cases of any seriousness, a prosecution will usually take place unless there are public interest factors tending against prosecution which clearly outweigh those tending in favour. Although there may be public interest factors against prosecution in a particular case, prosecutions for public justice offences should usually go ahead and those factors should be put to the court for consideration when sentence is being passed.

PERVERTING THE COURSE OF JUSTICE

(*Archbold*, 28-1 to 28-28; *Blackstone's CP 2005*, B14.26 to B14.32)

The offence of perverting the course of justice is committed when an accused:

- does an act or series of acts;
- which has or have a tendency to pervert; and
- which is or are intended to pervert;
- the course of public justice.

The offence is contrary to common law and triable only on indictment. It carries a maximum penalty of life imprisonment and/or a fine.

The course of justice must be in existence at the time of the act(s). The course of justice starts when:

- an event has occurred, from which it can reasonably be expected that an investigation will follow; or
- investigations which could/might bring proceedings have actually started; or
- proceedings have started, or are about to start.

In *R v Cotter and Others*, The Times, 29.05.02 it was held that 'the course of public justice included the process of criminal investigation following a false allegation against either an identifiable or unidentifiable individual'.

The offence of perverting the course of justice is sometimes referred to as 'attempting to pervert the course of justice'. It does not matter whether or not the acts result in a perversion of the course of justice: the offence is committed when acts tending and intended to pervert a course of justice are done. The words 'attempting to' should not appear in the charge. It is charged contrary to common (1990) law, not the Criminal Attempts Act 1981: *R v Williams* (1990) 92 Cr App R 158, CA.

The offence of perverting the course of justice overlaps with a number of other statutory offences. Before preferring such a charge, consideration must be given to the possible alternatives referred to in this Charging Standard and, where appropriate, any of the following offences:

- corruption: Prevention of Corruption Act 1906 and Public Bodies Corrupt Practices Act 1889;
- agreeing to indemnify a surety: s. 9 of the Bail Act 1976;
- making false statement: s. 89 of the Criminal Justice Act 1967, s. 106 of the Magistrates' Courts Act 1980, and s. 11(1) of the European Communities Act 1972;
- using documents with intent to deceive: s. 173 of the Road Traffic Act 1988;

- impersonating a police officer: s. 90 of the Police Act 1966;
- acknowledging a recognizance or bail in the name of another: s. 34 of the Forgery Act 1861; and
- concealing an arrestable offence: s. 5 of the Criminal Law Act 1967.

Perverting the course of justice covers a wide range of conduct. A charge of perverting the course of justice should, however, be reserved for serious cases of interference with the administration of justice. Regard must be had to the factors outlined in General Charging Practice, above, and in Charging Practice for Public Justice Offences, above, which help to identify the seriousness of the conduct.

Before deciding to proceed with a charge of perverting the course of public justice, you should consider whether the acts complained of can properly be dealt with by any available statutory offence, or any other offence mentioned in this charging standard. If the seriousness of the offence can properly be reflected in any other charge, which would provide the court with adequate sentencing powers and permit a proper presentation of the case as a whole, that other charge should be used unless:

- the facts are so serious that the court's sentencing powers would be inadequate; or
- it would ensure the better presentation of the case as a whole; for example, a co-defendant has been charged with an indictable offence and the statutory offence is summary only.

Note that in *R v Sookoo*, The Times, 10.04.02 the court cautioned against adding a count of perverting the course of justice when the conduct could properly be treated as an aggravating feature of the principal offence. However, consecutive sentences may be imposed when the conduct is a separate and subsequent act, in which case a count of perverting the course of conduct should be considered.

The following are examples of acts which may constitute the offence, although General Charging Practice, above, and Charging Practice for Public Justice Offences, above, should be carefully considered before preferring a charge of perverting the course of justice:

- persuading, or attempting to persuade, by intimidation, harm, or otherwise, a witness not to give evidence, to alter his evidence, or to give false evidence;
- interference with jurors with a view to influencing their verdict;
- false alibis and interference with evidence or exhibits, for example blood and DNA samples;
- providing false details of identity to the police or courts with a view to avoiding the consequences of a police investigation or prosecution;
- giving false information, or agreeing to give false information, to the police with a view to frustrating a police inquiry; for example, lying as to who was driving when a road traffic accident occurred;
- lending a driving licence to another to produce to the police following a notice to produce, thereby avoiding an offence of driving whilst disqualified being discovered;
- agreeing to give false evidence;

- concealing or destroying evidence concerning a police investigation to avoid arrest;
- assisting others to evade arrest for a significant period of time; and
- making a false allegation which wrongfully exposes another person to the risk of arrest, imprisonment pending trial, and possible wrongful conviction and sentence.

In deciding whether or not it is in the public interest to proceed, consideration should be given to:

- the nature of the proceedings with which the defendant was trying to interfere;
- the consequences, or possible consequences, of the interference.

A prosecution may not be in the public interest if the principal proceedings are at a very early stage and the action taken by the defendant had only a minor impact on those proceedings.

It is likely that perverting the course of justice will be the appropriate charge when:

- the acts wrongfully expose another person to risk of arrest or prosecution;
- the obstruction of a police investigation is premeditated, prolonged, or elaborate;
- the acts hide from the police the commission of a serious crime;
- a police investigation into serious crime has been significantly or wholly frustrated or misled;
- the arrest of a wanted person for a serious crime has been prevented or substantially delayed, particularly if the wanted person presents a danger to the public or commits further crimes;
- the acts completely frustrate a drink/drive investigation, thereby enabling the accused to avoid a mandatory disqualification;
- the acts strike at the evidence in the case; for example, influencing a vital witness to give evidence/altered evidence/false evidence, or destroying vital exhibits, or frustrating a scientific examination;
- the acts enable a defendant to secure bail when he would probably not have otherwise secured it;
- the acts strike at the proceedings in a fundamental way; for example, by giving a false name so as to avoid a mandatory disqualification or a 'totting' disqualification, giving false details which might significantly influence the sentence passed, giving details which may result in a caution instead of prosecution);
- there have been concerted attempts to interfere with jurors, attacks on counsel or the judge, or conduct designed to cause the proceedings to be completely abandoned;
- a concerted attempt has been made to influence significant witnesses, particularly if accompanied by serious violence;
- the sentencing powers of the court for an alternative offence would be inadequate.

Misrepresentation as to Identity

The most common example is when a suspect provides false details to an officer—whether it involves giving a false name, date of birth, address, or a combination of the three. Usually in such cases the facts of the basic offence (often motoring) are not in dispute.

In the absence of any other aggravating features, it is unlikely that it will be appropriate to charge perverting the course of justice in the following circumstances:

- giving a false name in circumstances in which no one else is exposed to the risk of prosecution;
- the attempt to avoid prosecution is inevitably doomed to failure;
- the misrepresentation is discovered before a significant period of time has elapsed.

In these circumstances, the alternative offences of wasting police time and obstructing the police should be considered, but may not be necessary in the public interest depending upon the nature of the misrepresentation and the circumstances of the offence.

Regard should be had to the case of *R v Sookoo*, The Times, 10.04.02, which cautioned against adding a charge of perverting the course of justice when the conduct could properly be treated as an aggravating feature of the principal offence, and *R v Cotter*, The Times, 29.05.02, which suggests the use of offences other than perverting the course of justice when other individuals are not exposed to risk.

Note that extended time limits apply to some summary only motoring offences and the principal offence can be prosecuted beyond the six months time limit. Note also s. 49 of the Road Traffic Offenders Act 1991. This allows a court to re-sentence an individual who has deceived it about circumstances which were, or might have been, taken into account in deciding whether, or for how long, to disqualify that person.

PERJURY

(Archbold, 28-152 to 28-174; Blackstone's CP 2005, B14.1 to B14.15)

By s. 1(1) of the Perjury Act 1911, perjury is committed when:

- a lawfully sworn witness or interpreter;
- in judicial proceedings;
- wilfully makes a false statement;
- which he knows to be false or does not believe to be true; and
- which is material in the proceedings.

The offence is triable only on indictment and carries a maximum penalty of seven years' imprisonment and/or a fine.

A conviction cannot be obtained solely on the evidence of a single witness as to the falsity of any statement. There must, by virtue of s. 13 of the Perjury Act 1991, be some other evidence of the falsity of the statement, for example a letter or account written by the defendant contradicting his sworn evidence is sufficient if supported by a single witness.

Perjury is regarded as 'one of the most serious offences on the criminal calendar because it wholly undermines the whole basis of the administration of justice': Chapman J in *R v Warne* (1980) 2 Cr App R (S) 42. It is regarded as serious whether it is committed in the context of a minor case, for example a car passenger who falsely states that the driver did not jump a red light as alleged, or a serious case, for example a false alibi witness in a bank robbery case.

In most cases, an offence of perjury will also amount to perverting the course of justice. If the perjury is the sole or principal act, then it will be normal to charge perjury. If the perjury is part of a much more significant series of acts aimed at perverting justice, then a charge of perverting the course of justice would be more appropriate.

A charge of perverting the course of justice cannot be brought simply to avoid the requirements of corroboration of the falsity of the evidence as required by s.13: *Tsang Ping Nam v R* (1981) 74 Cr App R 139, PC.

Perjury by a Prosecution Witness

Proceedings against a prosecution witness for perjury will depend on an assessment of the material effect of the perjured evidence. If a wrongful conviction is believed to have occurred because of the perjured evidence, a prosecution should follow, unless there are exceptional circumstances. If the witness has lied to protect his or her own interests rather than with an intent to pervert the course of justice, a prosecution may be unnecessary.

Perjury by a Defendant

If a defendant is convicted despite giving perjured evidence, the decision to prosecute must take note of the sentence imposed for the original offence. If you think a conviction for perjury is unlikely to result in a substantial increase in sentence, then the public interest probably does not require a prosecution.

Consider also the possible consequences to the original conviction of an acquittal of the defendant on a charge of perjury arising out of the earlier proceedings. You should, therefore, be satisfied that the evidence of perjury is exceptionally strong before instituting proceedings.

Evidence of premeditation is an important factor in coming to a decision on whether or not to prosecute. If the defendant's lies have been planned before the hearing, as opposed to arising on the spur of the moment during cross-examination, the public interest in prosecuting will be stronger.

Where a defendant is acquitted, wholly or partly because of false evidence given by him or her, a prosecution for perjury might be appropriate. Where there is clear evidence of perjury, which emerges after the trial, and which goes to the heart of the issues raised at the trial, a prosecution for perjury may be appropriate. A prosecution should not be brought, however, where it may give the appearance that the prosecution is seeking to go behind the earlier acquittal: see *dicta* by Lord Hailsham LC in *DPP v Humphrys* [1977] AC 1.

Perjury by a Defence Witness

The decision to prosecute a defence witness for perjury partly depends on whether the defendant in the earlier trial was convicted:

- If the defendant was convicted, and there is no clear evidence of collusion, a prosecution would not usually be appropriate.
- If the defendant was convicted and there is clear evidence of collusion between the witness and defendant to give perjured evidence, a prosecution may be appropriate. Where it is in the public interest to prosecute for perjury others involved in fabricating false evidence with the defendant, then the defendant should also be prosecuted, except in exceptional circumstances.
- In the event of an acquittal, in the absence of clear evidence of collusion, the evidential test for a prosecution is unlikely to be met. Where there is clear evidence of collusion, and where the perjured evidence is sufficiently material to the case, then careful consideration should be given to a prosecution.

OFFENCES AKIN TO PERJURY

(*Archbold*, 28-175 to 28-190; *Blackstone's CP 2005*, B14.16 to B14.25)

There are a number of offences akin to perjury in the Perjury Act 1911 which, though not detailed in this charging standard, should be considered, including:

- false statements on oath made otherwise than in a judicial proceeding: s. 2;
- false statements, etc. with reference to marriage: s. 3;
- false statements as to births or deaths: s. 4;
- false statutory declarations and other false statements without oath: s. 5;
- false declarations, etc. to obtain registration, etc. for carrying on a vocation: s. 6;
- subornation of perjury: s. 7.

These offences may overlap with other criminal offences, such as forgery or deception. The more flagrant the breach of the appropriate section of this Act, the more likely it will be that the defendant should be prosecuted for an offence under the Act as well as any other offences that arise.

Where the false evidence is tendered in written form under:

- s. 9 of the Criminal Justice Act 1967, an offence is committed under s. 89 of that Act;
- s. 5 of the Magistrates' Courts Act 1980, an offence is committed under s. 106 of that Act.

The Perjury Act does not cover making an untrue statement to obtain a passport. It is an offence contrary to s. 36 of the Criminal Justice Act 1925, and you will have discretion whether to charge under s. 36 or whether to charge for attempting to obtain a passport by deception. Where the defendant has not succeeded in obtaining a passport, you should normally favour charging the offence under s. 36.

OFFENCES CONCERNING WITNESSES AND JURORS

Intimidating or Harming Witnesses and Others—Criminal Proceedings

(*Archbold*, 28-142 to 28-150a; *Blackstone's CP 2005*, B14.34)

Attempts are often made to threaten or persuade a witness not to give evidence, or to give evidence in a way that is favourable to the defendant. Such offences go to the heart of the administration of justice. If there is sufficient evidence, the public interest requires that normally such cases be prosecuted.

Section 51 of the Criminal Justice and Public Order Act 1994 creates two offences:

- s. 51(1) creates an offence directed at acts against a person assisting in the investigation of an offence, or who is a witness or potential witness, or juror or potential juror, whilst an investigation or trial is in progress; and
- s. 51(2) creates an offence directed at acts against a person who assisted in an investigation of an offence, or who was a witness or juror, after an investigation or trial has been concluded.

The offences are triable either way. In the magistrates' court, the maximum penalty is six months' imprisonment and/or a fine to the statutory maximum. In the Crown Court, the maximum penalty is five years' imprisonment and/or a fine.

Section 51 is concerned with the protection of persons who are involved with criminal, as opposed to civil, investigations and/or trials. The section is not concerned with protecting evidence from being tampered with or fabricated, which may amount to the offence of perverting the course of justice, or one of the other statutory alternatives relating to written or other forms of evidence, referred to elsewhere in this charging standard.

Section 51(1): intimidation of witnesses/jurors

A person commits an offence contrary to s. 51(1) when doing to another person:

- an act which intimidates, and is intended to intimidate, that other person;
- knowing or believing the other person is assisting in the investigation of an offence, or is a witness/potential witness or a juror/potential juror in proceedings for an offence;
- intending thereby to cause the investigation or course of justice to be obstructed, perverted, or interfered with.

Note, there must be an investigation underway at the time of the alleged act. It is insufficient that the doer of the act believes this to be the case (*R v Singh (B) and Others* [1998] Crim LR 582). In a case in which the defendant believed (wrongly) that there was an investigation underway, it may be appropriate to charge him with attempting the s. 51(1) offence.

If a person does an act which intimidates another with the requisite knowledge or belief then he is presumed to have done so with the necessary intent unless the contrary is proved (s. 51(7)).

Examples of the type of conduct appropriate for a charge of intimidating include:

- orally or in writing threatening a witness not to make a statement to the police;
- damaging or threatening to damage the property of a potential witness in such a way that the witness will know or believe that it is linked to him assisting an investigation or giving evidence;
- staring at witnesses waiting to give evidence at court, or at jurors, in an intimidating manner;
- intending to intimidate a juror by following a juror away from the court building before the trial is concluded;
- assaulting or threatening to assault a relative or friend of a witness or juror in such a way that he/she will know that it is linked to him/her giving evidence or trying the case.

There is an overlap between conduct which amounts to an offence contrary to s. 51(1) and conduct which amounts to the more serious offence of perverting the course of justice. Regard must be had to the factors outlined in General Charging Practice, above, and Charging Practice for Public Justice Offences, above, which help to identify conduct too serious to charge as s. 51.

There may be an overlap between intimidating under s. 51 and contempt in the face of the court. A s. 51 offence should be considered unless the court deals with the behaviour as a contempt. When it does so, the court will act of its own motion.

Section 51(2): harming people who have assisted the police/given evidence/been a juror

A person commits an offence contrary to s. 51(2) when doing to another person:

- an act which harms and is intended to harm another person, or, intending to cause another person to fear harm, threatens to do an act which would harm that other person;
- knowing or believing the person harmed or threatened to be harmed (the victim), or some other person, has assisted in an investigation into an offence, or has given evidence or particular evidence in proceedings for an offence, or has acted as a juror, or concurred in a particular verdict in proceedings for an offence; and
- the act is done or the threat is made because of that knowledge or belief.

Note, if (within the relevant period) a person does or threatens to do an act to another person which harms or would harm that other person, with the required intent and knowledge or belief, he is presumed, unless the contrary is proved, to have done so with the necessary motive. (For definition of 'the relevant period', see s. 51(9).)

Harm done or threatened may be financial or physical, whether to person or property. Such cases apart, harm in this context is to be given its ordinary meaning of 'physical harm' (R v Normanton [1998] Crim LR 220). In that case the harm alleged was spitting in the face of the victim. Whilst that amounted to an assault, it was held the impact of the spittle would not, in itself, cause harm as required under the Act.

The s. 51(2) offence is directed at acts committed after an investigation or trial is concluded, and is aimed at those who wish to take revenge against witnesses, jurors, and those involved in the investigation of offences. It is unlikely, therefore, there will be an overlap with other public justice offences.

Examples of post-trial conduct appropriate for a s. 51(2) charge are:

- attacking or threatening to attack the home of someone who provided a police observation point, or police informant;
- attacking or threatening to attack the home or family of a police officer or other witness;
- assaulting or threatening to assault a former juror, or witness who gave evidence;
- scaring customers away from a former juror's business.

Application to set aside a 'tainted' acquittal

Where a person who has been acquitted of an offence is later convicted of an administration of justice offence involving interference with, or intimidation of, a juror or a witness (or potential witness) in the proceedings which led to their acquittal, application may be made to the High Court to have the acquittal set aside as 'tainted'—see ss. 54 and 55 of the Criminal Procedure and Investigations Act 1996. If granted, such an application opens the way to fresh proceedings for the original offence.

Intimidating or Harming Witnesses—Civil Proceedings

Two new offences were created by ss. 39 and 40 of the Criminal Justice and Police Act 2001:

- s. 39 creates the offence of intimidating a witness in the course of civil proceedings. An offence is only committed where an act of intimidation occurs after proceedings have been commenced;
- s. 40 creates the offence of harming a witness in civil proceedings. For this offence the act must be committed after the commencement of proceedings and within a year of proceedings being finally concluded.

The offences are triable either way. In the magistrates' court the maximum penalty is six months' imprisonment and/or a fine to the statutory maximum. In the Crown Court the maximum penalty is five years' imprisonment and/or a fine.

Section 39—intimidation

A person commits an offence contrary to s. 39 when doing to another person:

- an act which intimidates, and is intended to intimidate, another person (the victim);
- knowing or believing that the victim is, or may be, a witness in any relevant proceedings; and
- intending by his act to cause the course of justice to be obstructed, perverted, or interfered with; and
- the act is done after the commencement of those proceedings.

It is immaterial:

- whether the act is done in the presence of the victim;

- whether the act is done to the victim himself or to another;
- whether or not the intention to cause the course of justice to be obstructed, perverted, or interfered with is the predominant intention of the person doing the act.

A witness is defined as a person who provides, or is able to provide, information or documentation which might be used in evidence in proceedings, or might confirm other evidence which will or might be admitted in those proceedings, be referred to in the course of evidence given by another witness in those proceedings, or be the basis for any cross-examination during those proceedings.

There is a presumption that the defendant intended to pervert, obstruct, or interfere with the course of justice if it is proved that he did an act that intimidated and was intended to intimidate another person, and did the act knowing or believing that the person in question was, or might be, a witness in relevant proceedings.

Section 40—harming

A person commits an offence contrary to s. 40 when doing to another person:

- an act which harms and is intended to harm another person; or
- intending to cause another person to fear harm, he threatens to do an act which would harm that other person.

The offence is committed where the offender does the act knowing that the person harmed or threatened has been a witness in relevant proceedings, and he does or threatens to do that act because of that knowledge or belief. The act must be committed after the commencement of proceedings and within a year of proceedings being finally concluded.

It is immaterial whether the act in question is carried out in the presence of the person whom it is intended to harm, or whether a threat is made in the presence of that person; whether the motive set out in the offence is the predominating one, or whether the harm done or threatened is physical, financial, or harms a person or property.

For the purpose of s. 40 a witness is defined as a person who has provided information, a document or something else which was, or might have been, used in evidence in the proceedings, or which tended or might have tended to confirm other evidence which was, or could have been, given in those proceedings, was or might have been referred to in the course of evidence given by another witness in those proceedings, or was or might have been the basis for cross-examination during those proceedings.

For both s. 39 and s. 40, relevant proceedings are defined as proceedings in or before:

- the Court of Appeal;
- the High Court;
- the Crown Court;
- any county or magistrates' court;

which are not proceedings for an offence and which were commenced on or after the date these provisions came into force (1 August 2001).

Interference with Jurors

The common law offence of embracery covers any attempt to persuade a juror to be more favourable to one side or the other. It is generally regarded as obsolete. You should therefore regard allegations of interference with jurors as acts intended to pervert the course of justice. Where the alleged act amounts to the intimidation of a juror or potential juror, you should also consider the provisions of s. 51 of the Criminal Justice and Public Order Act 1994 outlined in Intimidating or Harming Witnesses and Others—Criminal Proceedings, above.

If it is alleged that a jury member has been approached with a view to influencing the verdict, and a full-scale investigation is needed to investigate the matter, the CCP should be consulted before further enquiries are made. This applies whether the allegation is in the form of a request by a trial judge for a police investigation, or arises from any other source.

Allegations of jury interference which do not involve an attempt to influence the verdict but are simply improper contact with a juror should be reported to the judge. He or she can then be reminded of the court's powers under the Contempt of Court Act 1981. Where the alleged interference is such that a full-scale investigation might be considered unwarranted because of the relatively minor nature of the interference, the court's powers to dispense immediate justice under the 1981 Act may avoid the necessity for such an enquiry.

Offences Committed by Jurors

Section 20 of the Juries Act 1974 (as amended)

(Archbold, 28-46; Blackstone's CP 2005, D12.6)

This section creates a range of summary offences that may be committed by persons summoned for jury service. Examples include making false representations for the purposes of evading jury service, or enabling another to do so; failure, without reasonable excuse, to answer questions under s. 2(5), or deliberately or recklessly giving false answers; and of serving on a jury when ineligible, disqualified, or not qualified.

The offence under s. 20(5)(a) of serving when disqualified (for instance because of a previous conviction) carries a fine not exceeding level 5 on the standard scale: all the other offences carry a fine not exceeding level 3 on the standard scale.

Public interest considerations

A prosecution should follow (unless there are exceptional circumstances) where there is clear evidence that:

- a defendant has knowingly made a false declaration as to disqualification by virtue of a previous conviction; and
- is part of a deliberate attempt to serve on a jury.

Where the false declaration is made knowingly, but with a genuine belief that the disqualifying period has elapsed, then you may take the following factors into account in deciding whether it is in the public interest to prosecute:

- what steps the defendant took to clarify the position;
- whether the defendant's belief was sincere;
- how long was the disqualifying period;
- how much of it was still to run.

OFFENCES CONCERNING THE POLICE

Obstructing a Police Officer—s. 89(2) of the Police Act 1996

(*Archbold*, 28-6; *Blackstone's CP 2005*, B2.27 to B2.30)

The offence of obstructing a police officer is committed when a person:

- wilfully obstructs;
- a constable in the execution of his duty; or
- a person assisting a constable in the execution of the constable's duty.

It is a summary only offence carrying a maximum penalty of one month's imprisonment and/or a level 3 fine.

A person obstructs a constable if he prevents him from carrying out his duties, or makes it more difficult for him to do so.

The obstruction must be 'wilful', meaning the accused must act (or refuse to act) deliberately, knowing and intending his act will obstruct the constable (*Lunt v DPP* [1993] Crim LR 534). The motive for the act is irrelevant.

Many instances of obstruction relate to a physical and violent obstruction of an officer in, for example, a public order or arrest situation. This standard only deals with conduct which can amount to an obstruction in the context of an interference with public justice.

Examples of the type of conduct which may constitute the offence of obstructing a police officer include:

- warning a landlord that the police are to investigate after hours drinking;
- warning that a police search of premises is to occur;
- giving a warning to other motorists of a police speed trap ahead;
- a motorist or 'shoplifter' who persists in giving a false name and address;
- a witness giving a false name and address;
- a partner falsely claiming that he/she was driving at the time of the accident but relenting before the breathalyzer procedure is frustrated;
- an occupier inhibiting the proper execution of a search warrant (if the warrant has been issued under the Misuse of Drugs Act, see also s. 23 of that Act);
- refusing to admit constables into a house when there is a right of entry under s. 4(7) of the Road Traffic Act 1988 (arrest for driving, etc. while unfit through drink or drugs).

Regard must be had to the factors outlined in General Charging Practice, above, and Charging Practice for Public Justice Offences, above, which identify conduct too serious to charge as an obstruction, when consideration should be given to charges of assisting an offender, or perverting the course of justice (refer to Misrepresentation as to identity, on page 116).

Wasting Police Time—s. 5(2) of the Criminal Law Act 1967
(*Archbold*, 28-224; *Blackstone's CP 2005*, B14.58)

The offence of wasting police time is committed when a person:

- causes any wasteful employment of the police by;
- knowingly making to any person a false report orally or in writing tending to:
  - show that an offence has been committed, or
  - give rise to apprehension for the safety of any persons or property, or
  - show that he has information material to any police inquiry.

It is a summary only offence carrying a maximum penalty of six months' imprisonment and/or a level 4 fine.

Proceedings may only be instituted by or with the consent of the Director of Public Prosecutions: s. 5(3). Consent may be granted after charge, but must be before a plea of guilty is entered or summary trial. Consent must be obtained before proceedings are started by way of summons.

Examples of the type of conduct appropriate for a charge of wasting police time include:

- false reports that a crime has been committed, which initiate a police investigation;
- the giving of false information to the police during the course of an existing investigation.

The public interest will favour a prosecution in any one of the following circumstances:

- police resources have been diverted for a significant period (for example, ten hours);
- a substantial cost is incurred, for example a police helicopter is used or an expensive scientific examination undertaken;
- when the false report is particularly grave or malicious;
- considerable distress is caused to a person by the report;
- the accused knew, or ought to have known, that police resources were under particular strain or diverted from a particularly serious inquiry;
- there is significant premeditation in the making of the report;
- the report is persisted in, particularly in the face of challenge.

There are statutory offences which involve wasting police time and which should be used instead of s. 5(2) when there is sufficient evidence. For example:

- perpetrating a bomb hoax—s. 51(2) of the Criminal Law Act 1977;
- false report to the Fire Service—s. 49 of the Fire and Rescue Services Act 2004;
- fraudulent insurance claims based on false reports of crime—deception.

There is an overlap between the offence of wasting police time and other, more serious, offences. Regard must be had to the factors outlined in General Charging Practice, above, and Charging Practice for Public Justice Offences, above, which help to identify conduct too serious to charge as wasting police time, when consideration should be given to a charge of perverting the course of justice.

Misrepresentation as to identity

In *R v Cotter and Others*, The Times, 29.05.02 it was held that 'the course of public justice included the process of criminal investigation following a false allegation against either an identifiable or unidentifiable individual'. In that case, the actions of the defendants in making the false allegations amounted to conspiracy to pervert the course of justice. See also *R v Bailey* [1956] NI 15 and *Rowell* [1978] 1 WLR 132, where it was held that s. 5(2) of the Criminal Law Act 1967 could be invoked where police time and resources had been wasted but where individuals (identified or otherwise) had been exposed to the risk of arrest, imprisonment, pending trial, and possible wrongful conviction and punishment that would amount to perverting the course of justice.

Impersonating a Police Officer

Section 90 of the Police Act 1996 (*Archbold*, 22-62; *Blackstone's CP 2005*, B11.16) creates several offences relating to the impersonation of police officers or the possession of articles of police uniform, namely:

- impersonating a police officer (including a special constable);
- making a statement or doing any act calculated falsely to suggest membership of a police force;
- wearing a police uniform calculated to deceive;
- possessing an article of police uniform.

The circumstances of the case may disclose more than one of these offences. It will seldom be necessary to charge more than one offence. You should select the most appropriate.

You should consider the motive of the defendant. Where the impersonation involves a threat to the safety of any person, or to property, or is done with a view to financial gain, then a prosecution should follow.

Refusing to Assist a Constable

At common law it is an offence to refuse to assist a constable when called on to do so. To establish the offence you need to prove that:

- the constable saw a breach of the peace being committed; and
- there was a reasonable necessity for calling upon the defendant for assistance; and

- when called on to do so the defendant, without any physical impossibility or lawful excuse, refused to do so.

The offence is triable on indictment but is rarely used.

OFFENCES CONCERNING PRISONERS AND OFFENDERS

Failing to Surrender to Bail

(Refer to Bail on the CPS website.)

Escape/Breach of Prison

(*Archbold*, 28-191 to 28-216; *Blackstone's CP 2005*, B14.54 to B14.57)

A person who, being in lawful custody either in prison or elsewhere on a criminal charge, escapes without the use of force, commits the common law offence of escape. Where any force is used, the common law offence of breaking prison should be considered. In this context, force can include damage to property such as locks or fences. For sentencing guidelines, see *R v Coughtrey* [1997] 2 Cr App R (S) 269, CA.

Section 39 of the Prison Act 1952 makes it an offence to assist a prisoner to escape. Unlike escape or breach of prison, this particular offence only applies to persons in prison, not, for example, making a remand appearance at a magistrates' court. Section 39 of the Act also makes it an offence to take things into prison, or to send things in by post, to facilitate an escape.

Where the defendant was in custody facing only summary offences (or either way offences where he has consented to summary trial), you should consider the availability of other charges, such as assault or obstruction.

However, where force has been used to break out of prison, the public interest will usually require a prosecution for breaking prison.

In relation to escape, the following factors are among those to be considered before deciding whether to prosecute:

- How successful was it?
- What were the charges the defendant originally faced?
- How carefully planned was the escape?

Where the escape is from prison, a prosecution should normally follow, but you should also consider:

- administrative prison procedures, such as loss of remission; and
- any lack of security, for example, an open prison.

Assisting a prisoner to escape is a serious matter and will usually require a prosecution in the public interest.

Harbouring Escaped Prisoners

The offence of harbouring is created by s. 22(2) of the Criminal Justice Act 1961. You need to prove that the person harboured had escaped from prison, or detention in a remand centre or Young Offenders' Institution, and such provisions are construed strictly: see *Nicoll v Catron* (1985) 82 Cr App R 339; *Moss* (1985) 82 Cr App R 116. The offence, therefore, cannot be committed in respect of a person who escapes from custody whilst in transit to or from prison, or from court, etc. In serious cases, however, an offence of perverting the course of justice might be considered.

When considering the public interest in prosecuting a person accused of harbouring, you should always bear in mind:

- What was the motive for harbouring?
- How serious was the offence for which the escapee was imprisoned?

Often, the public interest will not demand proceedings against a wife or parent who has been put under pressure to harbour a husband or son, especially if the offence for which the prisoner was incarcerated is not serious.

Assisting an Offender—s. 4(1) of the Criminal Law Act 1967

(*Archbold*, 18-34; *Blackstone's CP 2005*, B14.38)

The offence of assisting an offender ('the principal offender') is committed when:

- the principal offender has committed an arrestable offence;
- the accused knows or believes that the principal offender has committed that or some other arrestable offence;
- the accused does any act with intent to impede the apprehension or prosecution of the principal offender; and
- the act is done without lawful authority or reasonable excuse.

It is an offence triable only on indictment unless the principal offence is an either way offence, in which case the offence of assisting a principal offender is also triable either way. The maximum sentence for the offence varies from three to ten years' imprisonment, depending on the punishment applicable to the principal offence: s. 4(3).

Proceedings may only be instituted by or with the consent of the Director of Public Prosecutions: s. 4(4). Consent may be granted after charge, but must be before committal proceedings (indictable offences) or mode of trial (either way offences). Consent must be obtained before proceedings are started by way of summons. It is not an offence to attempt to commit an offence under s. 4.

Examples of the type of conduct appropriate for a charge of assisting an offender include:

- hiding a principal offender;
- otherwise assisting a principal offender to avoid arrest;
- assisting a principal offender to abscond from bail;

- lying to the police to protect principal offenders from investigation and prosecution;
- hiding the weapon used in an assault/robbery;
- washing clothes worn by a principal offender to obstruct any potential forensic examination.

There may be an overlap between the offence of assisting an offender and obstructing a constable, wasting police time, concealing arrestable offences (s. 5(1) of the Criminal Law Act 1967), and perverting the course of justice.

The courts have made it clear that assisting an offender is a serious offence and, if the statutory offence of assisting an offender can be charged, it should normally be preferred over common law offences.

However, the common law offence of perverting the course of justice should be considered when:

- the assisting is aimed at preventing or hindering the trial process (as opposed to the arrest or apprehension of an accused);
- the facts are so serious that the court's sentencing powers for the statutory offence are considered inadequate;
- admissible evidence of the principal offence is lacking.

Assisting an offender is sometimes not an easy offence to prove since it requires proof that the principal committed an arrestable offence and that the accused knew or believed this. In the absence of such proof, other public justice offences, such as obstruction or perverting the course of justice, can provide alternative charges.

OFFENCES CONCERNING THE CORONER

Obstructing a Coroner—preventing the burial of a body

Any disposal of a corpse with intent to obstruct or prevent a coroner's inquest, when there is a duty to hold one, is an offence. The offence is a common law offence, triable only on indictment, and carries a maximum penalty of life imprisonment and/or a fine.

The offence of preventing the burial of a body (indictable only, unlimited imprisonment) is an alternative charge. Proof of this offence does not require proof of the specific intent required for obstructing a coroner.

The offences of obstructing a coroner and preventing the burial of a body may arise, for example, when a person decides to conceal the innocent and unexpected death of a relative or friend, or prevent his burial. Such cases inevitably raise sensitive public interest factors which must be carefully considered.

When the evidence supports a charge of involuntary manslaughter, it may be necessary to add a charge of obstructing a coroner or preventing a burial if the disposal of the body is more serious than the unlawful act which caused the death.

Obstructing a coroner may also amount to an offence of perverting the course of justice. Regard must be had to the factors outlined in General Charging Practice, above, and Charging Practice for Public Justice Offences, above, which help to identify conduct too serious to charge as obstructing a coroner, when consideration should be given to a charge of perverting the course of justice.

7

Drug Offences, incorporating the Charging Standard

Drug Offences, incorporating the Charging Standard

PRINCIPLE

The legal restrictions placed on the use of controlled drugs are aimed at preventing drug abuse. The principal offences relating to the misuse of controlled drugs are contained in the Misuse of Drugs Act 1971 ('the Act') and most of the offences dealt with in this chapter are created by the Act. The primary objective of the Act is the control of the use and distribution of dangerous and harmful drugs. The Act classifies the drugs according to the degree of harm likely to be involved in their use. They are defined as 'controlled drugs' of Classes A, B, or C.

The purpose of the drug offences standard is to ensure that the most appropriate charge is selected for offences covered by the Act. The section provides standard guidance about the charges(s) which should be preferred in order to meet the criteria set out in the Code for Crown Prosecutors. The section does not cover importation or exportation offences under s. 3 of the Act and s. 170 of the Customs and Excise Management Act 1979, which are usually prosecuted by HM Customs and Excise.

The standard set out below:

- should not be used in the final determination of any investigatory decision, such as the decision to arrest;
- does not override any guidance issued on the use of appropriate alternative forms of disposal short of charge, such as cautioning or conditional cautioning;
- does not override the principles set out in the Code for Crown Prosecutors;
- does not override the need for consideration to be given in every case as to whether a charge/prosecution is in the public interest;
- does not remove the need for each case to be considered on its individual merits, or fetter the discretion to charge and to prosecute the most appropriate offence depending on the particular facts of the case.

Adoption of this standard should lead to a reduction in the number of times charges have to be amended, which in turn should lead to an increase in efficiency and a reduction in avoidable extra work for the police, CPS, and the courts.

The standard covers the following offences:

- possession offences:
  - possession—s. 5(1) of the Act,
  - possession with intent to supply—s. 5(3) of the Act;
- supply offences:
  - supplying a controlled drug—s. 4(3)(a) of the Act,
  - being concerned in a supply—s. 4(3)(b) of the Act,
  - offering to supply—s. 4(3)(a) of the Act,
  - being concerned in an offer to supply—s. 4(3)(c) of the Act;
- production offences:
  - production of a controlled drug—s. 4(2)(a) of the Act,
  - being concerned in the production—s. 4(2)(b) of the Act,
  - cultivation of the cannabis plant—s. 6(2) of the Act;

- occupier offences:
  - permitting premises to be used for producing—s. 8(a) of the Act,
  - permitting premises to be used for supplying—s. 8(b) of the Act,
  - permitting premises to be used for smoking cannabis, etc—s. (8)(d) of the Act;
- opium related offences:
  - smoking or using prepared opium—s. 9(a) of the Act,
  - frequenting a place used for opium smoking—s. 9(b) of the Act,
  - permitting premises to be used for preparing opium for smoking—s. 8(c) of the Act,
  - possessing pipes or other utensils in connection with the preparation or smoking of opium—s. 9(c)(i) and (ii) of the Act;
- supply of articles offences:
  - of articles for administering controlled drugs—s. 9A(1) of the Act,
  - of articles for preparing controlled drugs for administration—s. 9A(3) of the Act;
- obstruction offences:
  - s. 23 of the Act.

General Charging Practice

You should always have in mind the following general principles when selecting the appropriate charge(s):

(i)   the charge(s) should accurately reflect the extent of the accused's alleged involvement and responsibility, thereby allowing the courts the discretion to sentence appropriately;

(ii) the choice of charges should ensure the clear and simple presentation of the case, particularly when there is more than one accused;

(iii) there should be no overloading of charges by selecting more charges than are necessary just to encourage the accused to plead guilty to a few;

(iv) there should be no overcharging by selecting a charge which is not supported by the evidence in order to encourage a plea of guilty to a lesser allegation.

Public Interest Considerations: General

The public interest criteria may be prominent in drug cases, particularly where the drugs are of the so-called 'softer' variety and where the amounts involved are small. Among the factors to be taken into account are the following:

- Parliament has not acceded to pressure to 'decriminalize' cannabis; it has been reclassified as a Class C drug.
- The contents of the Home Office cautioning guidelines (refer to Cautioning and Diversion on the CPS website).

AIDS and Needle Exchange Schemes

It is well known that viruses including HIV and hepatitis C can be transmitted between drug users who use the same injecting equipment. A number of schemes have been established to provide counselling and exchange facilities where sterile equipment can be obtained.

These schemes need police and CPS cooperation because those who run and use them will necessarily commit offences under the Act. It is therefore not normally in the public interest to prosecute:

- a drug user retaining used needles;
- a drug user possessing sterile needles;
- bona fide operators of schemes.

Simple possession cases that are based on police surveillance at or near exchange centres should not normally be prosecuted. The need to prevent the spread of serious infections outweighs the normal requirement for prosecution.

Prosecution may be required when a scheme is not being operated properly, for example when:

- the provider of equipment was a party to the supply of drugs;
- the user has committed what may be a more serious offence, such as assisting with the supply of controlled drugs by giving X a needle to inject Y.

The Drug User as a Witness

There is no reason why a user of drugs should not be called as a witness against a supplier (refer to Evidential Considerations: The Drug User as a Witness, below).

GUIDANCE

Charging Standard: General

The Act creates a number of offences, and any one set of facts may give rise to more than one offence. You should ensure that the offence(s) charged is the most appropriate to reflect the criminality of the defendant. For example, in a case where there is a prima facie evidence of supplying, possession with intent to supply, being concerned in the supply and permitting premises to be used for supply, it will be unnecessary to charge all offences. The facts and the defendant's overall criminality require careful consideration before the appropriate allegation is made.

You must avoid more than one class of drug in a single charge. Such a charge would be bad for duplicity (*R v Courtie* [1984] 1 All ER 740; and refer to Drafting the Indictment on the CPS website). Charging cannabis or cannabis resin in the same count is not bad for duplicity (*R v Best and others* (1979) 70 Cr App R 21; **Blackstone's CP 2005**, B20.3).

It is best practice to charge different drugs from the same class in different counts.

Charging Standard: Use of Alternative Charges

Although an indictment should never be overloaded with unnecessary counts, you should always consider the use of alternative counts in cases where the defendant's culpability is uncertain. For example, where the evidence of intent to supply is not conclusive, an alternative count for simple possession may be justified. On the other hand, if the prosecution case is that the defendant is heavily involved in the supply of drugs, a count for simple possession would detract from that allegation.

It is impossible to be prescriptive when deciding upon the use of alternative counts. If a plea of guilty to the lesser alternative count would not be acceptable, you should think carefully before using such a charge.

Alternative counts should never be used in order to 'force' a plea from a defendant.

For further information, refer to Drafting the Indictment on the CPS website, and *Archbold*, 1-112; *Blackstone's CP 2005*, D10.33.

Charging Standard: Joint Charges

As with any offence involving more than one defendant, you must consider carefully the rules of joinder. Drug offences call for particular care where drugs are found in premises occupied by more than one person, or in a car in which there is more than one occupant. Mere knowledge of the existence of drugs is not enough to prove an allegation of joint possession; it is necessary to show that each defendant participated in the offence charged. The prosecution may have to prove either that the drugs have come from a 'pool' from which they all might draw, or by some other means that each defendant is liable as either a principal or secondary party (*Archbold*, 26-69 and 70; *Blackstone's CP 2005*, B20.12).

If you are considering charging conspiracy, then you will need to assess whether a conspiracy is the best way of presenting the case, or whether substantive offences are more appropriate. In cases involving supply where it is difficult to prove specific acts of supply, it may well be more appropriate to proceed by way of a conspiracy count in order to demonstrate the overall criminality of the case. Indictments may contain a conspiracy count as well as substantive counts, but the judge will require the prosecution to justify their joinder, and in the absence of such justification the prosecution will have to elect whether to proceed on the conspiracy or the substantive counts. Joinder is justified where the interests of justice demand it. This may occur where, for example, of three defendants two are husband and wife and there is a possibility of the third being acquitted. Joinder is not generally justified where the substantive counts are merely sample counts illustrative of the way the conspiracy was carried out.

For more guidance for indictments containing conspiracy counts, refer to *Archbold*, 34-41 to 59; *Blackstone's CP 2005*, A6.9 to A6.30.

Charging Standard: Sentencing Considerations

Awareness of the sentencing framework will often be of help when assessing the appropriate charge. You should be aware of the guidelines for cannabis in *R v Aramah* (1983) 76 Cr App R 190 and the basis for sentencing large-scale importation and the supply of certain Class A drugs in *R v Arunguren* (1994) 16 Cr App R (S) 211.

In *R v Arunguren*, the Court of Appeal departed from earlier considerations of street value and stated that weight and purity are to be the guiding factors, in so far as this part of the sentencing exercise in relation to cocaine and heroin is concerned. The court will calculate the weight of a consignment of 100% pure drug and sentence accordingly. The Court declined to give guidance for other Class A drugs such as LSD.

In major drug cases involving heroin and cocaine, you should take into account the information that the court requires for sentencing purposes when deciding on the charges to prefer and the evidence to be led in support of those charges.

You should also take into account the powers that the court may have to make a confiscation order under the Proceeds of Crime Act 2002. See s. 75 of that Act and Sch. 2, para. 1, which specifies the provisions in the 1971 Act where a conviction will bring the defendant within s. 75 (**Archbold**, 5-653; **Blackstone's CP 2005**, E21.3; and refer to Proceeds of Crime on the CPS website).

In the case of an offence contrary to s. 4(2) or s. 4(3) of the 1971 Act, you should also consider the possibility of the court making a Travel Restriction Order (ss. 33 and 34 of the Criminal Justice and Police Act 2001). (Note that the definition of a 'drug trafficking' offence is different for Travel Restriction Orders than under the Proceeds of Crime Act 2002) (**Blackstone's CP 2005**, E23.9).

Where an offender has been convicted of a 'drug trafficking offence' as defined in s. 34 of the Criminal Justice and Police Act 2001, the court is required to consider whether to make such an order, and to state its reasons if it decides not to make such an order.

Charging Standard: Mode of Trial Guidelines

The guidelines should not be used to determine the appropriate charge. They will only fall to be considered once the charge(s) have been decided upon and venue for the trial becomes relevant.

The following mode of trial and penalties apply:

Possession of a controlled drug

Possession of a controlled drug is an either way offence. The maximum penalty depends on both the trial venue and the class of drugs.

- Magistrates' courts:
  - Class A drug: £5,000 fine and/or six months' imprisonment;
  - Class B drug: £2,500 fine and/or three months' imprisonment;
  - Class C drug: £1,000 fine and/or three months' imprisonment.
- Crown Court:
  - Class A drug: unlimited fine and/or seven years' imprisonment;

- Class B drug: unlimited fine and/or five years' imprisonment;
- Class C drug: unlimited fine and/or two years' imprisonment.

Possession with intent to supply

Possession of a controlled drug with intent to supply it is an either way offence. The maximum penalty depends on both the trial venue and the class of drug.

- Magistrates' courts:
  - Class A drug: £5,000 fine and/or six months' imprisonment;
  - Class B drug: £5,000 fine and/or six months' imprisonment;
  - Class C drug: £2,500 fine and/or three months' imprisonment.
- Crown Court:
  - Class A drug: unlimited fine and/or life imprisonment;
  - Class B drug: unlimited fine and/or fourteen years' imprisonment;
  - Class C drug: unlimited fine and/or fourteen years' imprisonment.

Supplying controlled drugs

Supplying a controlled drug is an either way offence. The maximum penalty depends on both the trial venue and the class of drug.

- Magistrates' courts:
  - Class A drug: £5,000 fine and/or six months' imprisonment;
  - Class B drug: £5,000 fine and/or six months' imprisonment;
  - Class C drug: £2,500 fine and/or three months' imprisonment.
- Crown Court:
  - Class A drug: unlimited fine and/or life imprisonment;
  - Class B drug: unlimited fine and/or fourteen years' imprisonment;
  - Class C drug: unlimited fine and/or fourteen years' imprisonment.

Producing controlled drugs/cultivating cannabis

Producing a controlled drug or cultivating cannabis are either way offences. The maximum penalty depends on both the trial venue and the class of drug.

- Magistrates' courts:
  - Class A drug: £5,000 fine and/or six months' imprisonment;
  - Class B drug: £5,000 fine and/or six months' imprisonment;
  - Class C drug: £2,500 fine and/or three months' imprisonment.
- Crown Court:
  - Class A drug: unlimited fine and/or life imprisonment;
  - Class B drug: unlimited fine and/or fourteen years' imprisonment;
  - Class C drug: unlimited fine and/or fourteen years' imprisonment.

(The penalties for cultivating cannabis under s. 6 of the Act are identical to those shown above for producing a Class B controlled drug.)

Occupier offences

Occupier offences are either way offences. The maximum penalty depends on both the trial venue and the class of drug.

- Magistrates' courts:
  - Class A drug: £5,000 fine and/or six months' imprisonment;
  - Class B drug: £5,000 fine and/or six months' imprisonment;
  - Class C drug: £2,500 fine and/or three months' imprisonment.
- Crown Court:
  - Class A drug: unlimited fine and/or fourteen years' imprisonment;
  - Class B drug: unlimited fine and/or fourteen years' imprisonment;
  - Class C drug: unlimited fine and/or fourteen years' imprisonment.

Opium related offences

Opium related offences are triable either way. The maximum penalties are as follows:

- Magistrates' courts: £5,000 fine and/or six months' imprisonment.
- Crown Court: unlimited fine and/or fourteen years' imprisonment.

Section 9A offences

Offences under s. 9A are triable summarily only. The maximum penalty is as follows:

- Magistrates' courts: £5,000 fine and/or six months' imprisonment.

Obstruction offences

Obstruction offences under the Act are either way offences. The maximum penalties are as follows:

- Magistrates' courts: £ 5,000 fine and/or six months' imprisonment.
- Crown Court: unlimited fine and/or two years' imprisonment.

Charging Standard: Possession of Controlled Drug

The offence of possession of a controlled drug is committed when a person is unlawfully in physical possession or in control of any substance or product specified in Parts I, II, or III of Sch. 2 to the Act, and had knowledge of possession of the item even if he did not know it was a controlled drug. This includes anything subject to his control, even if it was in the custody of another.

A person found in possession of one form of drug, believing it to be another form of drug, should be charged with the substantive offence of possession of the actual drug. He should not be charged with attempted possession of the drug he believed it to be.

Crack cocaine is a Class A controlled drug, being a 'preparation or other product containing a substance' which is a controlled drug (Sch. 2, Part 1, para. 5 to the Act; *Archbold*, **26-33**; *Blackstone's CP 2005*, **B20.5**). It is cocaine for the purposes of the Act (*R v Russell* (1992) 94 Cr App R 351).

Cannabis, cannabis resin, cannabinol, and cannabinol derivatives are Class C drugs. The sentence for possession of cannabis is now reduced from five years' to two years' imprisonment; the sentence for Class C has been increased to fourteen years for trafficking, production, supplying, offering to supply, possession with intent to supply, and being an occupier of premises from which drugs are sold. The Policy Guidance states:

The maximum sentence for Class C offences is now the same as that for the comparable Class B offences. Accordingly, it would be appropriate in such Class C cases for prosecutors to seek committal unless there is only small-scale supply for no payment. This reflects the current guideline for Class B drugs.

The Court of Appeal has ruled that the prohibition of possession of cannabis did not infringe a defendant's rights under Articles 8 and 9 of the European Convention on Human Rights (*R v Taylor* [2002] 1 Cr App R 519) (refer to *ECHR Manual*; *Blackstone's CP 2005*, B20.38).

Public Interest Considerations: Possession of Controlled Drug

A prosecution is usual when a case involves the possession of a Class A drug.

A prosecution is also usual for the possession of more than a minimal quantity of Class B or C drugs. You should take into account the general public interest factors listed in the Code for Crown Prosecutors.

Charging Standard: Supply/Possession with Intent to Supply/Offering to Supply

Supplying includes distribution (s. 37(1)) and does not require proof of payment or reward. It must be unlawful, and where required, a controlled drug. For more detailed discussion, *Archbold*, 26-45 to 26-49; *Blackstone's CP 2005*, B20.32 to B20.38.

The definition of supply can be found in *R v Maginnis* [1987] 1 All ER 907, the House of Lords decision: it denotes more than mere transfer of physical control; the recipient is enabled to apply the thing handed over to purposes for which he desires or has a duty to apply it. A return of drugs to the 'trafficker' would be a supply.

In *R v Panton*, The Times, 27.03.01, the Court of Appeal held that the phrase 'supply' includes the retention and return of controlled drugs deposited with a 'custodier' by another person, applied notwithstanding the custodier's lack of consent to the arrangement.

The motive of the supplier is irrelevant and should not be confused with his intention (*R v X* [1994] Crim LR 827). Where two people agree to buy drugs for themselves, it is undesirable to charge one who happens to take physical possession of the drugs with the supply of drugs when he distributes the other's share to him. Although there is technically a supply, it was inevitable that a person convicted on the basis of such a distribution would be dealt with as for simple possession (*R v Denslow* [1998] Crim LR 566).

Where the evidence supports a charge of supplying or possessing controlled drugs of any class with intent to supply, such a charge should normally be proceeded with.

Possession with intent to supply a controlled drug under s. 5(3) of the Act, is a suitable charge in circumstances when a charge of possession would be justified together with evidence of an intent to supply.

As is the case with straight possession, a person found in possession of one form of drug but believing it to be another form of drug and intending to supply it to another, should be charged with possession with intent of the actual drug.

The intent must relate to a future supply of controlled drugs. If the evidence points to past supply, a charge of supplying may be appropriate.

You should always consider whether a charge for past supplying of drugs is more appropriate than a charge for possession with intent. This is particularly important where the evidence to establish a future intent is unclear.

In addition to the supply of a controlled drug, s. 4(3) of the Act creates offences of offering to supply, being concerned in the supply, and being concerned in the making of an offer to supply. An offence of offering to supply can be prosecuted simply by proving the existence of an offer. The prosecution does not have to prove either that the defendant intended to produce the drugs, or that the drugs were in his/her possession.

A defence under s. 28 of the Act will not be applicable as the offence is the making of the offer. In deciding whether there has been an offer you do not have to refer to Contract Law.

- *R v Dhillon* [2000] Crim LR 760: the fact that the drug is different/not controlled/ bogus is irrelevant, as is the fact that there is/was no intention to supply.
- *R v Goodard* [1992] Crim LR 588.
- *R v Mitchell* [1992] Crim LR 723: offer may be by words or conduct.
- *R v Showers* [1995] Crim LR 400: the exact identity of the substance is irrelevant.

The offences of being concerned will cover conduct which is preparatory to the actual supply, although the prosecution must prove that a supply, or an offer to supply, has been made. You must examine the actual conduct of the defendant carefully to decide which offence is the most appropriate.

If A injects B with a drug belonging to B, A is not supplying a drug in contravention of s. 4(1) (*R v Harris* [1968] 1 WLR 769).

However, consider offences under the Offences Against the Person Act 1861 and whether they could apply.

Sections 23 and 24 of the Offences Against the Person Act 1861

(*Archbold*, 19-223 to 231; *Blackstone's CP 2005*, B2.44 to B2.56).

Refer to Offences Against the Person, incorporating the Charging Standard in Chapter 3.

- s. 23: unlawfully and maliciously administer, or cause to be administered to or taken by, any other person any poison or other destructive or noxious thing so as to endanger the life of such person or thereby inflict upon any such person grievous bodily harm. Maximum sentence of ten years, indictable only.
- s. 24 unlawfully and maliciously administer or cause to be administered to or taken any poison or other destructive or noxious thing with intent to injure, aggrieve, or annoy such person. Maximum sentence of five years, indictable only.

Noxious thing is a question of fact and degree for the jury. A substance that may be harmless in small quantities may be noxious in the quantity administered. The meaning of the word is widely drawn. Heroin is a noxious thing, and the fact it is administered to a person with a high degree of tolerance is irrelevant (*R v Cato* (1976) 62 Cr App R 41).

Intent to injure may depend on the purpose for which the noxious substance was administered. Examples of an intent to injure include giving a baby methadone to keep it quiet where the child is born addicted because of the mother's addiction, to facilitate unwelcome advances, etc., as in date rape cases.

Public Interest Considerations: Supply/Possession with Intent to Supply/Offering to Supply

The supply of Class A drugs, their possession with intent to supply, or their importation will almost always justify a prosecution. These are the most serious offences in the Act and will often attract substantial custodial sentences. Circumstances where a prosecution for such an offence is not in the public interest will be very rare.

Similar considerations apply to drugs of Class B and C, although there may be exceptional circumstances where possession with intent to supply a small amount of drugs of these classes need not be charged on public interest grounds. For example, a charge of possession, or even a caution, may be appropriate where two young persons have pooled their resources and purchased cannabis which one shares with the other.

Charging Standard: Production Offences

An offence of production is committed when a suspect has some identifiable participation in the process of producing, by manufacture, cultivation, or any other method, a controlled drug specified in Parts I, II, or III of Sch. 2 to the Act (*Archbold,* **26-28 to 32;** *Blackstone's CP 2005,* **B20.5**).

An offence of being concerned in the production of a controlled drug requires:

- evidence that a controlled drug was produced; and
- evidence of some link between the suspect and the production process (for example, providing suitable premises or equipment); and
- evidence that the suspect knew that a controlled drug was being produced.

You should charge:

- production of a controlled drug under s. (4)(2)(a) when there is evidence of actual participation in the production;
- being concerned in the production of a controlled drug under s. 4(2)(b) when there is evidence of knowledge of commercial production and indirect participation in that production.

Production includes cultivation and, whilst there is a separate offence of cultivation of cannabis under s. 6 of the Act (*Archbold,* **26-79;** *Blackstone's CP 2005,* **B20.45**), a charge under s. 4(1)(a) of the Act of producing cannabis will usually be more appropriate. Technically, production also includes conversion of one drug to another, such as the production of 'crack' cocaine from cocaine hydrochloride (*R v Russell (P.A.)* (1991) 94 Cr App R 351, CA). See also **Archbold, 26-33; Blackstone's CP 2005, B20.42.**

Charging Standard: Occupiers or Managers of Premises

An occupier offence should be charged when the suspect is the occupier of the premises concerned, or is involved in its management.

A suspect is an 'occupier' if, whatever his legal status, he has a degree of control which would enable the exclusion of other people.

A suspect is concerned in the management of premises if he runs them, organizes them, or plans the running of them.

The fact that the suspect is a trespasser or squatter will not be a defence.

The suspect must knowingly permit (wilful blindness may be sufficient, but not mere suspicion), or suffer the taking place on those premises of, either the:

- production or attempted production of a controlled drug; or
- supply or attempted supply, or offer to supply a controlled drug; or
- preparing of opium for smoking; or
- smoking of cannabis, cannabis resin, or prepared opium.

The mere giving of permission will not be sufficient: the activity (smoking) must have taken place (*Auguste*, The Times, 15.12.03).

An occupier offence should be charged when the suspect is an occupier or is concerned in the management, and has permitted premises to be used to facilitate the commission of the offence of producing, supplying, or smoking a controlled drug; for example, the landlord of a public house when smoking occurs, or where the manager of a club has permitted the supply of drugs to take place within the club.

Production or supply of a controlled drug should be charged if the occupier or manager of the premises is a party to the production or supply of controlled drugs on the premises (s. 4 of the Act).

A possession offence should be charged when the occupier of premises is a party to consumption consistent with personal use, for example:

- the host who either smokes cannabis with his guests at a party in his home, or permits them to do so;
- one co-tenant of rented premises knowingly permitting the other co-tenant to smoke cannabis there (see s. 8 of the Act) (**Archbold, 26-84; Blackstone's CP 2005, B20.61**).

Where there is substantive evidence of supply or possession with intent to supply against the principal, an additional charge contrary to s. 8 of the Act will usually be unnecessary. Where an occupier or a person concerned in the management permits others to use the premises to produce, supply, or smoke drugs, such a charge will be proper provided that the requisite level of knowledge can be proved (*Archbold*, 26-87; *Blackstone's CP 2005*, B20.65).

In such cases, the defendant's belief that he had taken reasonable steps to prevent drugs being supplied, does not afford a defence to permitting premises to be used for supplying drugs (*R v Brock and Wyner* [2001] 2 Cr App R 3).

It is not necessary for the Crown to prove more than knowledge of the supply of a controlled drug even where the particular drug is specified (*R v Bett* [1999] 1 Cr App R 361; and see *Archbold*, 26-87; *Blackstone's CP 2005*, B20.67).

Charging Standard: Opium Related Offences

Preparing of opium for smoking, or smoking of cannabis, cannabis resin, or prepared opium, will be encountered rarely, but it is an offence for a person to:

- smoke or otherwise use prepared opium;
- frequent a place used for opium smoking;
- possess pipes or other utensils for use in connection with the preparation or use of opium for smoking.

See *Archbold*, 26-89; *Blackstone's CP 2005*, B20.52 to B20.55 and the possible application of s. 28 as to proof of lack of knowledge (*Archbold*, 26-123; *Blackstone's CP 2005*, B20.19).

(For the offences of preparing of opium for smoking and/or smoking of cannabis, cannabis resin, or prepared opium, refer to Charging Standard: occupiers or managers of premises, above.)

Charging Standard: Supply of Articles

Two offences under s. 9A of the Act are created (*Archbold*, 26-90; *Blackstone's CP 2005*, B20.56):

- to supply or offer to supply articles (other than a hypodermic syringe, or any part of one) for the purpose of administering a controlled drug, where the administration of the drug will be unlawful; and
- to supply or offer to supply articles to be used in the preparation of a controlled drug for unlawful administration.

Any administration of a controlled drug is treated as unlawful, except:

- the administration by any person of a controlled drug to another in circumstances where the administration of the drug is not unlawful under s. 4(1) of the Act; or
- the administration by any person of a controlled drug to himself in circumstances where having the controlled drug in his possession is not unlawful under s. 5(1) of the Act.

Charging Standard: Obstructing a Constable

The intentional obstruction of a police constable, or the concealment of items contrary to s. 23(4) of the Act (*Archbold*, 26-103; *Blackstone's CP 2005*, B20.77) are important offences. There is a strong public interest in prosecuting those who destroy or conceal evidence and thereby prevent the prosecution of others for serious drug offences.

The obstruction must be of an officer exercising his powers to search and obtain evidence. In the absence of such evidence, a charge of obstruction under the Police Act 1996 may be suitable (refer to Public Justice Offences, incorporating the Charging Standard, above).

Charging Standard: Importation

Section 3 of the Act (*Archbold,* 26-26; *Blackstone's CP 2005,* B17.11) prohibits importation and exportation of drugs. The offence of evading the prohibition is contrary to the Customs and Excise Management Act 1979. Most offences will be prosecuted by the Solicitor for the Customs and Excise, and in offences which the CPS prosecute, the consent of the Commissioners is required (refer to Relations with Other Prosecution Agencies on the CPS website).

Evidential Considerations: Proof of Possession

Proof of possession will often be difficult, especially where the drug has not actually been found on the defendant but in a room or car with which he/she has some association. Generally, proof of possession depends upon:

- actual physical possession;
- knowledge.

Section 37(3) of the Act provides that possession includes things subject to the defendant's control, which are in the custody of another. Possession includes the concepts of custody and control as well as physical possession.

The case of *R v Warner* [1969] 2 AC 256 illustrates the following points:

- a person should have possession of the substance rather than mere control;
- a person cannot be in possession of something of which he is completely unaware;
- mistake as to quality is no defence.

A more detailed discussion on the concept of possession can be found in *Archbold,* 26-59 to 61; *Blackstone's CP 2005,* B20.10 to B20.16.

Evidential Considerations: Proof of Intent to Supply

An intent to supply may be proved by direct evidence in the form of admissions or witness testimony, for example, surveillance evidence.

Another method of proving an intent to supply is by inference. Evidence from which an intent to supply may be inferred will include at least one or, more usually, a combination of the following factors:

- Possession of a quantity inconsistent with personal use.
- Possession of uncut drugs or drugs in an unusually pure state, suggesting proximity to their manufacturer or importer.

- Possession of a variety of drugs may indicate sale rather than consumption.
- Evidence that the drug has been prepared for sale. If a drug has been cut into small portions and those portions are wrapped in foil or film, then there is a clear inference that sale is the object.
- Drug related equipment in the care and/or control of the suspect, such as weighing scales, cutting agents, bags, or wraps of foil (provided their presence is not consistent with normal domestic use).
- Diaries or other documents containing information tending to confirm drug dealing, which are supportive of a future intent to supply, for example records of customers' telephone numbers together with quantities or descriptions of drugs.
- Money found on the defendant was considered in *R v Batt* [1994] Crim LR 592. It is not necessarily evidence of future supply. It may be evidence of supply in the past, but on its own the money is not evidence of a future intent to supply.
- Evidence of large amounts of money in the possession of the defendant, or an extravagant lifestyle which is only prima facie explicable if derived from drug dealing, is admissible in cases of possession with intent to supply if it is of probative significance to an issue in the case (*R v Morris* [1995] 2 Cr App R 69).
- Extravagant lifestyle, but only when that is of probative significance to an issue in the case. Evidence of this type is likely to be admitted by the courts only rarely, but for a detailed overview refer to **Archbold, 26-71 to 26-76; Blackstone's CP 2005, B20.37 and F1.9.**

Evidential Considerations: The Drug User as a Witness

The principles relating to accomplice evidence are usually relevant in these situations. The fact that a person is capable and willing to give evidence against an alleged supplier of drugs is a factor in deciding to prosecute. The following will be relevant:

- the quality of the evidence will need to be considered, as well as the quality of the witness;
- the value of the evidence to the police in an operation against a drug dealer may incline against prosecuting the witness;
- the gravity of the offence committed by the witness; generally, the more serious the offence, the more likely the witness himself or herself will be prosecuted.

Where it is proposed to call an accomplice for the prosecution it is the practice to:

(a) omit him from the indictment; or
(b) take his plea of guilty on arraignment.

For more guidance relating to accomplices, refer to **Archbold, 4-193 to 194; Blackstone's CP 2005, F4.8 and F5.8.**

- It should be further noted that ordinarily a participator in the crime of which the defendant is accused should not be called as a prosecution witness without a clear indication from that accomplice that he is willing to give evidence in favour of the Crown (*R v Sinclair*, The Times, 18.4.89, CA; and see **Archbold, 4-194**).

Evidential Consideration: Forensic Evidence

Difficulties are often experienced as a result of the lack of such evidence at an early stage in the case. Cases which are being committed or transferred to the Crown Court, or where there is a summary trial, must have a statement of a suitably qualified person giving evidence of the nature of the drugs in the case.

In heroin and cocaine cases, the statement should give the weight and purity of the drugs examined. This is to assist the sentencing court following the guidelines in *R v Arunguren* (see above).

In a charge of possession, the burden of proving that the drug falls outside the exception contained in the Regulations issued under the Act is upon the prosecution and not the defence. The forensic analyst should deal with the situation clearly if it appears that there is any possibility of the drug falling into an excepted category.

For further guidance, refer to Scientific Evidence on the CPS website.

Evidential Considerations: Drug Identification and Drug Testing Kits

There must be proper and admissible evidence of the nature and quantity of the drugs. Statements from police officers about the nature, quality, and quantity of drugs seized are not sufficient for Crown Court or contested cases.

Home Office Circular 40/1998, as amended by Home Office Circular 10/2005, states that in certain cases, drugs need not be sent for analysis, namely;

- Cannabis which has been identified by an experienced officer and of which the defendant admits possession and agrees that the drug is cannabis. The amount must be small and for personal use. There must be an indication of a guilty plea in the magistrates' court.
- Morphine, heroin, amphetamine, and cocaine identified as such by an approved FSS drug testing kit. The other circumstances above, must also apply.

(See POL 025/2004 on the CPS website.)

Evidential Considerations: Reverse Burdens of Proof

Under ss. 5(4) (*Archbold, 26-50; Blackstone's CP 2005, B20.18*) and 28 of the Act (*Archbold, 26-123; Blackstone's CP 2005, B20.19*), there are a number of statutory defences to drug offences in which the burden of proof is upon the accused to establish. The House of Lords, in an *obiter dicta* statement, considered whether such reverse burdens were compatible with Article 6 of the European Convention on Human Rights (*R v Lambert* [2001] 3 WLR 206). Their Lordships found that the reverse burden created in s. 28 was not proportionate to the public interest aims that were being pursued, and that by applying s. 3(1) of the Human Rights Act 1998 (*Archbold, 16-15; Blackstone's CP 2005, F3.6*), they 'read down' the legislation to read 'to give sufficient evidence' rather than 'prove'. This judgment has left open the question of European Convention on Human Rights compatibility and all reverse burden offences, and prosecutors should be aware of the potential challenges they could face in trials.

Evidential Considerations: Continuity

Establishing a proper chain of continuity of evidence is essential. You must look for evidence connecting the drug or other exhibit found to its eventual destination; for example, in the case of a drug found by the police, the chain might be:

- officer finding drug;
- officer to whom drug is passed, who places it in the drugs' cabinet;
- officer who removes drug from cabinet and takes it to laboratory;
- scientist who examines drug and makes statement.

There must be a clearly established link between each stage in order to avoid the danger of continuity being lost.

Confiscation

Refer to Confiscation on the CPS website.

Casework Location

Refer to Casework Directorate Criteria for Referral on the CPS website.

8

Driving Offences, incorporating the Charging Standard

INTRODUCTION

The offences dealt with in this section include the most serious of all road traffic offences. Their prosecution is not only vital to the enforcement and promotion of road safety and the protection of the public, but is also key to the public confidence of victims and their families in the criminal justice system.

CHARGING STANDARD—PURPOSE

The charging standard below gives guidance concerning the charge which should be preferred if the criteria set out in the Code for Crown Prosecutors are met.

The purpose of charging standards is to make sure that the most appropriate charge is selected, in the light of the facts which can be proved, at the earliest possible opportunity.

This will help the police and Crown Prosecutors in preparing the case. Adoption of this standard should lead to a reduction in the number of times charges have to be amended, which in turn should lead to an increase in efficiency and a reduction in avoidable extra work for the police and the Crown Prosecution Service.

The guidance set out in this charging standard:

- should not be used in the determination of any investigatory decision, such as the decision to arrest;
- does not override any guidance issued on the use of appropriate alternative forms of disposal short of charge, such as cautioning or conditional cautioning;
- does not override the principles set out in the Code for Crown Prosecutors;
- does not override the need for consideration to be given in every case as to whether a charge/prosecution is in the public interest;
- does not remove the need for each case to be considered on its individual merits.

GENERAL CHARGING PRACTICE

You should always have in mind the following general principles when selecting the appropriate charge(s):

- the charge(s) should accurately reflect the extent of the accused's alleged involvement and responsibility, thereby allowing the courts the discretion to sentence appropriately;
- the choice of charges should ensure the clear and simple presentation of the case, particularly when there is more than one accused;
- there should be no overloading of charges by selecting more charges than are necessary just to encourage the accused to plead guilty to a few;
- there should be no overcharging by selecting a charge which is not supported by the evidence in order to encourage a plea to a lesser allegation.

This standard covers the following offences:

- dangerous driving—s. 2 of the Road Traffic Act 1988;

- careless driving or inconsiderate driving—s. 3 of the Road Traffic Act 1988;
- murder and manslaughter;
- causing death by dangerous driving—s. 1 of the Road Traffic Act 1988;
- causing death by careless driving when under the influence of drink or drugs—s. 3A of the Road Traffic Act 1988;
- causing bodily harm by wanton or furious driving, etc.—s. 35 of the Offences Against the Person Act 1861.

GENERAL ISSUES ABOUT DRIVING OFFENCES

Consumption of Alcohol or Drugs

(*Wilkinson*, 5.53; *Blackstone's CP 2005*, C5)

Assessing the relevance of the consumption of alcohol (or drugs) is a difficult area. *R v Woodward (Terence)* [1995] 1 WLR 375, CA, which concerns alcohol consumption, set out two general principles:

1. The mere fact that the driver has consumed alcohol is not of itself relevant to or admissible on the question of whether his driving is careless or dangerous.
2. For such evidence to be admissible, it must tend to show that the amount of alcohol taken was such as would adversely affect a reasonable driver, or alternatively, that the accused was in fact adversely affected.

A similar approach should be followed with drugs.

Commission of a Number of Offences

Prosecutors will see cases in which the evidence shows a course of conduct, which involves the commission of a number of statutory or regulatory offences that are very close in time with one another. For example, a driver may drive through a red traffic light, ignore a pelican crossing, and fail to give way at a junction within the same course of driving. The court needs to be made aware of the link between what might otherwise appear as isolated incidents, which in reality form part of a more serious course of conduct. Where this type of situation arises, the manner of the driving has, in reality, fallen below or far below that expected of a competent and careful driver because of the driver's systematic failure to obey the relevant traffic directions. You should not simply charge a number of individual statutory or regulatory offences: prefer a charge of careless or dangerous driving according to the evidence.

'Nearest and Dearest' Cases

Causing death by dangerous driving is so serious that a prosecution is invariably required. Special considerations may apply when the deceased was in a close personal or family relationship with the accused driver—often referred to as 'nearest and dearest' cases. The considerations are unlikely to be relevant in any case where the evidence would support proceedings for manslaughter.

In each case, the particular circumstances and the nature of the relationship will have to be considered. The closer the relationship between the deceased and the accused driver, the more likely it will be that guidance which follows will apply. The police should provide information about the closeness of relationships when submitting the file.

1. Causing death by dangerous driving: In cases of causing death by dangerous driving involving the death of a 'nearest and dearest', where there is evidence to suggest an aggravating feature which imperilled other road users or that the accused is a continuing danger to other road users, the proper course will be to prosecute for dangerous driving under s. 2 of the Road Traffic Act 1988. The focus of the case will then be the imperilling of other road users.

   Additionally, if the accused drove in such a way as to show serious disregard for lives of the 'nearest and dearest' or other road users, notwithstanding that a 'nearest and dearest' has been killed, proceedings for causing death by dangerous driving should be considered.

   In cases of causing death by dangerous driving involving the death of a 'nearest and dearest', where there is no evidence to suggest an aggravating feature which imperilled other road users or that the accused is a continuing danger to other road users, careful consideration needs to be given as to whether there is a need for any prosecution at all.

2. Careless driving: In cases of causing death by careless driving while under the influence of drink, etc., involving the death of a 'nearest and dearest', the proper course will be to prosecute for careless driving and the appropriate drink/driving offence, rather than for a s. 3A of the Road Traffic Act 1988 offence. This will mark the public interest need for driving offences involving the consumption of alcohol to be properly punished, whilst acknowledging the need to deal with the culpable driver's bereavement sensitively.

   In cases of careless driving which caused the death of a 'nearest and dearest' where there is evidence to suggest that the accused is a continuing danger to other road users, the proper course is to prosecute for careless driving under s. 3 of the Road Traffic Act 1988.

   However, in cases of careless driving which caused the death of a 'nearest and dearest' where there is no evidence that the accused is a continuing danger to other road users, the proper course is not to prosecute.

3. Continuing danger to other road users: Evidence that an accused presents a continuing danger to other road users may be found in his/her previous convictions or medical condition. In such cases, the court may wish to make an order under s. 36 of the Road Traffic Offenders Act 1988, disqualifying the driver until he passes a driving test; or when it appears that the court ought to notify the Secretary of State that the driver may be suffering from any relevant disability within the meaning of s. 22 of the Road Traffic Offenders Act 1988.

4. Death(s) of others as well: If a person other than a 'nearest and dearest' is killed as a result of dangerous driving, notwithstanding the fact that a near relative

has also been killed, a charge for causing death by dangerous driving of the person other than the 'nearest and dearest' should normally follow. The case can be presented fully to the court without a separate charge for the death of the close relative.

It is wrong in principle for consecutive sentences to be imposed in respect of each death arising from a single piece of dangerous driving (*R v Peter Noble* [2002] EWCA Crim 1713), and therefore a charge in respect of the 'nearest and dearest' will not affect the court's powers of disposal. The guidance provided by the Court of Appeal in *R v Peter Noble* (para. [17]) is helpful:

... while, therefore, the total sentence should take account of the number of deaths, it cannot be determined by it, if only because of the chance nature of the number of deaths, as we have already emphasised. The fact that multiple deaths have been caused is not of itself a reason for imposing consecutive sentences. The main focus of the sentencing in such cases has to be on the dangerousness of the driving taking into account all the circumstances of the driving including the results.

In some circumstances the death of the 'nearest and dearest' may have to be reflected by inclusion in the indictment.

Drivers of Service Vehicles, and Drivers in Emergencies

Members of the emergency services do not enjoy any special exemption from prosecution when responding to emergency calls: they owe the same duty of care as anyone else would in all the circumstances of the case. Nevertheless, when a member of the emergency services commits an offence while responding to an emergency call, discretion should be used in deciding whether or not a prosecution is needed in the public interest. A prosecution is unlikely to be appropriate in cases of genuine emergency, unless the driving is dangerous or indicates a high degree of blameworthiness. In each case it is necessary to weigh all the circumstances of the case, particularly the nature of the emergency known to, or reasonably perceived by, the driver and the nature of the driving.

There will be cases when persons who are not members of the emergency services drive in an emergency situation. Examples include doctors who receive an urgent call for assistance and a driver taking a sick child to hospital. As with members of the emergency services, all the circumstances of the case must be weighed, particularly the nature of the emergency known to, or reasonably perceived by, the driver and the nature of the driving.

Injury to the Offender

The Court of Appeal (*R v Maloney* [1996] 1 Cr App R(S) 221) did regard the severity of the injuries to the offender as a relevant consideration for sentence. There was no suggestion that the severity of injury should have any influence on the decision to charge, and the general principles set out in the Code for Crown Prosecutors should be applied (*R v Cooksley*, The Times, 8.4.03).

Victims and their Families

Prosecutors must select the correct charge to enable the full gravity of the offence to be properly presented to the court. Where a death has occurred, it is difficult to think of an area of law where the consequences of a decision will have such importance to the relatives of the victim and to the defendant.

Prosecutors will be aware that any decision not to proceed on a s. 1, s. 2, or s. 3 charge, or to substitute a lesser charge, may bring about the need to write to a victim where one can be identified (refer to Direct Communication with Victims on the CPS website). In cases involving a fatality, a meeting should always be held with the victim's family if requested (refer to Meetings with Victims on the CPS website).

Irrelevant Factors

The following factors are not relevant when deciding whether an act of driving is careless or dangerous:

- the injury or death of one or more persons involved in a road traffic accident, except where Parliament has made specific provision for the death to be reflected in the charge. Importantly, injury or death does not, by itself, turn an accident into careless driving or turn careless driving into dangerous driving (but multiple deaths do aggravate the public interest consideration once a decision has been made to prosecute on the evidence, where the driving has deliberately put more than one person at risk, or where the occurrence of multiple deaths was reasonably foreseeable—see *R v Cooksley*, The Times, 8.4.03);
- the age or experience of the driver;
- the commission of other driving offences at the same time (such as driving whilst disqualified, or driving without a certificate of insurance or a driving licence);
- the fact that the defendant has previous convictions for road traffic offences;
- the disability of a driver caused by mental illness, or by physical injury or illness, except where the disability adversely affected the manner of the driving.

Fatality or Serious Injury Cases—Seizure of Vehicles

In cases where fatality or serious injury results during the period of the unauthorized taking of the vehicle, as a result of it being driven dangerously, then consideration should be given to the seizure and retention of the vehicle in its post-accident condition until the conclusion of the case, and any periods for an appeal. This allows an opportunity for expert examination of the vehicle.

This is because the condition of the vehicle involved in a road accident may be relevant in explaining why the accident happened, e.g. a mechanical defect. In this respect the Court of Appeal has stated in the case of *R v Beckford* [1996] 1 Cr App R 94 that the police should never give permission for a vehicle to be scrapped where serious charges are to be brought, which might involve the possibility of some mechanical defect to the vehicle as a potential issue in the case.

Prosecutors should also be aware of the need to balance the rights of the owner of vehicles under Article 1 of the First Protocol to the European Convention on Human Rights (right to peaceful enjoyment of property) against a defendant's right to a fair trial under Article 6 of the Convention—see Casework Bulletin 9 of 1999 and *ECHR Manual of Guidance*.

Compensation should be considered in appropriate cases. In particular, prosecutors should be aware that those involved in offences of taking vehicles contrary to ss. 12 and 12A of the Theft Act 1968 will not be insured. In such cases compensation should be claimed where appropriate. In this respect prosecutors should be aware of the scheme operated by the Motor Insurers Bureau and that under the scheme the victim has to meet the first £300 of a claim.

DANGEROUS DRIVING

Code for Crown Prosecutors

A charge of dangerous driving under s. 2 of the Road Traffic Act 1988 must only be allowed to proceed if it satisfies the tests laid down by the Code; in other words, that there is enough evidence to provide a realistic prospect of conviction on the charge of dangerous driving and, if so, whether it is in the public interest to prosecute the defendant in relation to that offence. In relation to the public interest test, it should be borne in mind the prosecution of traffic offences is vital to the promotion of road safety and the protection of the public.

The Law

Definition of dangerous driving

(*Archbold*, 32-17; *Wilkinson*, 5.04; *Blackstone's CP 2005*, C3.9)

A person drives dangerously when:

- the way he drives falls far below what would be expected of a competent and careful driver; and
- it would be obvious to a competent and careful driver that driving in that way would be dangerous.

Both parts of the definition must be satisfied for the driving to be 'dangerous' within the meaning of the Act (s. 2A(1) of the Road Traffic Act 1988).

There is no statutory definition of what is meant by 'far below', but 'dangerous must refer to danger of personal injury or of serious damage to property' (s. 2A(3)). Additionally, s. 2A(2) of the Road Traffic Act 1988 provides that a person is to be regarded as driving dangerously if it would be obvious to a competent and careful driver that driving the vehicle in its current state would be dangerous. When considering the state of the vehicle, regard may be had to anything carried by or attached to the vehicle (s. 2A(4)).

In the magistrates' court dangerous driving is an either way offence carrying a level 5 fine and/or six months custody; in the Crown Court the maximum penalty is two years' custody and/or an unlimited fine. Wherever the case is heard, the court must disqualify the driver from driving for at least a year and order him to pass an extended driving re-test, unless 'special reasons' are found for not disqualifying (in which case it must endorse the driver's licence with 3–11 penalty points unless there are, again, 'special reasons' for not doing so).

Charging Practice

The test of whether a driver has fallen far below the required standard is an objective one. It concerns situations when the manner of the driving in question is deliberate, and it also covers situations when the manner of the driving occurs as a result of an error of judgement, of incompetence, or inexperience. Dangerous driving can therefore cover a range of behaviours from a single error of judgement to a prolonged and deliberate course of driving with disregard for the safety of other road users. It is important to recognize that a single inadvertent act or omission may possibly fall so far below the standard of driving of a competent and careful driver that it constitutes dangerous driving.

Examples of cases which illustrate the latter principle include: *Attorney-General's Reference No. 32 of 2001* [2002] 1 Cr App R (S) 121 (offender failed to stop at a junction where there was a give way sign and collided with a taxi, failing to see it, that was being driven across the junction perfectly properly); and *Attorney-General's Reference No. 76 of 2002 (Hodges)* [2003] 1 Cr App R (S) 100 (offender drove across junction marked by a give way sign and collided with a car that was being driven along the major road, and had no explanation for his failure to see the car: 'This was a single mis-judgement. It was a bad mis-judgement but nevertheless a single one' (p. 524)). It is important to remember that the manner of the driving must be seen in the context of the surrounding circumstances in which the driving took place (e.g. amount of traffic, visibility).

It is not necessary to consider what the driver thought about the possible consequences of his actions: simply whether or not a competent and careful driver would have observed, appreciated, and guarded against obvious and material dangers.

In the case of a vehicle in such a state of disrepair as to be dangerous, consideration should be given to whether the vehicle should have been driven at all, as well as to how it was driven in the particular circumstances.

Although the test for 'dangerous' is an objective one, deliberate or persistent disregard of, say, traffic directions (be they 'stop', 'give way', or traffic lights) may be evidence that the manner of the driving has fallen far below the standard required, thus making a charge of dangerous driving appropriate.

The following are examples of driving which may support an allegation of dangerous driving:

- racing or competitive driving;
- speed, which is highly inappropriate for the prevailing road or traffic conditions;

- aggressive driving, such as sudden lane changes, cutting into a line of vehicles, or driving much too close to the vehicle in front;
- disregard of traffic lights and other road signs, which, on an objective analysis, would appear to be deliberate; or disregard of warnings from fellow passengers;
- overtaking which could not have been carried out safely;
- driving a vehicle with a load which presents a danger to other road users;
- where the driver is suffering from impaired ability, such as having an arm or leg in plaster, or impaired eyesight;
- driving when too tired to stay awake;
- driving with actual knowledge of a dangerous defect on a vehicle;
- using a mobile phone whether as a phone, or to compose or read text messages (see *R v Browning* [2001] EWCA Crim 1831; [2002] 1 Cr App R (S) 88).

In *R v Cooksley*, The Times, 8.4.03, the Court of Appeal gave detailed guidance as to sentencing in causing death by dangerous driving cases; this case nonetheless offers guidance as to what can constitute dangerous driving at the top end of the scale. In addition to some of the factors mentioned above, regard can be had to:

- callous behaviour at the time, such as throwing a victim off the vehicle or failing to stop;
- causing death (and presumably serious injury) in the course of an escape or an attempt to avoid detection.

CARELESS DRIVING AND DRIVING WITHOUT DUE CONSIDERATION—S. 3 OF THE ROAD TRAFFIC ACT 1988

Code for Crown Prosecutors

These apparently straightforward offences can cause substantial difficulties for prosecutors, particularly as the consequences of an incident may be much more serious than the offence suggests. The offences are summary only, and the only available penalties are a fine, penalty points, and/or disqualification.

You should focus on the extent to which the evidence proves that the accused's conduct fell below the standard required by law. Put another way, the test is: what did the defendant do, or fail to do? It is not what happened as a result of the defendant's action or inaction, even if this has serious consequences.

There will be times when another road traffic offence, such as failing to obey a traffic sign, will cover the same facts and may be easier to prove. At the other end of the scale, you will frequently have to consider this advice in conjunction with the advice on dangerous driving (refer to Dangerous Driving, above) in order to decide upon the appropriate charge.

Careless Driving—The Law

This offence is committed when the accused's driving falls below the standard expected of a reasonable, prudent, and competent driver in all the circumstances of the case (*Wilkinson*, 5.41 to 5.82; *Blackstone's CP 2005*, C6.1 to C6.3).

The maximum penalty is a level 4 fine (presently £2,500). The court must also either endorse the driver's licence with between 3 and 9 penalty points (unless there are 'special reasons' not to do so), or impose disqualification for a fixed period and/or until a driving test has been passed (*Wilkinson*, 19.01; *Blackstone's CP 2005*, C6.8).

The test of whether the standard of driving has fallen below the required standard is objective. It applies both when the manner of driving in question is deliberate and when it occurs as a result of incompetence, inadvertence, or inexperience.

Occasionally an accident occurs but there is no evidence of any mechanical defect, illness of the driver, or other explanation to account for why the accident happened. In these cases, a charge of careless driving may be appropriate, but you should exercise caution. If you can prove how an incident occurred (e.g. a collision), the case can be put on the basis that there is a very strong inference that the defendant was driving below the standard expected of a reasonable, prudent, and competent driver. In the absence of any explanation by the defendant as to the cause of the accident, a court may infer that the offence was committed; but where the defendant does provide an explanation for the accident, however unlikely, you will have to consider whether to proceed. The civil law doctrine of *res ipsa loquitur* (the thing speaks for itself) has no direct application to the criminal law. (But see *Wilkinson*, at 5.50: 'In the absence of any explanation by the defendant, if the only conclusion which is possible to draw is that the defendant was negligent or had departed from what a reasonably prudent and confident driver would have done in the circumstances, a court should convict.')

In some cases, particularly where there has been a collision, the evidence will show that more than one driver was at fault. It will be necessary to establish that there is evidence from an independent source against any driver who is to be charged, but the possibility of charging more than one driver remains if both have failed to comply with the statutory standard.

Due Care—Public Interest Considerations

When considering the public interest test you should look at the degree of blameworthiness: the greater the blameworthiness, the greater the public interest in favour of prosecution. There are specific reasons to proceed where the defendant has not passed a driving test, particularly where he/she is unfit to drive because of a disability, or is driving otherwise than in accordance with the conditions of a provisional licence. See s. 36 of the Road Traffic Offenders Act 1988 for power to disqualify the driver until he passes a driving test, and s. 22 of the Road Traffic Offenders Act 1988 where, if the defendant may be unfit to continue to drive, the court has power to notify the Secretary of State about any relevant disability.

Conversely, the public interest does not call for a prosecution in every case where there is, evidentially, a realistic prospect of conviction for careless driving. A prosecution should not be commenced because of technical lapse from the statutory standard where a case is likely to attract only a nominal penalty and will have no deterrent effect on a defendant or other motorists. It will not necessarily be appropriate to prosecute in every case where a minor collision occurs. What matters is the extent of the error, not the extent of any damage. It is not the function of the prosecution (or the criminal courts) to conduct proceedings in order to settle questions of liability for the benefit of individual motorists or insurance companies. Therefore, the public interest will tend to be against a prosecution for careless driving where the incident is of a type such as frequently occurs at parking places or in traffic queues, involving minimal carelessness.

A prosecution may not be necessary where the only or main loser (in terms of personal injury or damage) was the proposed defendant (refer to 'Nearest and Dearest' cases, above).

Charging Practice

The following are examples of driving which may amount to driving without due care and attention:

- overtaking on the inside;
- driving inappropriately close to another vehicle;
- driving through a red light;
- emerging from a side road into the path of another vehicle;
- conduct whilst driving, such as:
  - using a hand-held mobile telephone while the vehicle is moving,
  - tuning a car radio,
  - reading a newspaper/map,
  - selecting and lighting a cigarette/cigar/pipe,
  - talking to and looking at a passenger.

The above examples are merely indicative of what can amount to careless driving. It is necessary to put the facts in context and consider whether the particular facts of the case warrant a charge of careless or dangerous driving.

The reason for the driver's behaviour is not relevant to the choice of charge: it is the acts or omissions of the driver, or conduct whilst driving, which determine whether the driver has fallen 'below' (careless driving) or 'far below' (dangerous driving) the standard required.

Consider whether a defendant has failed to observe a provision of the Highway Code. This does not itself render that person liable to criminal proceedings, but a failure, particularly a serious one, may constitute evidence of careless or dangerous driving. Section 38(7) of the Road Traffic Act 1988 is the statutory authority for this point.

Where there is an overlap between careless driving and some other offences, such as driving with excess alcohol, a regulatory offence, an offence of strict liability, or a 'Construction and Use' offence, the merits of the individual case may often be adequately met by charging the specific statutory or regulatory offence. In short, a prosecutor may ask: what does the 'due care' allegation add to the case—and what additional penalty is likely? In practice, there will need to be some further evidence to show that the manner of the driving fell below that which is to be expected in order to justify proceedings under s. 3 of the Road Traffic Act 1988.

Driving without Reasonable Consideration—the Law

This offence is committed when a vehicle is driven on a road or other public place 'as a result of which other persons using the road or place are inconvenienced'. 'Other persons' may include persons in or on the driver's vehicle itself. The penalties are the same as for 'careless driving'.

Generally, prosecutors prefer 'careless driving' to 'driving without due consideration', as the former is easier to prove—there is no need to show that an actual road user is inconvenienced, etc. But 'due consideration' is more appropriate where the real harm done is aimed at, or suffered by, a particular person.

The accused must be proved:

- to have fallen below the standard of a reasonable, prudent, and competent driver in the circumstances of the case; and
- to have done so without reasonable consideration for others; and
- to have inconvenienced an actual road user.

Note, the essential difference between the two offences under s. 3 of the Road Traffic Act 1988 is that in cases of careless driving the prosecution need not show that any other person was inconvenienced. In cases of inconsiderate driving, there must be evidence that some other user of the road or public place was actually inconvenienced.

This offence is appropriate when the driving amounts to a clear act of incompetence, selfishness, impatience, or aggressiveness. There must, however, also be some inconvenience to other road users, for example forcing other drivers to move over and/or brake as a consequence. Examples of conduct appropriate for a charge of driving without reasonable consideration are:

- flashing of lights to force other drivers in front to give way;
- misuse of any lane to avoid queuing or gain some other advantage over other drivers;
- unnecessarily remaining in an overtaking lane;
- unnecessarily slow driving or braking without good cause;
- driving with un-dipped headlights which dazzle oncoming drivers;
- driving through a puddle causing pedestrians to be splashed;
- driving a bus in such a way as to scare the passengers.

Note that you must decide which version of the offence to charge as the section creates two separate offences and there is no alternative verdict provision in the magistrates'/youth court (*R v Surrey Justices, ex parte Witherick* [1932] 1 KB 450).

Driving without Due Consideration—Public Interest Factors

The public interest considerations for the two offences created by this section are largely the same. You may be more inclined to prosecute where you have decided that due consideration is the appropriate charge and you will be calling evidence to show that the defendant caused harm, annoyance, or distress (e.g., the example regarding the pedestrians and the puddle above).

Relationship between s. 2 and s. 3 Offences

The manner of the driving must be considered objectively. In practice, the difference between the two types of bad driving will depend on the degree to which the driving falls below the minimum acceptable standard. If the manner of the driving is below that which is expected, the appropriate charge will be careless driving; if the manner of the driving is far below that which is expected, the appropriate charge will be dangerous driving. There is no statutory guidance about what behaviour constitutes a manner of driving which is 'below' and 'far below' the required standard. The appropriate charge will therefore have regard to the extent of departure from the required standard, rather than to the consequences of that departure.

There is no clear-cut dividing line between acts of careless driving and acts of dangerous driving. The factual examples set out in this standard are merely indicative of the sort of behaviour which may merit prosecution under s. 2 or s. 3 of the Road Traffic Act 1998.

It is important to put the facts of the case in context. Although the test is objective, the manner of the driving must be seen in context of the circumstances in which the driving took place. Behaviour which may not be criminal in certain conditions may merit proceedings in other conditions, for example a safe lane change in slow-moving traffic may become unsafe on a motorway where speeds are faster, there is less time to react, and the consequences of any accident are likely to be more serious. Similarly, behaviour which might merit proceedings under s. 3 in certain conditions, may merit a prosecution under s. 2, for example, if there is poor visibility; increased volume of traffic; adverse weather conditions; or difficult geography, such as blind corners.

MURDER AND MANSLAUGHTER

Code for Crown Prosecutors

Murder and manslaughter are so serious that a prosecution is almost certainly required where the evidence is sufficient.

The personal circumstances of a defendant may be a relevant public interest factor in exceptional circumstances.

The Law

If the vehicle was intentionally used as a weapon to kill then a charge of murder may be considered. If the killing was involuntary then it may amount to manslaughter either by way of 'constructive manslaughter', or by way of 'gross negligence manslaughter'.

'Motor manslaughter' is an obligatorily disqualifiable offence (Part II of the Road Traffic Offenders Act 1988, Sch. 2).

Constructive Manslaughter

(*Archbold*, 19-98; *Blackstone's CP 2005*, B1.34)

This may also be termed 'unlawful act manslaughter'.

It must be proved that:

- the defendant's act caused the death of the victim;
- the defendant's act constituted a criminal offence in itself, requiring proof of mens rea;
- the defendant had the mens rea appropriate to the unlawful act which caused the victim's death;
- the defendant's unlawful act would objectively be recognized as subjecting the victim to the risk of some physical harm, albeit not serious harm.

In the context of a road traffic fatality, the unlawful act complained of cannot be another driving offence.

Gross Negligence Manslaughter

(*Archbold*, 19-108; *Blackstone's CP 2005*, B1.37)

It must be proved that:

- the defendant owed the victim a duty of care;
- the defendant's act or omission amounted to a breach of that duty;
- the defendant's act or omission caused the death of the victim; and
- the jury must be satisfied that the conduct of the defendant was so bad in all the circumstances as to amount in their judgement to a criminal act or omission.

In respect of gross negligence manslaughter, the driver must be shown to have been in breach of a duty of care towards the person who died. The ordinary principles of the law of negligence apply to ascertain whether there is such a duty. There is a general duty of care on all persons not to do acts imperilling the lives of others.

To show a breach of a duty of care will require proof that the driving:

- fell far below the minimum acceptable standard of driving; and
- involved a risk of death; and
- was so bad in all the circumstances as, in the opinion of the jury, to amount to a crime: *R v Adomako* [1994] 3 All ER 79.

Manslaughter is also discussed at **Wilkinson's**, **5.61**. At **5.65**, Wilkinson argues that in one factual scenario a 'hit and run' driver might be guilty of manslaughter. Consideration should be given to this in appropriate cases where there is clear evidence to satisfy all the above elements.

The examples of driving which fall far below the minimum acceptable standard of driving (see Dangerous Driving, above) apply here as well.

Corporate Manslaughter

On occasion it will be apparent that working regimes, dangerous or illegal practices, or negligence have contributed to the death. In these circumstances liability may arise either in respect of corporate bodies, or in respect of officers within those bodies.

The normal principles of 'gross negligence manslaughter' must be followed to determine liability. A clear line of causation must be shown from the directing or controlling mind through to the unlawful act or omission. The following are examples of where corporate or individual 'officer' responsibility may arise:

- An operator has no regular system of preventative checks, showing indifference to an obvious risk of injury.
- A company director knows about a defect in the vehicle and allows it to go out before the defect has been repaired, showing an appreciation of the risk but a determination to run that risk.
- A substandard repair is done to a defective part.
- An operator fails to ensure that drivers of vehicles work proper hours and have appropriate rest periods.

Charging Practice

Prosecutors, when deciding whether the appropriate charge is manslaughter, must therefore consider whether there is sufficient evidence to prove gross negligence on the part of the alleged offender.

Manslaughter will very rarely be appropriate in road traffic fatality cases because of the existence of the statutory offences. It should be reserved for a 'very grave case' (*R v Governor of Holloway, ex parte Jennings* [1983] RTR 1), where on the facts there was a very high risk of death (*R v Pimm* [1994] RTR 391).

Manslaughter should be considered when a vehicle has been used as an instrument of attack (but where the necessary intent for murder is absent) or to cause fright and death results.

Manslaughter may be considered where the death did not arise from the manner of the defendant's driving but where he did not comply with his positive duty under s. 170 of the Road Traffic Act 1988. If he knew that serious injury had been occasioned and that there would be a risk of death if medical assistance was not called, his failure to stop and report the accident may found a manslaughter charge if the victim consequently dies (*Wilkinson*, 5.40).

Manslaughter should also be considered where the driving has occurred other than on a road or other public place, or when the vehicle driven was not mechanically propelled, and death has been caused. In these cases the statutory offences do not apply.

Prosecutors should not include counts of manslaughter and death by dangerous driving together on one indictment (one being a common law and the other a statutory offence) (refer to Alternative Verdicts, below).

All corporate manslaughter cases should be referred to Casework Directorate (with a recommendation) via the Chief Crown Prosecutor.

CAUSING DEATH BY DANGEROUS DRIVING — S. 1 OF THE ROAD TRAFFIC ACT 1988

The Law

Definition of the offence

(Archbold, 32-2; Wilkinson, 5.22; Blackstone's CP 2005, C3.7)
This offence is committed when:

- the driving of the accused was a cause of the death of another person; and
- the driving was dangerous within the meaning of s. 2A of the Act (see Dangerous Driving, above).

The defendant's driving must have been a cause of the death and 'something more than de minimis'. Subject to that it need not be 'a substantial cause or a major cause or any other description of cause, of the accident' (*R v Hennigan* [1971] 3 All ER 133).

The examples given in relation to dangerous driving apply to this offence (see Dangerous Driving, above).

It is an offence triable only on indictment and carries a maximum penalty of fourteen years' imprisonment, by virtue of the Criminal Justice Act 2003, and/or an unlimited fine. The court must disqualify the driver for driving for at least two years (three years if there is a relevant previous conviction) and also order him to be disqualified until he passes an extended driving test, unless special reasons are found for not disqualifying (in which case it must endorse the driver's licence with 3–11 penalty points again unless there are special reasons not to do so).

The Sentencing Advisory Panel recommends that the occurrence of more than one death should be treated as a seriously aggravating factor, where the offender has knowingly put more than one person at risk, or where the occurrence of multiple deaths was reasonably foreseeable.

CAUSING DEATH BY CARELESS DRIVING WHEN UNDER THE INFLUENCE OF DRINK OR DRUGS — S. 3A OF THE ROAD TRAFFIC ACT 1988

The Law

This offence is committed when:

- the driving was without due care and attention, or without reasonable consideration for other roads users; and
- the driving has caused the death of another person; and
- the driver is either unfit through drink or drugs, or the alcohol concentration is over the prescribed limit, or there has been a failure to provide a specimen in pursuance of the Road Traffic Act 1988 (***Wilkinson, 5.83 to 5.92; Blackstone's CP 2005,*** C3.14 to C3.20).

The defendant's driving must have been a cause of the death and 'something more than de minimis'. Subject to that it need not be 'a substantial cause or a major cause or any other description of cause, of the accident' (*R v Hennigan* [1971] 3 All ER 133).

The examples given in respect of careless driving apply to this offence (see Careless Driving, above).

The offence is triable only on indictment and carries a maximum penalty of fourteen years' imprisonment, by virtue of the Criminal Justice Act 2003, and/or an unlimited fine.

The court must disqualify the driver from driving for at least one year (three years if there is a relevant previous conviction), unless special reasons are found for not disqualifying (in which case it must endorse the driver's licence with 3–11 penalty points), again unless there are special reasons not to do so.

Charging Practice

Proper procedures have to have been adopted in the requesting and/or obtaining of any sample of breath, blood, or urine. In cases where the procedures are flawed, there is a risk that the evidence may be excluded. Where this is possible, careful consideration must be given to whether the remaining evidence will support an alternative allegation of causing death by careless driving while unfit to drive through drink/drugs, in which case evidence other than that from an intoximeter machine can be relied upon to demonstrate the defendant's unfitness to drive.

It is not necessary to add a further charge relating to drink/driving when the defendant is charged with a s. 3A offence, because a guilty verdict to the relevant drink/drive offence can be returned by the jury under the statutory provisions (refer to Alternative Verdicts, later in this chapter).

Relationship between s. 1 and s. 3A of the Road Traffic Act 1988

Offences under s. 1 and s. 3A carry the same maximum penalty, so the choice of charge will not inhibit the court's sentencing powers. The courts have made it clear that for sentencing purposes the two offences are to be regarded on an equal basis (*Attorney-General's Reference No. 49 of 1994* [1995] 16 Cr App R (S) 837; *R v Brown* [1995] Crim LR 437; *R v Locke* [1995] Crim LR 438).

The court will sentence an offender in proportion to his criminality. The consumption of alcohol is an aggravating feature increasing the criminality of the offender and therefore the sentence passed. The consumption of alcohol is an aggravating feature within the definition of s. 3A. The consumption of alcohol is not part of the definition of s. 1, but may be treated as an aggravating feature in appropriate cases.

Where a s. 1 offence can be proved, it should be charged. However, you may on occasions have to decide which is the more appropriate charge: s. 1 or s. 3A. This will almost always occur when the manner of the driving is on the borderline between careless and dangerous. The prosecution is likely to be put to election if the two offences are charged in the alternative. Where this is the case, s. 3A should be chosen, provided all the other elements of that offence can be proved. The prospects of a conviction will be greater and the court's sentencing power remains unaffected

Alternative Counts

There may be rare occasions where the only issue to be decided is the degree to which the driving fell below the required standard and there is a genuine triable factual issue between the prosecution and the defence. As s. 3A is not an available alternative verdict to s. 1, it may be necessary to put both counts on the indictment to give effect to the ability of a jury to reach a verdict. Such situations will be rare and must be capable of justification (refer to Alternative Verdicts, later in this chapter).

CAUSING BODILY HARM BY FURIOUS OR WANTON DRIVING— S. 35 OF THE OFFENCES AGAINST THE PERSON ACT 1861

Code for Crown Prosecutors

A charge under s. 35 can only be pursued if it satisfies both tests laid down by the Code; in other words, that there is sufficient evidence to provide a reasonable prospect of conviction on the charge of wanton or furious driving and, if there is, whether it is in the public interest to proceed with the charge. It should be borne in mind that this offence is not strictly a road traffic offence and will generally be under consideration when a victim suffers physical harm as a result of the misuse of a vehicle. It will often be in the public interest to proceed in these circumstances.

The Law
Definition of wanton or furious driving
(*Archbold*, 19-248e; *Wilkinson*, 5.93; *Blackstone's CP 2005*, C3.28 to C3.32)
It is an offence for anyone:

- to be in charge of a vehicle; and
- to cause or cause to be done bodily harm to any person;
- by wanton or furious driving, racing; or
- other wilful misconduct;
- by wilful neglect.

It is an offence triable only on indictment (except when committed by a youth).

The offence carries a maximum penalty of two years' imprisonment and/or an unlimited fine.

The offence can only be committed if the driver has a degree of subjective recklessness so far as the foreseeability of causing injury is concerned. In other words, he must appreciate that harm was possible or probable as a result of the bad driving: see *R v Okosi* [1996] Crim LR 666.

Charging Practice
This offence should be used rarely as it does not carry endorsement or disqualification. It should normally be used only when it is not possible to prosecute for an offence under the road traffic legislation, for example:

- when the driving was not on a road or other public place;
- when the vehicle used was not a mechanically propelled vehicle (such as a bicycle or horse-drawn vehicle);
- when the statutory notice of proposed prosecution was not given.

When a vehicle has been deliberately used as a weapon and has caused injury, alternative charges of dangerous driving under s. 2 of the Road Traffic Act, or s. 18 of the Offences Against the Person Act 1861 (refer to Offences Against the Person, above) should be considered if all the elements of the offence are present and can be proved.

TAKING A CONVEYANCE WITHOUT AUTHORITY, CONTRARY TO S. 12 OF THE 1968 THEFT ACT
(*Archbold*, 21-141; *Blackstone's CP 2005*, B4.90)
This offence is committed when a person takes a conveyance without the owner's consent or other lawful authority for his own or another's use, or, knowing that any conveyance has been taken without such authority, drives it or allows himself to be carried in it or on it.

It is a summary offence, which carries a penalty of imprisonment for a term not exceeding six months and/or a fine not exceeding level 5 on the standard scale and discretionary disqualification from driving. Note that as a result of s. 37 of the Vehicle (Crime) Act 2001 (*Archbold*, 21-141). S. 12(4A) now provides that when there is a certificate setting out the date on which sufficient evidence came to the knowledge of the person responsible for commencing the prosecution, proceedings should be commenced within six months from the date specified, but that no proceedings may be brought after three years from the date of the taking of the motor vehicle.

In addition, a charge of taking a conveyance without consent is one of the specified offences for the purposes of s. 40 of the Criminal Justice Act 1988. As a result, in appropriate cases such offences can be placed as a count on the indictment, e.g. where a vehicle has been taken to facilitate the main offence (refer to Summary Offences and the Crown Court, on the CPS website).

Prosecutors should also note that a jury is able to bring an alternative verdict convicting an offender of taking without the owner's consent as an alternative to a count alleging theft of the conveyance (**Archbold, 21-145; Blackstone's CP 2005, B4.4 and B4.91**).

The taking of a pedal cycle or the riding of a pedal cycle, knowing it to have been taken without the owner's consent, is not within the provisions of s. 12(1) of the 1968 Act, but is covered by s. 12(5) of the 1968 Act—the penalty for this offence is a fine not exceeding level 3 on the standard scale.

The elements of the offence are:

- Taking.
  There must be some element, but more than mere movement—the vehicle should be used as a conveyance.
- A conveyance.
  This means a conveyance constructed or adapted for the carriage of a person or persons whether by land, water, or air. It does not include a conveyance constructed or adapted for use only under the control of a person not carried in or on it.
- Without the consent of the owner or other lawful authority.
  Section 12(7) of the 1968 Act provides that when a vehicle which has been taken is the subject of a hiring agreement or a hire purchase agreement, a person in the possession of the vehicle under such an agreement is deemed to be the owner for the purposes of s. 12.
- Knowing that such a conveyance has been taken without consent, drives it or allows himself to be carried in it or on it.
  Note that this requires knowledge that the vehicle has been taken, and the accused has either driven the vehicle or been a passenger.

Statutory Defence

Section 12(6) of the 1968 Act provides that a person does not commit an offence under s. 12 by anything done in the belief that he has the lawful authority to do it, or that he would have the owner's consent if the owner knew of his doing it and the circumstances of it.

Examples when it would be Appropriate to Charge this Offence

- When an accused takes a conveyance and then later abandons it.
- When a motor vehicle is legitimately borrowed for a particular purpose and is used thereafter for a wholly different purpose—for example, when the accused is given the use of his employer's vehicle to drive from London to Cardiff on business, but decides to visit friends in Liverpool instead.
- When a vehicle has been stolen or taken without the owner's consent by one person, abandoned and subsequently taken without consent by another person.
- When the evidence is not clear as to whether a driver or passenger was a party to the taking of the vehicle, you should consider whether to charge the offence of driving it or allowing oneself to be carried, provided that the necessary evidence is available to show that the person knew that it has been previously taken without the owner's consent.
- When a victim has been forcibly deprived of his vehicle, but there is insufficient evidence to support robbery, because an intention to permanently deprive cannot be proved (refer to Theft Acts, incorporating the Charging Standard, in Chapter 4 of this book).

Examples when it is not Appropriate to Charge this Offence

- When there is a minor deviation from a proper route by a person who has an otherwise authorized use of the vehicle.
- When a vehicle has been moved only a short distance because it was causing an obstruction.
- When consent to the taking was obtained by fraud, for example by providing false particulars at the time of the hiring of a motor vehicle. In these circumstances, you should consider whether an offence of obtaining property or services by deception is made out.

Charging Considerations

- When there are any evidential difficulties in proving an offence under s. 12 of the 1968 Act, you should consider charging an offence of vehicle interference contrary to s. 9 of the Criminal Attempts Act 1981.
- Where there is fingerprint or DNA evidence, you need to consider carefully where this is located on the vehicle. You cannot assume, for example, that a fingerprint on an outside wing mirror is evidence of taking a motor vehicle. However, traces of blood on the ignition barrel will be different.
- Note that taking a motor vehicle where force is used may amount to robbery, when the evidence supports the inference that the offender did not intend the victim to recover the car intact (for example, the car is not recovered, or is recovered but seriously damaged or burnt out). Refer to Theft Acts, incorporating the Charging Standard, in Chapter 4 of this book.

Attempts

Section 12 of the 1968 Act is a summary only offence. There is no longer an offence of attempting to commit a summary offence, and thus no offence of attempting to commit an offence under s. 12 of the 1968 Act. Actions by an accused, which fall short of the full offence under this section, are likely to be covered by a charge of vehicle interference (refer to Interference with a Motor Vehicle, Contrary to s. 9 of the Criminal Attempts Act 1981, on page 164).

AGGRAVATED TAKING OF CONVEYANCES WITHOUT OWNER'S CONSENT OR BEING CARRIED IN A CONVEYANCE SO TAKEN, CONTRARY TO S. 12A OF THE 1968 THEFT ACT

(*Archbold*, 21-158; *Blackstone's CP 2005*, B4.99)

The offence of aggravated vehicle taking is committed if a person commits an offence under s. 12(1) of the 1968 Act in relation to a mechanically propelled vehicle and it is proved that at any time after the vehicle was unlawfully taken (whether by that person or another) and before it was recovered, the vehicle was driven, or death, injury, or damage was caused, in one or more of the circumstances set out in paras (a) to (d) of s. 12A(2):

- that the vehicle was driven dangerously on a road or other public place;
- that, owing to the driving of the vehicle, an accident occurred by which injury was caused to any person;
- that, owing to the driving of the vehicle, an accident occurred by which damage was caused to any property, other than the vehicle;
- that damage was caused to the vehicle.

Aggravated vehicle taking is an either way offence which carries a penalty on conviction on indictment of imprisonment for a term not exceeding two years; or if, in the circumstances of s. 12A(2)(b) above, an accident results in the death of another, then a person guilty of the offence shall be liable to imprisonment for a term not exceeding fourteen years (by virtue of the Criminal Justice Act 2003). On summary conviction, it carries a penalty of imprisonment for up to six months and/or a fine of up to the statutory maximum.

When the only aggravated element of an offence under s. 12A is the allegation of damage being caused to the vehicle and/or other property, the offence will be triable summarily only, if the value of the damage does not exceed the relevant sum under s. 22 of the Magistrates' Court Act 1980 (*Archbold*, 1-52; *Blackstone's CP 2005*, B4.100).

Offences under s. 12A of the 1968 Act are subject to obligatory disqualification (for a minimum period of twelve months) and endorsement of the offender's driving licence with 3–11 penalty points when, for special reasons, disqualification is not imposed.

Charging Considerations

Since the prerequisite for an offence under this section is that the accused must have committed the basic offence of taking the vehicle without the owner's consent, you should apply the guidance set out above in Taking a Conveyance without Authority, contrary to s. 12 of the 1968 Theft Act, before proceeding any further. If there is a realistic prospect of conviction on the evidence for an offence under s. 12(1) then you should consider whether any of the additional circumstances referred to in s. 12A(2) of the 1968 Act exist, which would make it appropriate for the aggravated form of vehicle taking to be charged.

In cases involving an accident and damage or injury, prosecutors should be aware that it is not a requirement to show that the standard of driving is at fault. What is required to be established is a causal connection between the driving of the vehicle and the occurrence of the accident from which the damage or injury results (*R v Marsh* [1997] 1 Cr App R 67).

It should be appreciated that a person who either takes a vehicle without authority, or allows himself to be carried in it, may commit the aggravated offence if the vehicle is driven or damaged by someone else so as to come within the specified circumstances as set out in s. 12A of the Theft Act 1968. In this respect, reviewing lawyers should be aware of the two statutory defences provided by s. 12A(3) of the Theft Act 1968.

Section 12A of the 1968 Act creates two offences, one with a maximum penalty of two years' imprisonment on indictment and the second, when the additional facts under s. 12A(2)(b) are proved and death results, with a maximum penalty of fourteen years' imprisonment. A sentence of fourteen years is only available to a judge if the indictment alleges that a death occurred. Thus any charge and any indictment must make it clear which of the two offences is being charged.

If the evidence is that a vehicle has been taken by the use of force or threat of force, but there is insufficient evidence to prove an intention to permanently deprive the owner of the vehicle, it may be appropriate to charge aggravated vehicle taking or blackmail (refer to Theft Acts, incorporating the Charging Standard, above).

Public Interest Considerations

Reviewing lawyers should have in mind that unauthorized takings of motor vehicles causes distress and can result in great inconvenience to those relying on that vehicle, e.g. the owner and his/her family. It follows that, in the absence of clear reasons to the contrary, a prosecution should normally follow a decision that sufficient evidence exists to support the evidential test in respect of basic offences under s. 12(1) of the Theft Act 1968.

In the case of aggravated offences, it is more likely that the public interest will require a prosecution because of the serious nature of such offences in terms of risk to other road users and to the general public.

Where one or more defendant is being carried in a conveyance it is necessary to establish each knew that the vehicle had been taken without authority. For this reason, it is best practice to charge each occupant of the vehicle separately.

Alternative Verdicts

The 1968 Act also provides for alternative verdicts in two circumstances:

Offences	Alternative verdicts
Theft of a motor car (s. 1)	Taking without the owners consent (s. 12);
Aggravated vehicle taking (s. 12A)	Taking without the owner's consent (s. 12).

INTERFERENCE WITH A MOTOR VEHICLE, CONTRARY TO S. 9 OF THE CRIMINAL ATTEMPTS ACT 1981

(*Wilkinson*, 15.54 to 15.60; *Blackstone's CP 2005*, B4.107 to B4.110)

The offence is committed when a person interferes with a motor vehicle or a trailer, or with anything carried in it or on it, with the intention that an offence specified in sub-s. (ii) shall be committed by that person or some other person. The offences under sub-s. (ii) are:

- theft of the motor vehicle or trailer or part of it;
- theft of anything carried in or on the motor vehicle or trailer;
- an offence under s. 12(1) of the 1968 Act (refer to Taking a Conveyance without Authority, Contrary to s. 12 of the 1968 Theft Act, above).

If it can be shown that the accused intended to commit one of those offences, it is immaterial that it cannot be shown which it was.

Motor vehicle interference is a summary only offence, which carries a penalty on conviction of imprisonment for a term not exceeding three months and/or a fine not exceeding level 4 on the standard scale.

The elements of the offence are:

- Interference.

The Act does not define what constitutes interference. The mere placing of a hand on a door may not be an act of interference. Putting pressure on a vehicle's door handle is an act of interference.

- With a motor vehicle or trailer or anything in it or on it.
- With an intention to commit one of the three offences specified in sub-s. (ii).

Examples when a Charge of Vehicle Interference would be Appropriate

- When the acts of the accused fall short of what is required for attempted theft of the vehicle/trailer or content, for example because they are acts merely preparatory to theft.

- When the accused attempts to take a motor vehicle without the owner's consent but does not succeed.
- When the accused's fingerprint or DNA is found on the interior of a vehicle that he did not have authority to enter or use.

Charging Considerations

- This offence should be charged when there is insufficient evidence to prove the full offence contrary to s. 12 of the 1968 Act.
- When from the available evidence the accused's intention is not clear, you should consider charging motor vehicle interference.

ACCEPTABILITY OF PLEAS

Plea to Careless Driving from a Charge of Dangerous Driving, when there has been a Fatality

Before accepting a plea to careless driving on a charge of dangerous driving, ensure that:

1. the investigating officer has been consulted;
2. the CPS is satisfied that there is insufficient evidence to continue with dangerous driving; and
3. where there has been a fatality, that the family of the victim has been consulted.

Plea to Causing Death by Careless Driving Whilst under the Influence of Drink or Drugs (s. 3A of the Road Traffic Act 1988) from Causing Death by Dangerous Driving

The victim's family will be concerned at any reduction in the seriousness of the charge. Before accepting a plea under s. 3A of the Road Traffic Act to a count under s. 1 of the Road Traffic Act, ensure that:

1. the investigating officer has been consulted;
2. the CPS and counsel are satisfied that there is insufficient evidence to continue with the s. 1 count;
3. the family of the victim have been consulted.

Plea to Dangerous Driving from a Count of Causing Death by Dangerous Driving

It will never be appropriate to accept a plea to simple dangerous driving from a count of causing death by dangerous driving unless the 'causing death' element can no longer be proved.

PROCEDURE (GENERAL APPLICABILITY)

Inquests

Where an inquest has been opened in relation to a case in which summary criminal proceedings have been commenced (usually careless driving where a death has occurred as a consequence of the driving), as a matter of good practice the justices ought not to proceed with the case until after the inquest. Prosecutors should in such cases apply for the case to be adjourned: *Smith v DPP* [2000] RTR 36.

The rationale for this approach is to avoid the possibility of two tribunals arriving at incongruous results and to ensure that the prosecution is not deprived of the opportunity to reconsider the decision to proceed with careless driving, rather than a more serious offence, if a coroner's court reaches a finding of unlawful killing: *Re Beresford* (1952) 36 Cr App R 1.

This does not mean the summonses for careless driving should not be issued prior to the conclusion of an inquest (to do otherwise would, in many cases, result in the offence becoming statute-barred), merely that, once listed, application should be made for the case to be adjourned to await the outcome of the inquest. If a verdict of unlawful killing is returned, the case should be re-reviewed to consider whether or not a more serious charge is appropriate.

Prosecutors should note that the position as regards the following indictable-only offences is reversed by virtue of s. 16 of the Coroners Act 1988:

- murder, manslaughter, or infanticide;
- causing death by dangerous driving, or causing death by careless driving when under the influence of drink or drugs;
- aiding, abetting, counselling, or procuring the suicide of the deceased.

Where a person has been charged with one of the above offences, the coroner must, on being so informed by the relevant magistrates' court, adjourn the inquest pending the outcome of the criminal proceedings unless there is any reason to the contrary. The inquest will not usually be reconvened after the trial has been concluded.

Notices of Intended Prosecution

Refer to Road Traffic Offences on the CPS website.

Dangerous Driving

If a s. 2 of the Road Traffic Act 1988 allegation is being committed to the Crown Court and there is sufficient evidence of a s. 4, 5, or 7 of the Road Traffic Act 1988 offence, then that summary offence should be committed to the Crown Court pursuant to s. 41(1) of the Criminal Justice Act 1988 if it arises out of circumstances which appear to the magistrates to be the same as or connected with the circumstances of the s. 2 of the Road Traffic Act 1988 offence (refer to Summary Offences and the Crown Court, ss. 40 and 41 of the Criminal Justice Act 1988).

Causing Death by Careless Driving when under the Influence of Drink or Drugs

Where a s. 3A of the Road Traffic Act 1988 offence can be proved and there is sufficient evidence of a s. 4, 5, or 7 of the Road Traffic Act 1988 offence, the appropriate summary offences should be 'sent' to the Crown Court provided they meet the conditions specified in s. 51(11) of the Crime and Disorder Act 1998 (refer to Summary Offences and the Crown Court, ss. 40 and 41 of the Criminal Justice Act 1988; s. 51 of the Crime and Disorder Act 1998, Sch. 3, para. 6, on the CPS website).

Death by Dangerous Driving

Where a s. 1 of the Road Traffic Act 1988 offence can be proved and there is sufficient evidence of a s. 4, 5, or 7 of the Road Traffic Act 1988 offence, the appropriate summary offences should be 'sent' to the Crown Court provided they meet the conditions specified in s. 51(11) of the Crime and Disorder Act 1998 (refer to Summary Offences and the Crown Court, ss. 40 and 41 of the Criminal Justice Act 1988; s. 51 of the Crime and Disorder Act 1998, Sch. 3, para. 6, on the CPS website).

Alternative Verdicts

(*Archbold*, 4-453; *Blackstone's CP 2005*, C2.12)

Section 24 of the Road Traffic Offenders Act 1988 allows for the return of alternative verdicts where the allegations in the indictment amount to, or include, an allegation of an offence specified in the table set out in that section. The section applies to magistrates' courts as well as to juries, provided the magistrates' court has jurisdiction to try the 'Offence charged'. The relevant statutory provisions are:

Offence charged	Alternative verdicts
Section 1: death by dangerous driving	Section 2: dangerous driving Section 3: careless, and inconsiderate, driving
Section 2: dangerous driving	Section 3: careless, and inconsiderate, driving
Section 3A: causing death by careless driving while under the influence of drink or drugs	Section 3: careless, and inconsiderate, driving and/or the relevant offence from: Section 4(1): driving whilst unfit Section 5(1)(a): driving with excess alcohol Section 7(6): failing to provide a specimen

Where the accused is charged with an offence under s. 3A of the Road Traffic Act 1988, he may not be convicted as an alternative with any offence of attempting to drive: s. 24(2) of the Road Traffic Offenders Act 1988.

Death by dangerous driving is not an alternative verdict to a charge of manslaughter; if the jury do not find that there is sufficient evidence to convict of manslaughter, they cannot substitute a verdict of guilty to an offence of causing death by dangerous driving, even if they thought the evidence was sufficient to prove such a charge. Furthermore, it is not open to the prosecutor to include both charges on the indictment as the trial judge will not allow the trial to proceed on both counts but will require the prosecution to elect on which of the two they wish to proceed (*R v Seymour* [1983] RTR 455 per Lord Roskill). The same principle would apply to a charge under s.3A of the Road Traffic Act 1988.

It is essential that the charge which is the most appropriate in all the circumstances of the case is always preferred. It will never be appropriate to charge a more serious offence in order to obtain a conviction (whether by plea or verdict) to a lesser offence.

PART 3

Crown Prosecution Service Guidance and Policy Documents

9

Guidance on Prosecuting Cases of Domestic Violence

1 INTRODUCTION

1.1 We have updated our public policy statement, CPS Policy for Prosecuting Cases of Domestic Violence, to reflect changes in legislation, new trends and initiatives.

1.2 This updated Guidance is designed to give more detail about some of the key areas of the Policy.

1.3 The Policy and Guidance needed to be updated to address a number of factors including:

- new legislation and the implementation of existing legislation (e.g. Domestic Violence, Crime and Victims Act 2004, Sexual Offences Act 2003, Criminal Justice Act 2003, Part II Youth Justice and Criminal Evidence Act 1999);
- recent CPS initiatives in charging, witness care, and the Effective Trial Management Programme;
- the recommendations made by Her Majesty's Crown Prosecution Service Inspectorate (HMCPSI) and Her Majesty's Inspectorate of Constabulary (HMIC) in the Joint Thematic Inspection of the Investigation and Prosecution of Cases Involving Domestic Violence (February 2004);
- the non-legislative proposals in the Government's consultation paper 'Safety and Justice';
- the work on domestic violence within the CPS, including the development of CPS Area Domestic Violence Coordinators, the CPS Domestic Violence Project, and work with the Home Office Violent Crime Unit Domestic Violence section;
- the recommendations from the 'Evaluation of Domestic Violence Specialist Courts and Fast-Track Systems' report, jointly commissioned by CPS and the Department for Constitutional Affairs (DCA).

1.4 As before, we have consulted colleagues across the criminal justice system, other government departments, and the voluntary and community sector with whom we work. By doing this we have gained a better knowledge of the issues that are important to them.

1.5 The Policy and Guidance demonstrate our continuing efforts to raise awareness of issues relating to domestic violence and our determination to improve the prosecution of domestic violence cases and the service we provide to victims and witnesses.

2 THE DEFINITION OF DOMESTIC VIOLENCE

2.1 The Government has agreed a definition of domestic violence to replace the various definitions used by government departments and other agencies. A common definition was needed to improve joint working and monitoring but does not mean that agencies will be required to deal with incidents of domestic violence that fall outside their sphere of responsibility. The CPS will still deal only with criminal offences.

2.2   The definition is:

> any incident of threatening behaviour, violence or abuse (psychological, physical, sexual, financial or emotional) between adults who are or have been intimate partners or family members, regardless of gender or sexuality.

> An adult is defined as any person aged 18 years or over. Family members are defined as mother, father, son, daughter, brother, sister, and grandparents whether directly related, in-laws, or step-family.

2.3   The definition is supported by an explanatory text:

> The definition acknowledges that domestic violence can go beyond actual physical violence. It can also involve emotional abuse, the destruction of a spouse's or partner's property, their isolation from friends, family or other potential sources of support, control over access to money, personal items, food, transportation, the telephone and stalking. Violence will often be witnessed by children and there is an overlap between the abuse of women and abuse (physical and sexual) of children. The wide adverse effects of living with domestic violence for children must be recognised as a child protection issue. They link to poor educational achievement, social exclusion and to juvenile crime, substance misuse, mental health problems and homelessness from running away. It is acknowledged that domestic violence and abuse can also manifest itself through the actions of immediate and extended family members through the perpetration of illegal activities, such as forced marriage, so-called 'honour crimes' and female genital mutilation. Extended family members may condone or even share in the pattern of abuse.

2.4   Previously, we worked to the following definition:

> any criminal offence arising out of physical, sexual, psychological, emotional or financial abuse by one person against a current or former partner in a close relationship, or against a current or former family member.

> That definition reflected our involvement with criminal proceedings (rather than incidents) and included abuse regardless of the age of either the victim or defendant. This captured many cases that we also classify as child abuse/child witness cases.

2.5   When prosecuting cases of domestic violence, we will apply our policy to those cases falling within our original definition, i.e. where there is current or former partner or family abuse, irrespective of the age of the perpetrator or the victim.

2.6   However, when monitoring for Government purposes, we will count as domestic violence only the cases that fall into the Government's definition. For the purpose of our own domestic violence monitoring, we will flag the cases that accord with our original definition as both domestic violence and child abuse/child witness (and any other appropriate flag) where those situations arise. We will then also be able to see the number of cases that fall within the category of domestic violence child abuse, and those perpetrated by youth offenders.

3   THE IMPACT AND DYNAMICS OF DOMESTIC VIOLENCE

3.1   We have published our policy statement because we want victims, as well as the general public, to be confident that we understand the serious nature of domestic violence and the real and lasting effects it has on them, their children, and wider families, and on society as a whole. By letting people know what they can expect from us when we prosecute cases of domestic violence, we aim to improve confidence in the criminal justice system.

3.2   The most recent research estimates that domestic violence costs the state around £23 billion per year.[1] One billion pounds is spent within the Criminal Justice System, which is 25% of the total CJS budget spent on violent crime. The 2001 British Crime Survey's Inter-Personal Violence Module shows that one in four women and one in six men have suffered domestic violence at some point in their lives, though women form the overwhelming majority of those subject to the greatest abuse in terms of frequency, range of violence, and severity of injury.[2]

3.3   Domestic violence is widely recognized as being a pattern of behaviour to exert coercive control. It is often a series of incidents, including those of greater and lesser severity but usually increasing in frequency and seriousness, which has a cumulative impact on the victim.

3.4   The impact of domestic violence on children is examined in paragraph 14 [below], but its effects are likely to be devastating. Pregnancy itself is likely to be a trigger for the beginning or acceleration of violence. The short-, medium-, and long-term consequences for children of chronic exposure to domestic violence can include:

- emotional disturbance;
- relationship problems;
- aggressive behaviour and the use of aggression to solve problems;
- self-esteem problems and school failure;
- increased psychiatric problems and, in some children, post-traumatic stress disorder;
- in the long term, a greater likelihood of involvement in violent relationships, especially boys.

3.5   The act of leaving does not automatically make the victim safe. Research shows that victims can be most at risk of being subjected to further violence when they are on the point of seeking help or leaving. Stalking, harassment, and threats are common. The violence does not necessarily stop when the

---

[1] *The Cost of Domestic Violence* (Walby, 2004).

[2] *Domestic violence, sexual assault and stalking: Findings from the British Crime Survey* (Walby and Allen, 2004). Data gathered for the Module for the year 2000–2001 reveals that 125 people were killed in a domestic homicide (102 female, 23 male), 428,000 were subjected to non-sexual severe domestic force (242,000 female, 186,000 male), 584,000 subjected to non-sexual minor domestic force (410,000 female, 174,000 male), and 517,000 were stalked (446,000 female, 71,000 male). The victims of sexual assault were exclusively female, with 37,000 being the victim of serious penetrative assault (of which 28,000 were victims of rape), and 26,000 victims of non-penetrative assault.

victim leaves—many violent 'domestic' assaults occur after the victim has left the abuser.

4 TERMINOLOGY

The term 'victim' is perceived by some as negative. 'Survivor' is perceived to convey a more positive outcome for adults and children and, as such, is the preferred terminology for some of our partner agencies. However, our policy reflects the CPS role in domestic violence criminal proceedings and so the term 'victim' (victim of a crime, victim of an offence) is retained. For similar reasons, the policy refers mainly to a 'defendant' rather than to an 'abuser'.

5 GENDER

Overwhelmingly it is women who experience domestic violence, and almost always at the hands of their male partners or former partners.[3] However, it is recognized that domestic violence also takes place within same-sex relationships, that men can be abused by women, and that family members can be abused by siblings, children, grandchildren, and other relatives.

6 AVOIDING ASSUMPTIONS

6.1 When dealing with members of groups that traditionally experience discrimination (e.g. women, black and minority ethnic people, disabled people, older people, lesbians, gay men, transgender people, bisexuals, and transsexuals), prosecutors should avoid making stereotypical assumptions.

6.2 Where appropriate, expert advice should be sought on religious, cultural, or other issues from relevant agencies, and particularly from specialist black and minority ethnic women's groups that deal with domestic violence. In some cases, these agencies may already be involved with the victim and playing an important role as advocates and supporters.

6.3 Specialist advice can also be sought from the Equality and Diversity Unit at CPS Headquarters in London. (See CPS Directory for contact details.)

7 ABUSE WITHIN SAME-SEX OR TRANSGENDER RELATIONSHIPS

7.1 The basic dynamics of violence within same-sex or transgender relationships are similar to those within heterosexual relationships, but the manifestations

---

[3] *Domestic violence, sexual assault and stalking.* Eighty-nine per cent of victims facing four or more incidents since the age of 16 were women; women on average faced 20 incidents compared with seven by men; women were injured in 75% of incidents compared to 50% of incidents involving male victims; 42% of women suffered mental health problems following domestic violence compared with 11% of men.

may differ. For example, any pre-existing isolation from the family due to the person's sexuality and/or lifestyle may be exploited by the abuser.

7.2　The victim may fear 'outing', or removal of children by Social Services, or loss of legal rights that would be afforded to a heterosexual person in the same position (e.g. tenancy rights, or rights of access to children). The potential to use the new reporting restrictions (s. 46 of the Youth Justice and Criminal Evidence Act 1999) may go some way to alleviating worries about publicity of any court proceedings.

7.3　In particular, victims may fear homophobic or transphobic reactions from the statutory services when reporting incidents (e.g. assumptions that gay men and lesbians favour sadomasochistic sex). These fears or previous experience of negative reactions can make it more difficult to report the violence.

7.4　It is also important to be aware that victims of domestic violence within same-sex relationships may not have the same access to places of safety as do heterosexual women. There are few refuges for men, and whilst women may access refuges, lesbians may be subjected to homophobia within the refuge and the abusive partner may be able to gain access to the refuge herself.

8　ELDER ABUSE

8.1　Some older victims of domestic violence may be mentally or physically frail. Abusers often have significant problems of their own, and there may be a mutually dependent relationship between abuser and victim. Where this situation exists, victims may fear that by reporting the abuse and supporting a prosecution, they will be left without a carer.

8.2　Abuse can be in many forms, for example:

- financial (theft or misappropriation of assets, etc.);
- psychological (infliction of mental/emotional suffering, e.g. by sustained verbal abuse);
- physical (wilful infliction of pain, injury, sexual abuse, or unreasonable confinement);
- sexual;
- or a combination (inadequate provision of care services necessary to maintain the physical and/or psychological well-being of the elderly person).

8.3　The age of a witness is a factor that the court can take into account when determining whether a witness is intimidated under s. 17, Part II of the Youth Justice and Criminal Evidence Act 1999. Where a witness is elderly, consideration should always be given to applying for special measures, although it should not be assumed that because a witness is elderly, special measures should automatically be applied for. In particular, prosecutors should actively consider early special measures meetings, issues arising from Achieving Best Evidence, and remote television links if a witness is not able to leave home.

9   DISABILITY ISSUES

9.1   Many disabled people already face problems of negative attitudes towards impairment, isolation from participation in 'mainstream' society, limited access to services, low self-esteem, and enforced dependence on others to carry out physical tasks necessary for daily living and often survival. This social and physical dependence can increase a victim's vulnerability to domestic abuse.

9.2   Abuse can be in many forms, for example:

- withdrawing physical assistance;
- withdrawing medication/care/mobility aids;
- denying visitors access to the disabled person;
- verbal abuse and name-calling;
- threats to withdraw care/place the victim in residential care/gain custody of any children.

9.3   Disabled victims of domestic violence often remain in abusive relationships. They often feel they cannot leave, because, for example, they have limited economic opportunities, they may lack transport, they feel they are responsible for financial and social tensions within the relationship/family, they fear loneliness and think no one else would want them, fear losing their independence and having to move into residential care, or fear losing their children. Even if a disabled victim wants and is able to leave, there is little emergency accommodation and few refuges available.

9.4   Often the abuser is the carer, with the ability to monitor the victim's movements and conceal and obstruct detection of abusive behaviour. They may be continually present, making it almost impossible for a victim to report abuse. Disabled victims in these circumstances may be reluctant to disclose abuse or support a prosecution because they fear losing personal assistance or worry about finding appropriate community care.

9.5   Witnesses with disabilities may be eligible for special measures (s. 16, Part II of the Youth Justice and Criminal Evidence Act 1999), although no assumptions that these will be wanted should be made and applications will not automatically be granted. Careful consideration will need to be given to how to support a disabled witness. Measures, other than special measures, that may be appropriate include, for example, wheelchair access to court, hearing loop systems,[4] a supporter during the trial, and a pre-court familiarization visit. Some of these measures will be entitlements under the Disability Discrimination Act 1995 and are the responsibility of the court.

9.6   If a witness has a learning disability or a mental disorder within the meaning of s. 16 of the Youth Justice and Criminal Evidence Act, it is vital, under s. 53 of the same Act, that they can understand questions put to them and give answers that can be understood (the Competency Test). This can be with the

---

[4] Also a special measure, being an aid to communication, but unlikely to require a special measures application.

assistance of special measures. The use of statutory intermediaries is currently being piloted, but prosecutors are able to apply now for an intermediary under the inherent jurisdiction of the court. Consideration should also be given to holding an early special measures meeting to assess a witness's needs.

10 BLACK AND MINORITY ETHNIC COMMUNITIES INCLUDING GYPSIES AND TRAVELLERS

10.1 Perceptions or experience of racism and lack of confidence in the criminal justice system may make it difficult for victims of domestic violence in minority ethnic communities to report an offence or support a prosecution. Pressure from within the immediate and extended family and the wider community, together with other cultural differences, can also act as barriers to reporting offences of domestic violence.

10.2 Domestic violence may take different forms within minority ethnic communities. Some examples of these are forced marriage (as distinct from arranged marriage, where the marriage is based on free consent), dowry-related violence, and female genital mutilation.

10.3 There is often a great degree of pressure exerted upon women to remain within the marriage or family rather than leave because of domestic violence. This pressure can come from a variety of sources, including both male and female members of the immediate and extended family, religious leaders, and other leading members of the wider community. In Gypsy and Traveller communities[5] it can be particularly difficult for victims to leave and live in an alien environment where they may be expected to use furniture, linen, and utensils that are not their own.

10.4 Within some South Asian communities there exist complex and powerful strictures about honour and shame that extend beyond the immediate family and often encompass the extended family and wider community. If these strictures are not observed or are broken, it can lead to ostracism, harassment, violence, and ultimately, in some cases, death. The term 'honour killing' is often used to describe a murder that results from this.

10.5 Some Asian families may need to maintain the reputation and respectability that is vital if their children are to be married within the Asian community in this country or abroad. Fear of transferring dishonour to children or other family members is very strong amongst many Asian women and can act as a powerful disincentive to making a complaint or bringing proceedings.

10.6 Family members should never be used as interpreters. Interpreters should, wherever possible, be selected from the National Register of Public Service Interpreters to ensure that the interpreter is properly qualified and subject to

---

[5] Gypsies and Travellers are recognized as racial groups for the purposes of the Race Relations Act 1976 (RRA), i.e. Romany Gypsies and Irish Travellers. Other Gypsies and Travellers who are ethnic or national in origin may come within the definition of a racial group under RRA.

a professional Code of Conduct. Checks should be made to ensure that the interpreter does not have any connections with the victim or the family, and some victims may express a preference for the interpreter to be the same sex. Interpreters from within the local community should be avoided as this may sometimes place victims in additional danger. Correspondence with victims may also need translating. Further information about interpreters may be found in 'The Trials Issues Group Agreement: Arrangements for the Attendance of Interpreters in Investigations and Proceedings within the Criminal Justice System'.[6]

10.7 Assumptions that cultural practices must be respected can lead to a refusal or failure by professional agencies to intervene. The CPS view is that cultural difference is not an acceptable reason for failing to protect victims of domestic violence.

10.8 Where appropriate, advice should be sought from specialist local or national groups (see Annex E).

11 REFUGEES AND ASYLUM SEEKERS

11.1 Women and children constitute 80% of the refugee population across the globe. Many of the women who enter Britain as refugees are not independent applicants for asylum but family members dependent on a husband, father, or older male members of the family for immigration purposes.

11.2 Few of these women receive independent advice or information about their rights and the legal provisions of the host country. They are often unaware of the support systems available and how to access these provisions if they need to do so.

11.3 Lack of independent immigration status can create an additional barrier preventing women from leaving an abusive relationship. They may fear being deported themselves; they may fear their family being deported. Hostility shown towards refugees in host countries also deters women from finding the courage and confidence to get help from appropriate agencies. Racism too plays its part. It polarizes the communities, making it more difficult for a woman to leave her community to access outside help.

11.4 When reviewing a domestic violence case in which the victim is a member of the refugee community or an asylum seeker, a prosecutor should take into account the combination of social and cultural factors, communication difficulties, lack of information in their own language, and lack of access to informal and formal support, which may make it difficult for the victim to support

---

[6] The Trials Issues Group Agreement: Arrangements for the Attendance of Interpreters in Investigations and Proceedings within the Criminal Justice System. See Casework Bulletin No. 10 dated 8 April 2002. The Agreement reflects the introduction of the Human Rights Act 1998 and emphasizes the requirement to check the competence of an interpreter.

or take part in a prosecution. The review note should deal with potential problems and possible solutions and set out what steps need to be taken if the victim is to give evidence, for example, special measures, community support, Victim Support, etc.

11.5 Where appropriate, advice should be sought from specialist local or national groups (see Annex A) and the CPS Equality and Diversity Unit.

12 IMMIGRATION

12.1 A person from abroad is granted two years' leave to enter or remain in the UK on the basis of marriage to a person settled here, or as an unmarried partner of a person settled here. This is known as the probationary period. If the relationship breaks down within this period, the person is required to leave the UK unless he or she qualifies to remain on another basis.

12.2 The Home Office incorporated what was known as the Domestic Violence Concession into the Immigration Rules in April 2004. As a result, a woman or man who experiences domestic violence during the probationary period may apply for indefinite leave to remain in the UK. The person should make the application within the validity of the probationary period, but it is recognized by the Home Office that a victim of domestic violence may not make regularizing immigration status the first priority. The Home Office will consider applications from 'overstayers' sympathetically. However, only a person who has leave to enter or remain in the UK as a spouse or unmarried partner may benefit under this rule. It does not affect foreign nationals who have entered in a different capacity.

12.3 In order to qualify under the Rules the applicant will have to show that he or she is no longer living with the sponsor, that domestic violence was the cause of the breakdown of the relationship, and that the relationship was subsisting at the time. Qualification under the Rules also depends on the applicant producing one or more of the following forms of evidence that domestic violence has taken place:

- an injunction, non-molestation order, or other protection order made against the sponsor (other than a 'without notice' or interim order); or
- a relevant court conviction against the sponsor; or
- full details of a relevant police caution issued against the sponsor.

12.4 Where a prosecution is pending against the sponsor, the applicant may be granted further periods of six months' limited leave to remain, subject to the same conditions, until the outcome of the prosecution is known. Pending a hearing for the grant of an injunction, non-molestation, or other protection order, the application will be delayed until the outcome of the hearing is known.

12.5 It is often difficult for victims of domestic violence to produce the documentary evidence of violence described above, and there is often an unwillingness or insufficient evidence to take the matter to court. Where it is not possible to obtain police or court evidence of confirmation of domestic violence, the Home Office will accept evidence in the form of more than one of the following:

- a medical report from a hospital doctor confirming that the applicant has injuries consistent with being a victim of domestic violence;
- a letter from a family practitioner who has examined the applicant and is satisfied that the applicant has injuries consistent with being a victim of domestic violence;
- an undertaking given to a court that the perpetrator of the violence will not approach the applicant who is the victim of the violence;
- a police report confirming attendance at the home of the applicant as a re-sult of a domestic violence incident;
- a letter from a social services department confirming its involvement in con-nection with domestic violence;
- a letter of support or report from a women's refuge.

12.6 Where an applicant has suffered domestic violence from another member of the family, an application will be considered if this is the reason for leaving the partner and if the partner is unwilling to offer protection.

13 SEX WORKERS

13.1 As with other victims of domestic violence, sex workers can fall into some or all of the vulnerable groups discussed in this document—they may have insecure immigration status, be a child, come from a minority ethnic background, or have a disability.

13.2 Research shows that many have been abused as children and, in order to cope with their chaotic lifestyles, or as a result of them, many misuse alcohol or other substances. Sex workers are one of the groups most at risk of domestic violence from a partner, particularly if, as in many instances, their partner is also their 'pimp'.

13.3 When dealing with cases of domestic violence where the victim is a sex work-er, it is especially important that we make enquiries of the police to satisfy ourselves as far as possible that he or she is supported during the proceedings, as continuing with a prosecution against a pimp can be difficult and dangerous for the sex worker. Sex workers may also face repercussions from other pimps or sex workers. A key factor for sex workers considering whether to support a domestic violence prosecution against the 'pimp' will be the arrangements made to ensure their safety.

13.4 It is possible that sex workers may already have experiences of the criminal justice system and that many of them will themselves have been defendants. Therefore, it is particularly important for them to be offered the chance to obtain support from and talk things through with a specialist domestic violence advocate.

13.5 If a sex worker decides to withdraw the initial complaint, as with any complainant, the safety of the victim will be a primary consideration when deciding whether to continue the prosecution. Prosecutors should seek information through the police from the sex worker or someone who knows the sex worker well and who can give an opinion on the risks attached to, for example, compelling the victim to give evidence.

14 CHILDREN

14.1 Prosecutors must take the rights and interests of children into full account in domestic violence cases.[7] The safety, physical and emotional well-being of children are, rightly, pivotal issues for those making decisions in cases of domestic violence. The Code for Crown Prosecutors states that a prosecution is likely to be needed if the offence was committed in the presence of, or in close proximity to, a child.[8]

14.2 Some victims say that they stayed for the children's sake, others that they left for the children's sake. Often when abuse is directed at a child, it is a trigger for a victim to make a first complaint of abuse or decide to leave, despite having endured abuse upon themselves for some time.

14.3 Research shows that exposure to domestic violence can have a devastating effect on children. Ninety per cent of children are in the same or next room during the assault.[9] One third of children actively intervene or run to get help.[10] Nearly three quarters of the children on the 'At Risk' registers of local authority social services departments are experiencing or witnessing domestic violence, which means at least 750,000 children a year. It is not possible to shield children from the adverse effects of living with domestic violence.[11] This is why the presence of children is treated as an aggravating factor when applying the public interest test.

14.4 Prosecutors should always seek information from the police regarding the presence of children in the household, the extent to which they have been exposed to the domestic violence, and whether the children are the subject of any orders, for example child protection register, contact, non-molestation orders. We should also explore whether any child wishes to give evidence.

14.5 Prosecutors must take children's interests into account at all stages of the review process and address their safety and welfare as a primary consideration,

---

[7] *Violence at Home: A Joint Thematic Inspection of the Investigation and Prosecution of Cases Involving Domestic Violence*, Chapter 4 (HM CPSI and HMIC), February 2004.

[8] The Code for Crown Prosecutors, para. 5.9j (2004).

[9] *Impact of Spouse Abuse on Children of Battered Women Violence Update, 1* (Hughes, 1992).

[10] *The Hidden Victims: Children and Domestic Violence* (Abrahams, 1994).

[11] *Children's Needs—Parenting Capacity. The Impact of Parental Mental Illness, Problem Alcohol and Drug Abuse and Domestic Violence on Children's Development* (Cleaver, Unell, and Aldgate, 1999).

especially when deciding whether children should be warned to give evidence. Prosecutors need to take into consideration any escalation of violence, whether children were assaulted, any threats to harm children, and the willingness of the child to give evidence. Children ought to be informed, consulted, and involved in any matter concerning them, according to their age and understanding.

14.6 Child witnesses must be afforded as much protection as is necessary and available to enable them to give their evidence in a way that both maintains the quality of that evidence and minimizes the trauma suffered. For example, a child witness to an offence of sex, violence, neglect, or abduction can give evidence in chief in the form of a video-recorded statement, but where a video-recording has not been made, that evidence may be given instead, both in chief and cross-examination, on a live television link.

14.7 There may be cases in which a child who witnessed the incident wishes to give evidence but the victim will not permit the police to interview the child. In such cases, we will need to consider the ECHR implications (child's rights), as well as the evidential and public interest factors that arise. An approach to the local Social Services department may be appropriate for the police to make arrangements to interview a child.

15 INTER-AGENCY WORKING

15.1 It is now recognized that in order to meet the full range of social, welfare, economic, safety, accommodation, criminal, and civil justice needs that victims of domestic violence have, a multi-agency partnership approach is required. We are committed to working nationally and locally within a multi-agency approach to address domestic violence both generally and case-specifically.

15.2 As well as the police and courts, other agencies, including local authority departments (Housing, Social Services, Education), the National Health Service, the National Probation Service, refugee and women's support and outreach projects, and the voluntary sector, all have roles to play. Evaluation of specialist domestic violence courts indicated the importance of partnership working across agencies,[12] and DCA have issued guidance on the development of further specialist courts, based on a model drawn up from the evaluation.

15.3 The Crime and Disorder Act 1998 placed a statutory duty on local crime reduction partnerships to create Local Criminal Justice Boards (LCJBs) to develop strategies to tackle and reduce the incidence of domestic violence. The Children Act, when implemented, will establish Local Safeguarding Children Boards and will require local authorities to work in partnership with public, private, and voluntary organizations to protect children.

---

[12] *Evaluation of Specialist Domestic Violence Courts/Fast Track Systems* (Cook, Burton, Robinson, and Vallely, March 2004).

15.4 Responsible information-sharing plays a key role in enabling organizations and professionals to protect victims of domestic violence and their children and to save lives. Casework, advocacy, conducting risk assessments, and providing general support and protection may all require information about individuals to be shared with other agencies. ACPO is about to publish 'Guidance: Identifying, Assessing & Managing Risk in the context of Policing Domestic Violence'. The Home Office has published information and advice for practitioners who work with victims of domestic violence which can be accessed on its website.[13] A national CPS/ACPO/Social Services Protocol exists, and a police/family court protocol is currently being piloted in Manchester.

15.5 We are sometimes asked to supply to third parties copies of documents held in prosecution files. The request might be made, for example, for the purpose of civil proceedings, or by local authorities in child care cases. Detailed guidance on such disclosure issues is available on the CPS Intranet.

15.6 Where information is held by us, the duty to consider disclosing unused material to the defence under common law and the provisions of the Criminal Procedure and Investigations Act 1996 arises. Again, detailed guidance is available on the CPS Intranet.

16 CASE MANAGEMENT ISSUES

Charging

16.1 In all Areas, we are operating either the shadow charging scheme or the statutory scheme, and currently CPSDirect covers the fourteen Areas where the statutory scheme is currently in place. National coverage is anticipated by Spring 2006.

16.2 All alleged offences of domestic violence are to be referred to duty prosecutors where and when the charging scheme is in place once the Threshold Test has been met. Prosecutors will need to satisfy themselves that evidence has been, or is being, effectively gathered and that the MG2 and MG11 will include sufficient details to enable witness care issues to be comprehensively assessed. Guidance for the police on the background information to be provided on prosecution files has now been published by Centrex[14] and forms the substance of most local Service Level Agreements (SLAs).

16.3 Duty prosecutors, when giving advice on domestic violence cases, should ensure that they have available, in addition to other legal resources, the updated domestic violence Policy and Guidance, The Code for Crown Prosecutors, any appropriate charging standards, and Centrex police guidance. Annex D outlines an interpretation of domestic violence offences.

---

[13] Safety and Justice: sharing personal information in the context of domestic violence—an overview, www.homeoffice.gov.uk/rds.

[14] *Guidance on Investigating Domestic Violence 2004* (National Centre for Policing Excellence), Checklist 19: File preparation, p. 54.

16.4 All available charges should be considered and full reasons for decisions recorded. Evidence from the Joint Thematic Inspection, supported by CPS annual monitoring, showed that, in some instances, an offence under the Protection from Harassment Act 1997 could properly have been charged. Such offences have the advantage of legitimately introducing background material into the case and providing protection for the victim by means of a restraining order (see paragraph 18 [below] for restraining orders under the Domestic Violence, Crime and Victims Act 2004). Unfortunately there were many occasions when this avenue was not explored and file endorsements were reported to be often inadequate or, in some cases, non-existent. Prosecutors should actively consider charges under ss. 2 and 4 where circumstances permit, and should examine as wide a range of appropriate charging options as possible in accordance with The Code.

16.5 Charging standards are designed to assist prosecutors in selecting the most appropriate charge, in the light of the facts that can be proved, at the earliest possible opportunity. When deciding whether a battery in a domestic violence case should be a common assault (s. 39 of the Criminal Justice Act 1988) or an ABH (s. 47 of the Offences Against the Person Act 1861), prosecutors should have regard to the circumstances when the presence of serious aggravating features means that ABH is the appropriate charge, for example, where a victim is vulnerable.

Identification and Flagging

16.6 Cases falling within the Government definition of domestic violence (see paragraph 2 [above]) should be identified both on the file jacket and flagged on COMPASS as Domestic Violence. Some cases will need more than one flag. There may be cases with racist or homophobic elements, for example, and instances of rape. Cases falling within the categories of Domestic Violence and Child Abuse/Child Witness should be identified and flagged as both.

16.7 We will apply our Policy for Prosecuting Cases of Domestic Violence to all these cases particularly with regard to safety issues, retractions, and effective evidence gathering.

16.8 Note that when prosecuting cases of domestic violence, the policy will also apply to those cases falling within our original definition, i.e. where there is current or former partner or family abuse, irrespective of the age of the perpetrator or the victim.

Bail

16.9 Our prime concern is the safety of the victim and any children. We look to the police to supply us with sufficient information, including the victim's views, to help us make our decisions.

16.10 It is the defendant who is subject to bail conditions, not the victim. Care should be taken when formulating bail conditions to ensure that the victim retains as much freedom of movement as possible by curbing the ability of the defendant to approach or intimidate the victim at home, work, or on the way to school, etc. Magistrates should be encouraged to make it clear to defendants that bail conditions apply to them, not victims, and that any breaches will be taken very seriously. Magistrates, of course, will be aware that it is for the family court to make arrangements regarding child contact, and generally it should not be a matter to be considered within a bail hearing.

16.11 Where a defendant is on bail with a condition not to contact the victim, it is common, especially where there is reconciliation, for the victim either to come to court to ask for the condition to be removed or to do so through the defence. The appropriate step is to seek an adjournment in order for the victim to speak freely and for the police to take a full statement. A withdrawal of support for the prosecution case does not mean that the case will automatically be discontinued, and nor should it be an automatic trigger for the relaxation of bail conditions.

16.12 Prosecutors should insist that the defence gives proper notice of any application to vary bail in order that enquiries can be made of the victim to seek views and check whether any court orders already exist or are pending. Where the proposed variation concerns child contact, prosecutors should be aware that they rarely have the necessary information or training to deal with this—family courts do, along with CAFCASS, Social Services, and specially trained benches. Contact with a child may permit opportunities to intimidate the child and/or victim, and in the worst cases can result in murder or suicide.

16.13 The Joint Thematic Inspection found that there were many instances where no action was taken in relation to breaches and no consideration that the breach itself amounted to the commission of a further offence. Where bail conditions are breached, prosecutors should consider applications for remanding the defendant into custody if circumstances merit, and should review the evidence to see whether any new offence has been committed.

16.14 The Joint Thematic Inspection also found that file endorsements recording bail representations and conditions were often inadequate. It is essential that whoever may be involved in reviewing a case or taking it into court can readily establish what has been done at what stage. We are taking more responsibility for keeping victims and witnesses informed, which is difficult to achieve in the absence of a clear record. File endorsements should be clear, full, and accurate, and must include conditions imposed with supporting grounds and reasons under the Bail Act 1976 for every file that each defendant has. Advocates must satisfy themselves that they are familiar and comply with local arrangements for notifying victims promptly of the remand status of the defendant. If no system exists, urgent consideration should be given to creating one in consultation with the Witness Care Unit.

Review

16.15 Prosecutors are required to keep all files under continuous review and make full endorsements recording work done and decisions made. In cases of domestic violence there is a particular need to keep informed of the victim's current view regarding the prosecution, because of the safety issues for the victim and any children, and also because the victim is usually the main witness.

16.16 Full and timely information is required to enable proper and continuous review. The prosecutor will need to consider not just the incident in question, but the totality and long-term aspect of any domestic violence suffered by the victim and any children of the family and inflicted by the defendant. Some defendants will have perpetrated domestic violence in more than one of their relationships and information of this nature will always be relevant to the prosecutor reviewing the case. In some instances, it may amount to admissible evidence.

16.17 The Code for Crown Prosecutors requires us to 'take into account the consequences for the victim of whether or not to prosecute and any views expressed by the victim or the victim's family'.

16.18 A key feature of domestic violence cases is often the difficult task of balancing the victim's wishes against the public interest. However, individual acts must be put in the context of the wider social picture.

16.19 It is often difficult to achieve the right balance between what is seen by some as empowering and by others as burdening the victim with the 'responsibility' for the prosecution. On the one hand, it is our decision whether or not to proceed with any prosecution, and this may be a relief to some victims. On the other, some victims of domestic violence feel that they are continuing to be 'controlled' and have no influence over what is to happen to them and their families. Prosecutors need to be alert to these issues and aware of the views of the victim. The availability of support from a specialist domestic violence agency will often be invaluable in these situations.

16.20 In any event, defendants need to know that the prosecution will not rely simply on a victim's willingness to give evidence. Where possible, cases should be constructed on the basis of evidence other than that of the victim, so that the victim's evidence is the 'icing on the cake' rather than the cake itself. The police are aware of the need to gather evidence in this way and close liaison with them is essential.

16.21 When deciding whether and how to proceed, matters to be taken into account should include the following:
  • effective evidence gathering, for example, res gestae;[15]

---

[15] *Centrex Module 3 Workbook 2003*, p. 15: 'For effective evidence gathering, you should consider: preserving 999 tapes, preserving any relevant CCTV footage, preserving forensic evidence, recording observations at the scene, e.g. furniture overturned, broken ornaments, damaged telephone etc., taking instant pictures of, or sketching, the scene and/or any injuries, making use of all call recording/intelligence/crime recording systems

- any formal risk assessment;
- the Victim Personal Statement, and if not on the file, information as to whether one was requested and consideration given to obtaining one if possible;
- use of hearsay evidence (currently s. 23 of the Criminal Justice Act 1988, but replaced by Chapter 2 of the Criminal Justice Act 2003), possibility of calling doctors/probation officers/voluntary agency supporters to provide information or give evidence as to fear, etc., witness summonses, facilities available under the Youth Justice and Criminal Evidence Act 1999;
- use by victim or other agency of civil proceedings, information or evidence from other key agencies, for example, housing departments about requests for emergency accommodation, or repairs to doors or windows, etc.

Direct Communication with Victims

16.22 Prosecutors will be aware of the circumstances in which letters are sent and meetings are offered. Further information is available on the CPS Intranet in the Legal Guidance section. Particular attention must be given to letters written to victims of domestic violence as there is a strong likelihood that they will be read by the abuser. It is especially important that where a case is being stopped, it is made clear that it is a CPS decision, not that of the victim, and that any subsequent incident will be judged individually and proceeded with accordingly. Suitable formats will need consideration, e.g. large print, Braille, audio tapes, and translated materials.

Victim's Withdrawal of Support for the Prosecution

16.23 A senior lawyer, experienced in domestic violence issues, should be consulted in any case where the victim indicates a wish to withdraw support for the prosecution and/or consideration is being given to investigating whether the victim will proceed if special measures could be provided.

16.24 A senior lawyer, experienced in domestic violence issues, must be consulted where the victim indicates a wish to withdraw support for the prosecution and consideration is being given to:
- proceeding without using the victim's evidence;
- making an application under s. 23 of the Criminal Justice Act 1988;

---

to check for previous incidents, bail conditions, injunctions, restraining orders, child contact orders or PNC circulations, speaking to neighbours, friends, work colleagues, speaking to any other potential witnesses e.g. people in nearby business premises or trades people who may have called at the premises, interviewing children in the household who may have witnessed the incident, arranging for physical checks on any children who may have been harmed, checking child at risk registers, arranging medical examinations of both suspect and victim, researching medical records at accident and emergency departments and doctors' surgeries, preserving correspondence from suspect to victim, taking a victim statement, taking a Victim Personal Statement, obtaining a victim impact statement from a third party, obtaining other expert witness statements, collating statements from police officers.'

- compelling the victim to give evidence;
- discontinuing as a result of the victim withdrawing support for the prosecution.

16.25 The police must be asked to send a withdrawal statement in the format described in this document at Annex A, as there cannot be an informed decision about the next steps without it. As a result of the police officer's report, prosecutors may need to consider whether further charges, e.g. witness intimidation, are appropriate. It may also be appropriate to ask the police to offer the victim the services of a specialist support agency, if this has not already occurred.

16.26 Prosecutors should assess at an early stage whether there is sufficient evidence to proceed without the victim, for example, the 999 tape, admissions in interview, CCTV, and officers' statements. If there is, and providing the public interest test continues to be met, there may be no need to consider a witness summons if the victim subsequently withdraws support.

16.27 Prosecutors will also need to consider any Victim Personal Statement. There can be advantages to victims regarding these where victims state that they do not support the prosecution so that it is clear to the court—and the defendant—that the decision to proceed rests with the CPS.

16.28 Where we are considering proceeding against the victim's wishes, we must consider all parties' human rights issues (including children's) and endorse fully and clearly the decision-making process on file.

Witness Summonses

16.29 Before a decision to issue a summons is taken, prosecutors must make enquiries to satisfy themselves, as far as possible, that the safety of the victim and any children will not be endangered by their decision. Through the police, prosecutors should check that the victim has been made aware of available specialist support and whether it has been offered and accepted or declined. Police and advocacy services should be asked to advise on their assessment of safety.

16.30 Summonses will be appropriate in some circumstances and can be very successful. They can support victims and assist their attendance at court by 'removing' the decision from them. Where a witness attends as a result of a summons, there is often a guilty plea. However, it is also possible that a witness will still not attend, or may come to court but refuse to give evidence. Table 1 [below] sets out factors that will tend to support or militate against the decision to issue a witness summons.

16.31 If a witness refuses to attend as a result of a summons, we must go on to consider whether a warrant is appropriate. It is a difficult decision but one that must not be avoided. Again, a senior experienced lawyer should be consulted, safety issues must be considered and then reference made to Table 1. The intention is not to penalize or criminalise victims, but to assist their

Table 1

If going ahead with the prosecution against the victim's wishes, consider the following and any combinations:[16]	Summons more desirable	Summons less desirable
The seriousness of the offence in the context of that case:		
1. Serious offence	✔	
2. Minor offence and isolated event		✔
Victim's injuries (including psychological)		
1. Serious injuries	✔	
2. No or minor injuries		✔
Use of a weapon	✔	
Any subsequent threats by defendant	✔	
Whether attack planned	✔	
Whether incident witnessed (seen or heard) by children	✔	
Whether offence committed in presence of, or in close proximity to a child	✔	
Effect (including psychological) on any children living in the household	✔	
Recurrence likely	✔	
Threat to the health and/or safety of the victim or any other person involved	✔	
Pregnancy	✔	
Current state of victim's relationship with defendant		
1. Further incidents	✔	
2. Relationship assessed as 'unstable'	✔	
3. No divorce proceedings	✔?	
4. No further incidents		✔?
5. No further police call-outs		✔?
6. No ongoing civil proceedings	✔?	
7. No history of a volatile relationship		✔
8. Relationship assessed as 'stable'		✔
History of relationship		
1. Violent relationship and/or pattern of offending	✔	
2. Mostly harmonious relationship		✔
Defendant's criminal history (particularly if previous violence)—(See Bad Character form, Police MoG 2004/5)	✔	
Information from any other agencies supporting proceeding, e.g. Social Services, Housing, Health, Women's Aid, voluntary sector (including perpetrator services) etc	✔	

[16] A combination of factors may be present which may make a summons more or less desirable. Options must be balanced. Where ✔? appears on the Table, these factors may tend in either direction and *must* be viewed within the context of the case as a whole.

attendance at court. (Note: the Joint Thematic Review found that in many instances prosecutors and police failed to ensure conduct/service money was provided when serving summonses. Local SLAs should cover this provision.)

Compelling a Witness to Give Evidence

16.32 A witness before the court can be compelled to give evidence under the threat of being in contempt of court and subject to imprisonment. Each case must be judged on its merits, taking into account the factors in Table 1, the individual circumstances of the victim, and the wider public interest. Prosecutors may be reluctant to make this choice because of the threat of imprisonment, but it should be remembered that a tiny minority of victims are imprisoned as a consequence of refusing to give evidence. Safety issues (including those of any children) are key in this decision-making process.

'Bind Overs'

16.33 Where the victim withdraws support for the prosecution and all avenues for continuing the case have been explored and discounted, a 'bind over', which affords the victim some protection, may be an acceptable option. 'Bind overs' should not be routinely used and should be viewed as a last resort.

Deciding to Discontinue

16.34 If a senior experienced lawyer has considered whether it is possible to proceed without the victim, decided that it is but that it would not be right to do so in the particular circumstances, the case will be discontinued. These cases will be rare and should be marked as discontinued for failing the public interest test.

16.35 Where it is not possible to continue without the victim and the decision is made not to compel attendance, again the decision to discontinue is on public interest grounds.

Dealing with Self-Defence and/or Counter Allegations

16.36 In cases where a counter allegation has been made, police officers should have noted and recorded the following information:
- comparative severity of injuries;
- threats of future harm to others made by either party;
- any prior history of violence;
- any previous counter allegations;
- whether either party acted defensively to protect himself, or herself, or a third party from injury.

Where self-defence is raised, prosecutors should request from the police as much of this information as is appropriate, especially if considering discontinuing the case because of insufficient evidence.

Sentencing

16.37 Prosecutors need to be aware of their duties in relation to sentencing issues, particularly with regard to appeals, potentially unduly lenient sentences (ensuring they are cognisant of recent sentencing case law), and correcting derogatory defence assertions. The Code contains a section on the prosecutor's role in sentencing. Newton hearings may be necessary in some circumstances. Prosecutors can and should guide the court in relation to orders available and draw attention to relevant cases. Applications for compensation should be made where appropriate, bearing in mind that where the parties remain together such orders will probably be met from family money. Victim Personal Statements should always be brought to the court's attention.

Agents and Counsel

16.38 Staff will need to ensure that agents and counsel instructed by us are familiar with the CPS Instructions for Prosecuting Advocates (2004) as well as CPS Policy and Guidance documents. Agents and counsel must be made aware that decisions relating to acceptability of pleas and issues affecting witnesses' attendance at court, including compelling their attendance, must be referred to CPS staff.

Training

16.39 A national CPS domestic violence training package has been prepared in association with Centrex (Central Police Training and Development Authority) in readiness for February 2005.

Monitoring

16.40 We monitor cases of domestic violence because they are included in CPS Hate Crime performance indicators as well as new government performance indicators, and monitoring enables us to assess our performance. Flagging of domestic violence cases on COMPASS is key to providing data for Areas and monitoring performance indicators. Detailed analysis is also currently conducted by means of an annual 'snapshot' in December.

17 ECHR ISSUES

- Affect the way in which the police conduct their investigation.

- Affect our decisions to prosecute or not to prosecute—particularly when the victim withdraws support for the prosecution.
- Affect the manner in which we decide to conduct the case.

17.1 Prosecutors will be used to considering the impact of ECHR issues on both the defendant's and victim's rights within criminal proceedings generally. Given that many domestic violence cases involve repeat incidents and/or close personal relationships, and children, particular ECHR issues arise for consideration.

17.2 A victim of domestic violence has rights under, for example, Articles 2, 3, 6, and 8, as would any children of the family.

17.3 The rights of the victim, any children, the public (in the narrowest as well as widest sense, e.g. including extended family or neighbours), and the defendant have to be balanced.

17.4 For example, a victim who did not support the prosecution might argue that our decision to prosecute breached Article 8—the right guaranteeing a family life. On the other hand, depending on the circumstances of the case, it might be argued that we had not only a positive duty to protect the victim and any children whose lives were at risk from the criminal acts of another, but also to respect the children's right to a family life free of violence or other forms of abuse.

Article 2—Right to Life

Osman v UK (1999) 29 EHRR 245

17.5 There is a positive obligation on public authorities, in some well-defined circumstances, to take preventative operational measures to protect an individual whose life is at risk from the criminal acts of another individual. The public authority must do all that can reasonably be expected to avoid a 'real and immediate risk' to life.

17.6 Although this could be applied to justify a prosecution against the victim's wishes, it could also, arguably, be applied to justify a request not to prosecute.

Article 3—Prohibition of Torture, Inhuman, or Degrading Treatment

Z v UK (2002) 34 EHRR 3

17.7 This article may be taken to include physical assaults or mistreatment relating to mental and physical suffering. It can be applied to the positive duty on a public authority not to allow an individual to apply such treatment to another. Or, it could be applied to the manner in which a public authority compels a victim to give evidence against another family member against their will. Vulnerable individuals are entitled to 'protection by way of effective deterrence' against serious breaches of their personal integrity, and the authorities are under an obligation to take reasonable steps to prevent ill-treatment of which they had, or ought to have had, knowledge.

Article 6—Right to a Fair Trial

17.8 This article includes a victim's right to pursue civil proceedings. The ability to pursue this right can be affected by the manner in which the investigation or prosecution are conducted. Children, other family members, and even other persons could be considered 'victims' in accordance with ECHR terminology. Thus, in any particular case, there may be a number of people with different views and wishes, all of whom are entitled to have their rights taken into consideration.

Article 8—Right to Respect for Private and Family Life

17.9 These rights and freedoms may be limited if it is necessary to achieve an important objective such as prevention of crime or disorder, or for the protection of health or safety.

Article 14—Prohibition of Discrimination

17.10 The rights set out above apply without discrimination on any grounds—for example sex, race, colour, language, or association with a national minority.

18 NEW LEGISLATION

See Annex F for further information.

18.1 Female Genital Mutilation Act 2003

This came into force on 3 March 2004.

- The Act makes it illegal for female genital mutilation (FGM) to be performed in the UK and, for the first time, it is also an offence for UK nationals or permanent UK residents to carry out, or aid, abet, counsel, or procure the carrying out of FGM abroad on a UK national or permanent UK resident, even in countries where the practice is legal.
- The maximum penalty is fourteen years' imprisonment.
- FGM constitutes all procedures that involve partial or total removal of the external female genitalia, or injury to the female genital organs.
- It is reportedly practised in twenty-eight African countries from the Gambia to Somalia and parts of the Middle and Far East. It has been reported in immigrant African populations in Europe, Australia, New Zealand, Canada, and the USA.

18.2 Sexual Offences Act 2003

This came into force on 1 May 2004.

The Act repeals almost all the existing statute law in relation to sexual offences. The main provisions of the Act relevant for cases of domestic violence are:

- rape is widened to include oral penetration;
- significant changes to the issue of consent;
- specific offences relating to children under 13, 16, and 18;
- familial child sex offences;
- familial adult sex offences.

The elements of rape (s. 1) are:

- penetration of V's vagina, anus, or mouth with D's penis, where
- V does not consent to the penetration, and
- D does not reasonably believe that V consents.

Rape is a crime of basic intent and drunkenness is no defence. It is triable only on indictment with a maximum penalty of life imprisonment.

Section 74 defines consent as 'if s/he agrees by choice, and has the freedom and capacity to make that choice'.

Two fundamental questions need to be answered. First, whether the complainant had the capacity (i.e. the age and understanding) to make a choice about whether to take part in the sexual activity at the time in question. Second, whether s/he was in a position to make that choice freely, which is not constrained in any way. Assuming that the complainant had both the freedom and capacity to consent, the crucial question is whether the complainant agreed to the activity by choice. This potentially has application for victims of domestic violence who may not be able to make free choices because of, for example, the nature of the abuse within the household, or fears of/for the wider family.

Sections 5–8 apply the main non-consensual offences (rape, assault by penetration, sexual assault, and causing a person to engage in sexual activity) to children under 13, except that consent in these offences is irrelevant. A child under 13 does not, under any circumstances, have the legal capacity to consent to any form of sexual activity.

The Act provides that the age of consent is 16. Sections 9–13 clarify that any sexual activity involving consenting children under 16 is illegal.

Familial sex offences reflect the modern family unit and take into account situations where someone is living within the same household as a child and assumes a position of trust or authority over that child, as well as relationships defined by blood ties, adoption, fostering, marriage, or living together as partners.

18.3 Youth Justice and Criminal Evidence Act 1999: Special Measures Implementation in England and Wales

See implementation charts at Annexes B and C.

In addition, s. 46 (reporting restrictions for adults) came into force in October 2004, and guidance can be found on the CPS Intranet (see Annex F).

18.4 Powers of Criminal Courts (Sentencing) Act 2000

Section 46 of the Criminal Justice and Courts Act 2000 provides for a new s. 40A to be inserted in the Powers of Criminal Courts (Sentencing) Act 2000, providing for exclusion orders on conviction that prohibit a person from entering a place specified in the order for a specified period. The section is not yet in force, but is being piloted for prolific offenders and domestic violence offenders in Hampshire and the West Midlands, as well as sex offenders in Greater Manchester, by means of satellite tracking. For further information, see http://www.probation.homeoffice.gov.uk/output/page244.asp.

18.5 Criminal Justice Act 2003

The Act received Royal Assent on 20 November 2003. Legal guidance is available on the CPS Intranet. Evidence of bad character was implemented in December 2004 and the provisions relating to evidence of hearsay were implemented on 4 April 2005.

The Act is designed to introduce reform in court procedure and sentencing. Provisions of particular interest in cases of domestic violence are highlighted below.

Court procedure

Management of cases through the courts will be improved by:

- following the Criminal Case Management Framework (issued in July 2004);
- involving the CPS in charging decisions and providing for a new method of instigating prosecutions (Part 4 of the Act);
- amending some of the provisions relating to disclosure in the Criminal Procedure and Investigations Act 1996 for both prosecution and defence (Part 5);
- reforming the system for allocating cases to court by making magistrates aware of the defendant's previous convictions, if any, and allowing defendants to seek a broad indication of sentence were they to plead guilty at that point (Sch. 3);
- increasing magistrates' sentencing powers;
- breaches of bail will be reduced because of a new presumption against bail in some cases.

Criminal trials will be run more efficiently as:

- rules on evidence will be changed to allow the use of previous convictions where relevant (Part 11);
- rules of evidence will be changed to allow the use of hearsay evidence where there is good reason why the original source cannot be present, or the judge considers it appropriate;
- any witness will be able to give evidence via a live link (Part 8);
- it will be possible in certain very serious cases for a retrial to take place despite an earlier acquittal if there is new and compelling evidence of an accused's guilt (Part 10).

Evidence

Part 11, Chapter 1 of the Act deals with evidence of bad character. Section 101 sets out the grounds for a defendant's bad character being admissible, and, of particular interest for cases of domestic violence, s. 103(2) provides:

a defendant's propensity to commit offences of the kind with which he is charged may... be established by evidence that he has been convicted of (a) an offence of the same description as the one with which he is charged, or (b) an offence of the same category as the one with which he is charged.

Part 11, Chapter 2 of the Act deals with hearsay evidence. The main provisions in ss. 114 and 115 remove the old common law rule against the admissibility of hearsay and provide that such evidence will be admissible provided certain safeguards are met. Section 118 preserves certain common law categories of admissibility, most notably for domestic violence cases, res gestae:

any rule of law under which in criminal proceedings a statement is admissible as evidence of any matter stated if (a) the statement was made by a person so emotionally overpowered by an event that the possibility of concoction or distortion can be disregarded, (b) the statement accompanied an act which can be properly evaluated as evidence only if considered in conjunction with the statement, or (c) the statement relates to a physical sensation or mental state (such as intention or emotion).

Sentencing

The Act aims to provide a sentencing framework which is clearer and more flexible than the current one. The purposes of sentencing adults are identified as punishment, crime reduction, reform and rehabilitation, public protection, and reparation. Previous convictions, if they are recent and relevant, should be regarded as an aggravating factor which may increase the severity of the sentence.

Sentences will be reformed as follows with a phased introduction over three years from 2005:

- the range of community orders for adults will be replaced by a single community order with an improved range of possible requirements;
- custodial sentences of less than twelve months will be replaced by a new sentence (described in the Halliday report as 'custody plus') which will always involve a period of at least twenty-six weeks' post-release supervision in the community;
- custodial sentences of over twelve months will be served in full, half in custody, half in the community, with supervision extended to the end of the sentence;
- serious violent and sexual offenders will be given new sentences to ensure they are kept in prison or under supervision for longer periods than currently.

Other Provisions

Part 3 of the Act allows for a caution with specific conditions attached to it to be given where there is sufficient evidence to charge a suspect with an offence which s/he admits and the suspect agrees to the caution. If the suspect fails to comply with the conditions, s/he is liable to be prosecuted for the offence. It is for the prosecutor to decide whether a conditional caution is appropriate, which in cases of domestic violence is likely to be rare but not impossible. Where, for example, the incident appears to be isolated, out of character with minor injuries being inflicted, and the victim's views have been sought and approval given, a conditional caution may be the appropriate remedy.

The Act establishes a new scheme under which the court, rather than the Home Secretary, will determine the minimum term to be served in prison before eligibility for parole by a person convicted of murder and sentenced to life imprisonment.

In relation to youths, the Act extends the use of parenting orders by making them available at an earlier stage, and introduces individual support orders, requiring young people with anti-social behaviour orders to undertake education-related activities.

18.6 Children Act 2004

Section 58 (reasonable punishment) came into effect on 15 January 2005. It removes the defence of reasonable chastisement in any proceedings for an offence of s. 47, 20, or 18 of the Offences Against the Person Act 1861, or cruelty to a child (s. 1 of the Children and Young Persons Act 1933). It also prevents the defence being relied upon in any civil proceedings where the harm caused amounts to actual bodily harm. The defence would still be available in proceedings for common assault on a child.

18.7 Domestic Violence, Crime and Victims Act 2004

The Act is divided into four parts: domestic violence, criminal justice, victims, etc., and supplementary. The first two parts contain the main provisions with relevance to cases of domestic violence. In due course, guidance will be published on certain aspects of this proposed legislation, for example, prosecuting breaches of non-molestation orders and drafting restraining orders.

Domestic Violence

- Section 1: Breach of a non-molestation order to be a criminal offence.
  This amends the Family Law Act 1996 by inserting a new s. 42A. The offence may be punished either as a criminal offence with a maximum penalty of five years' imprisonment, or as a civil contempt of court.

  The 'associated persons' criteria of the Family Law Act are widened to give same sex couples who are cohabiting the same level of protection as cohabiting heterosexual couples, and to include relationships where the couple has never lived together.

  There has been some debate about how and by whom the choice of venue will be made, especially if the police are able to arrest for breach, and what the standard of proof will be in order to prove a breach.

- Section 5: Causing or allowing the death of a child or vulnerable adult.

  This section creates an offence where a child or vulnerable adult dies as the result of the unlawful act of a person who was a member of the same household as the victim *and* who had frequent contact with the victim. A person may be classed as a member of the victim's household if he or she visits so often and for such periods of time that it is reasonable to regard the person as a member of it.

  Liability for an offence of 'familial homicide' arises if it can be proved that either the defendant caused the victim's death, or that the defendant failed to take reasonable steps to protect the victim in circumstances where he or she was aware, or ought to have been aware, that there was a significant risk of serious physical harm being caused to the victim by a member of the victim's household who also had frequent contact with the victim, and that the act occurred in circumstances of the kind that the defendant ought to have foreseen. This offence will be applicable in circumstances where it is possible to show that the death of a child or vulnerable adult was caused by *a* member of the household as defined above, but there is no evidence to show who in particular actually caused the death. This new offence is, however, a stand-alone offence that creates a duty to protect children and vulnerable adults. All members of a household who have frequent contact with a child or vulnerable adult will have that duty, and liability will arise in respect of all those who failed to take reasonable steps to protect the victim from risk, regardless of whether or not it can be proved that one particular individual was responsible for the actual death.

  What steps a person might reasonably have taken will depend on that person's situation. It must be proved that the defendant failed to take such steps as he or she could reasonably have been expected to take to protect the victim from risk. It will ultimately be a matter for the court, and a judgement will need to be made in the circumstances of each case as to whether a court would be likely to hold particular steps to have been reasonable. In cases where defendants have also been victims of violence, the courts may be prepared to accept that the steps they could reasonably have been expected to take were limited by their own experience of victimization. However, it should always be borne in mind that the Act is premised on the basis of a duty to protect children and other vulnerable people from harm. The fact that the defendant may be young and uncertain, feel intimidated, or have suffered violence, will not of itself be conclusive evidence that it was reasonable for the defendant *not* to take any steps to protect the victim. In most cases (although not necessarily all) there will be steps, however limited, which the defendant could have taken.

  Again this section has provoked considerable debate, and some organizations have expressed anxiety that some adult victims of domestic violence may be liable to charge under this section for failing to protect their children from domestic violence that results in the child's death.

  The offence carries a maximum term of imprisonment of fourteen years.

- Section 9: Domestic homicide reviews.
  This section establishes that a domestic homicide review may take place where a death of a person aged 16 or over (V) has, or appears to have, resulted from violence, abuse, or neglect by (a) a person to whom V was related or with whom V was or had been in an intimate personal relationship, or (b) a member of the same household as V. The purpose of the review is to identify lessons to be learned from the death.

Criminal Justice

- Section 10: Common assault to be an arrestable offence.
  This will prevent the hitherto common situation where a police officer would arrest for an offence of assault occasioning actual bodily harm and the charge later be 'reduced' or 'downgraded' to common assault with predictable negative perceptions by victims and witnesses.
- Section 11: Common assault becomes a statutory alternative verdict.
  Common assault will be an alternative verdict to more serious offences of assault even if the count has not yet been preferred in the indictment.
- Section 12: Restraining orders.
  This section extends the availability of restraining orders. A restraining order may be made when sentencing for any offence. It also, controversially, extends their availability to cases where there has been an acquittal but the court considers it necessary to make a restraining order to protect a victim.

19 CIVIL PROCEEDINGS

19.1 The needs of individual victims vary and, to ensure their safety, criminal and civil law may need to be used in conjunction. Prosecutors therefore should be aware of the options open to victims or other agencies under civil procedures so that a holistic approach can be taken in safeguarding and supporting victims.[17] Where there are concurrent criminal and civil proceedings (and prosecutors will need to make enquiries to see if this is the case), prosecutors will need to ensure that courts have the appropriate information to enable them to make orders that prioritize the safety of victims and children and are consistent.

19.2 If it is not already contained within the file, the police should be asked to provide information about any relevant civil proceedings past, current, or pending (see Annex A).

19.3 There are complex policy and legal issues regarding the use within criminal proceedings of evidence arising from civil proceedings—particularly family court proceedings, which are generally held in chambers. Further guidance will be issued in due course but, in the meantime, prosecutors should not be deterred from making appropriate use of information about civil proceedings

---

[17] *Domestic Violence: A Guide to Civil Remedies and Criminal Sections*, DCA (February 2003).

in the course of their review or prosecution of cases of domestic violence. For example, the fact that a non-molestation injunction was issued/breached is likely to be relevant to review and bail decisions, and breaches of non-molestation orders will be criminal offences when new legislation is implemented—see the Domestic Violence, Crime and Victims Act 2004 at paragraph 18.

19.4 The availability of civil proceedings does not diminish a defendant's criminal behaviour and is not therefore a reason, in itself, to discontinue.

Section 3 of the Protection from Harassment Act 1997

19.5 Proceedings under s. 3 may be founded on the basis of one act and anticipated further breaches of s. 1 (in contrast to criminal proceedings under s. 2 or s. 4 that require at least two incidents in order to constitute a course of conduct). Breach of an order is a criminal offence. However, no power of arrest can be attached to this civil order and, in order to enforce it, the victim will need to return to court to apply for a warrant of arrest.

Housing Act 1996

19.6 This Act revised the grounds for repossession on the basis of nuisance (including domestic violence). Local authorities and housing associations now have greater powers to repossess properties as a result of nuisance or annoyance for which the tenant is responsible. Local authorities may also apply for injunctions, to which a power of arrest can be attached, to protect tenants from similar conduct.

Part IV of the Family Law Act 1996

19.7 This part of the Act came into force in October 1997 and concerns domestic violence and occupation of the family home. It provides a set of remedies available in all courts with a family jurisdiction (including magistrates' courts). Orders available include non-molestation and occupation orders. Applications under the Act can be made without notice.

19.8 Where a court has the power to make a non-molestation or occupation order, it can accept an undertaking from the respondent (e.g. not to molest, not to go within a certain distance of the home, etc.). A power of arrest cannot be attached to an undertaking and the court must not accept an undertaking where otherwise it would be appropriate to attach a power of arrest. If the undertaking is breached, it can be enforced as if it were an order of the court.

19.9 Unless the court is satisfied that the applicant and any relevant child will be adequately protected without such a power, a power of arrest must be attached to a non-molestation or occupation order made following an application on notice and where the court is satisfied that the respondent has used or threatened violence against the applicant or relevant child. (The Domestic

Violence, Crime and Victims Act 2004 makes changes to this provision—see paragraph 18.)

19.10 Where the court makes a without notice order, it may attach a power of arrest if the respondent has used or threatened violence and there is a risk of significant harm to the applicant or child, attributable to the conduct of the respondent, if the power of arrest is not attached immediately.

19.11 Part IV gives powers of remand and bail to the county courts, exercised by circuit or district judges.

Family Law Act 1996

19.12 Section 60 provides for designated third parties to take proceedings on behalf of victims of domestic violence who are unwilling or unable to take proceedings on their own behalf. A decision was made in 2002 not to implement this section as research indicated that complex issues arose from it requiring further consideration.

Children Act 1989

19.13 This Act was amended by Part IV of the Family Law Act 1996. Formerly, where a court made an emergency protection order or an interim care order for the protection of a child, it was the child, not the suspected abuser, who was removed from the home. Now, the court can attach an exclusion order (with a power of arrest if necessary) permitting the removal of the suspected abuser from the home, rather than the child.

Adoption and Children Act 2002

19.14 Section 120 came into force on 31 January 2005. It amends the definition of 'harm' in the Children Act 1989 to make it clear that harm includes any impairment of a child's health or development as a result of hearing or seeing the ill-treatment of another person. This amendment provides guidance for the courts that adds to existing guidelines on contact and domestic violence.

Anti-Social Behaviour Orders (ASBOs)—Crime and Disorder Act 1998 and Anti-Social Behaviour Act 2003

19.15 Anti-Social Behaviour Orders (ASBOs) came into effect on 1 April 1999 and were designed to target activities that disrupt the lives of individuals, families, and communities. They are civil orders containing prohibitions to prevent anti-social behaviour.

19.16 Use of ASBOs in the context of domestic violence is viewed as a message to abusers that their behaviour has an effect on neighbours and the community that will not be tolerated.

19.17 Note that anti-social behaviour is to be understood by reference to the term 'anti-social manner', which is defined in s. 1 (1)(a) as 'acting in a manner that caused or was likely to cause harassment, alarm or distress to one or more persons not of the same household' as the perpetrator. Clearly, therefore, ASBOs can only be considered in cases where the domestic violence has had the necessary impact on persons 'not of the same household'. This provision was not intended to cover separated partners—it is intended to cover neighbours and members of the local community—but where partners (or former partners) are maintaining separate households, the legislation does apply and the obtaining of an ASBO is a valuable tool for protecting the victim and the public.

19.18 The court may make an order if it is satisfied that a person has acted in an anti-social manner, and that the ASBO is necessary to protect the public from further acts of anti-social behaviour by that person. An ASBO can be applied to any person aged 10 years or over and is for a period of not less than two years or until further order.

19.19 When the Crime and Disorder Act was first introduced, only the police or a local authority could apply for an order, after having consulted each other ('stand-alone ASBOs'). In such cases, the application is made to the magistrates' court within six months of the behaviour, although earlier incidents can be used as background information to support the need for an order.

19.20 The Police Reform Act 2002 introduced 'orders upon criminal conviction' but did not specify who could apply for such orders. This was clarified by the Anti-Social Behaviour Act 2003, which states that such orders can be made if either the prosecutor asks for an order, or the court itself is of the view that an order is necessary.

19.21 The same criteria apply to the making of an order upon conviction, but in addition, the court must be satisfied that the person has been convicted of a relevant offence (one committed after 2 December 2002). For the purpose of deciding whether to make an order upon conviction, the court may consider evidence led by the prosecution and the defence, and it is immaterial whether such evidence would have been admissible in the proceedings in which the offender was convicted. As proceedings are civil, not criminal, hearsay evidence is admissible (which may be useful when the victim will not give evidence). Magistrates will apply the criminal standard of proof in relation to s. 1(1)(a) of the Crime and Disorder Act 1998—whether a person has acted in an anti-social manner. The enquiry under s. 1(1)(b)—whether an order is necessary to protect one or more persons—does not involve a standard of proof but is an exercise of judgement or evaluation.[18]

19.22 The key to both stand-alone and orders upon conviction is a pattern of behaviour causing or likely to cause harassment, alarm, or distress, continuing over a period of time and having an adverse effect on neighbours or the community.

---

[18] *R (on the application of McCann and others) v Crown Court at Manchester and another; Clingham v Kensington and Chelsea Royal London Borough Council* [2002] UKHL 39, [2003] 1 AC 787.

19.23 The purpose of an ASBO is not to punish the defendant but to prevent further harassment, alarm, or distress being caused to the community.

19.24 Breach of an ASBO is a criminal offence punishable by fine and/or imprisonment of up to five years.

ANNEX A: EVIDENCE AND ISSUES CHECK LIST

Issue to be considered	Decision/Comment	Information Dated
1. INFORMATION NEEDED FROM THE POLICE		
History of relationship		
Previous incidents		
Ability/willingness of victim to give evidence		
Composition of family		
Details of gender, age, faith, ethnicity, disability, sexuality, special needs		
Effect of proceedings on any children		
Whereabouts of children during the incident		
Current domestic arrangements and information or police view on future relationship		
Likelihood of recurrence		
Views on safety of victim and any children		
Formal risk assessment if any		
Information from other agencies, e.g. Social Services, Health Dept, etc.		
Details of any support from a specialist domestic violence agency		
Need for special measures		
Civil orders made or pending and any breaches		
Any other information, e.g. medical or photographic evidence		

Issue to be considered	Decision/Comment	Information Dated
2. BAIL		
Police view on victim's and children's safety		
Victim's view on own and children's safety		
Method by which victim to be informed promptly of bail decision		
Information about location, for example children's school, usual shopping area, victim's place of work, and social areas		
Child contact issues		
Previous breaches of bail		
Victim Personal Statement?		
3. EFFECTIVE EVIDENCE		
Any photos of scene/photos of injuries/medical/ admissions/res gestae/ 999 record/forensic/ independent witnesses/ children/similar fact evidence?		
4. RETRACTION		
Has an experienced prosecutor been consulted?		
Statement from victim giving full reasons?		
Original complaint true or false?		
Duress?		
Any other relevant information?		

Guidance on Prosecuting Cases of Domestic Violence

Issue to be considered	Decision/Comment	Information Dated
Police officer's:		
View on veracity and general assessment of reasons given		
View on how case should be dealt with, including proceeding against victim's wishes		
View on how victim might react to being compelled		
View on victim's and children's safety and whether any other support agency has expressed a view		
Victim's:		
Views on case proceeding?		
Any other relevant information?		
Consider:		
Seriousness of offence		
Victim's injuries (including psychological and emotional)		
Use of a weapon		
Any subsequent threats by defendant		
Whether attack planned		
Whether incident witnessed (seen or heard) by children		
Whether incident occurred in presence of, or near, a child		
Effect (including psychological and emotional) on any children living in the household		
Chances of recurrence		

Issue to be considered	Decision/Comment	Information Dated
Threat to health/safety of victim or any other person involved		
Pregnancy		
Current state of victim's relationship with defendant and assessment of its stability		
Effect on that relationship of continuing with the prosecution against the victim's wishes		
History of relationship (particularly if previous violence)		
Defendant's criminal history (particularly if previous violence)		
Effect of 'outing' a LGBT person		
Information from any other agencies, e.g. Social Services, Housing, Health, Women's Aid, voluntary sector (including perpetrator services) etc.		
Where victim's evidence is not vital:		
Sufficient other evidence and in public interest to proceed?		
Where victim's evidence is vital:		
Witness summons appropriate? (see next section)		
Arrest warrant appropriate?		
Section 23 of the Criminal Justice Act 1988 procedure appropriate?		

Guidance on Prosecuting Cases of Domestic Violence

Issue to be considered	Decision/Comment	Information Dated
Any witness protection measures necessary?		
5. TRIAL		
Defence invited to accept any s. 10s?		
Victim, child, or any witness vulnerable and/or intimidated?		
Witness Service or other supporting agency involved?		
Waiting arrangements?		
Pagers?		
Specialist support agency?		
Safe entrance/waiting area?		
Eligible for any special measures Youth Justice and Criminal Evidence Act 1999?		
Early special measures meeting		
Meeting with prosecutor		
Reporting restrictions		
Screens		
Live TV link		
Video evidence		
Clear public gallery		
'Bind over'		
Appropriate? Discussed with police/victim?		
Sentence		
Restraining order appropriate?		
Any other order appropriate?		

Issue to be considered	Decision/Comment	Information Dated
Providing information		
Method of notifying victim promptly of results/decisions		
Contact details of police DVOs and CPS DVCs available for all CPS staff		
6. CIVIL PROCEEDINGS AND ORDERS		
Previous/current/pending		
Family Law Act 1996 non-molestation?		
Family Law Act 1996 occupation?		
Children Act 1989 interim care order?		
Children Act 1989 undertaking?		
Children Act 1989 emergency protection?		
Children Act 1989, s. 8 contact?		
Children Act 1989 exclusion?		
Crime and Disorder Act 1998 ASBO?		
Housing Act 1996 injunction?		
Protection from Harassment Act 1997, s. 3 injunction?		
Child Protection Register?		
Any breaches?		

ANNEX B: SPECIAL MEASURES IMPLEMENTATION CHART 1

Part II, Youth Justice and Criminal Evidence Act 1999

Vulnerable Witnesses		Children—automatically eligible		Intimidated Witnesses (s. 17)
Adults				
All Offences Always Quality Tested Mentally Disordered (per MHA 1983) Intellectually and Socially Impaired Physically Disabled		All offences—Primary Rule presumes video evidence & live link, but remains subject to Quality Test for children in cases other than sex or violence and for all other measures Children (Under 17 yrs) only	For Children deemed in need of Special Protection, i.e. in Violence, Abduction, Neglect or Sex offences No Quality Test Required for video evidence and live link Children (Under 17 yrs) only	All Offences Always Quality Tested Automatic eligibility for complainants in sexual cases Quality of Evidence Diminished by Fear or Distress

Special Measure	YJCE Act 1999	Crown Court		Magistrates' Court		Addl. Info
		Vulnerable (s16)	Intimidated (s17)	Vulnerable (s16)	Intimidated (s17)	
SCREENS	s.23	24 July 2002	24 July 2002	3 June 2004	3 June 2004	
VIDEO LINK	s.24	24 July 2002	24 July 2002	24 July 2002—Child (Sex, Violence, Threats & Cruelty)8*	2003–2004 pilot evaluation in Crown Court	*For ALL other s. 16 wits after evaluation in Crown Ct.
EVIDENCE IN PRIVATE	s.25	24 July 2002	24 July 2002	3 June 2004	3 June 2004	
WIGS & GOWNS OFF	s.26	24 July 2002	24 July 2002	Not Applicable	Not Applicable	
VIDEOTAPED EVIDENCE IN CHIEF	s.27	24 July 2002	2003–2004 Awaits evaluation of s. 16	24 July 2002—Child (Sex, Violence, Threats & Cruelty)*	Not yet available as of 1 January 2005	*For ALL other s. 16 wits after evaluation in Crown Ct.
VIDEOTAPED X-EXAM	s.28	No current plans to implement	No current plans to implement	No current plans to implement		
INTERMEDIARY	s.29	Awaits evaluation of Pilot	No current plans to implement	Awaits evaluation of Pilot	No current plans to implement	Live pilots began Feb 2004
AIDS TO COMMUNICATION	s.30	24 July 2002	Not Available See s18 (1)(b)	3 June 2004	Not Available See s18 (1)(b)	

ANNEX C: SPECIAL MEASURES IMPLEMENTATION CHART 2
Youth Justice and Criminal Evidence Act 1999: Special Measures Implementation (England & Wales)

* = currently available (June 2004) ■ = not currently available (June 2004)	Crown Court		Magistrates' Court	
	Section 16 witnesses	Section 17 witnesses	Section 16 witnesses	Section 17 witnesses
Section 23 screening witness from accused	*(24/7/02)	*(24/7/02)	*(3/6/04)	*(3/6/04)
Section 24 evidence by live link	*(24/7/02)	*(24/7/02)	*(24/7/02 for child witnesses in need of special protection only) (note 1)	*(note 1)
Section 25 evidence given in private	*(24/7/02)	*(24/7/02)	*(3/6/04)	*(3/6/04)
Section 26 removal of wigs and gowns	*(24/7/02)	*(24/7/02)	Not applicable	Not applicable
Section 27 video recorded evidence in chief	*(24/7/02)	■(note 2)	*(24/7/02 for child witnesses in need of special protection only) (note 2)	■Not yet available as of 01/1/05
Section 28 video recorded cross-examination/re-examination	■(note 3)	■(note 3)	■(note 3)	■(note 3)
Section 29 examination through an intermediary	*(23/2/04 in Merseyside only)	Not applicable	*(23/2/04 in Merseyside only) (note 4)	Not applicable
Section 30 aids to communication	(note 4) *(24/7/02)	Not applicable	*(23/2/04—Merseyside) *(3/6/04—all other courts)	Not applicable

Note 1: to be made more widely available once sufficient facilities are in place, we are planning to implement from 1 April 2005.
Note 2: wider implementation pending investigation of alternatives to transcription in less serious cases which will be piloted in 2004/2005, and if successful the Home
Office is planning to implement from 1 September 2005.
Note 3: we are currently reviewing the workability of this measure in the context of a review of child evidence.
Note 4: will be piloted before national roll out; Merseyside pilot went live 23/2/04, other pilots to be phased in by late Summer 2004 and run for 12–18 months.

ANNEX D: OFFENCES CHECK LIST

Examples of Behaviour	Possible Offences
Pressuring a victim/witness to 'drop the case' or not to give evidence.	Witness intimidation, obstructing the course of justice, conspiracy to pervert the course of justice.
Physical violence, with or without weapons, including punching, slapping, pushing, kicking, headbutting, and hair pulling.	Common assault, actual/grievous bodily harm, wounding, attempted murder.
Violence resulting in death.	Murder, manslaughter.
Violence resulting in miscarriage.	Child destruction, procuring a miscarriage or abortion.
Choking, strangling, suffocating.	Common assault, actual/grievous bodily harm, attempting to choke, strangle, or suffocate.
Spitting at a person.	Common assault.
Threatening with an article used as a weapon, e.g. a knife, tool, telephone, chair.	Threats to kill, common assault, affray, threatening behaviour.
Throwing articles, e.g. crockery, even if they miss their target.	Common assault, actual/grievous bodily harm, wounding, criminal damage, affray, threatening behaviour.
Tying someone up.	Common assault, actual bodily harm, false imprisonment.
Threatening to kill someone.	Threats to kill, harassment.
Threats to cause injury.	Common assault, affray, threatening behaviour.
Threats seriously to damage or undermine social status.	Harassment, blackmail.
Damaging or destroying property, or threatening to damage or destroy property.	Criminal damage, threatening to cause criminal damage, harassment.
Harming or threatening to harm a pet.	Criminal damage, threatening to cause criminal damage, cruelty to animals, harassment.
Locking someone in a room or house, or preventing him or her from leaving.	False imprisonment, harassment.
Preventing someone from visiting relatives or friends.	False imprisonment, kidnapping, harassment.

Examples of Behaviour	Possible Offences
Preventing someone from seeking aid, e.g. medical attention.	False imprisonment, actual bodily harm.
Preventing someone from dressing as they choose, or forcing them to wear a particular make-up, jewellery, and hairstyles.	Actual bodily harm,** harassment.
Racial abuse.	Racially aggravated threatening behaviour,* disorderly conduct,* or harassment.
'Outing', e.g. sexual orientation or HIV status.	Harassment, actual bodily harm,** blackmail.
Enforced financial dependence or unreasonably depriving someone of money.	Harassment.
Dowry abuse.	Blackmail, harassment, common assault, actual/grievous bodily harm.
Unreasonable financial demands.	Blackmail, harassment.
Forced marriage.	Kidnap, blackmail, false imprisonment, common assault, actual/grievous bodily harm, rape, indecent assault.
Enforced sexual activity.	Rape, indecent assault, harassment, living off immoral earnings.
Persistent verbal abuse, e.g. constant unreasonable criticism.	Harassment, actual bodily harm.**
Offensive/obscene/menacing telephone calls, text messages, or letters.	Improper use of public telecommunication systems, malicious communications, actual/grievous bodily harm,** harassment.
Excessive contact, e.g. numerous telephone calls to check someone's whereabouts.	Harassment, false imprisonment.
Secret or enforced administration of drugs.	Common assault, actual bodily harm, grievous bodily harm, administering poison.
Neglecting, abandoning, or ill-treating a child.	Child cruelty.
So-called 'honour crimes'.	Murder, aiding and abetting suicide.
Female circumcision.	Female genital mutilation.
Forcing entry into a house.	Using violence to secure entry.

* If the threatening or disorderly words/behaviour are used in a dwelling house, the offence can only be committed if the other person is not inside that or another dwelling.
** Actual physical or mental harm must be proved to have resulted from the behaviour.

215

ANNEX E: CONTACT DETAILS FOR SOME OF THE ORGANIZATIONS THAT PROVIDE HELP OR INFORMATION TO VICTIMS OF DOMESTIC VIOLENCE

They should be able to give contact details for local organizations.

Organization	Role of organization	Contact Details
24-hour Domestic Violence Helpline	The confidential 24-hour national domestic violence freephone helpline is run in partnership by Refuge and Women's Aid. The helpline provides support, information, and a listening ear to women experiencing (or who have experienced) domestic abuse and to those seeking help on a woman's behalf and, if appropriate, refer callers on to refuges and other sources of help and information.	The 24-hour freephone number is: 0808 2000 247
Broken Rainbow & hold tight tight hold	Broken Rainbow provides assistance to lesbians, gay men, bisexual, and transgender (LGBT) people in Britain who are affected by homophobic, transphobic, and same-sex domestic violence.	Broken Rainbow Hotline Number: 07812 644 914 Email: lgbtdv@btopenworld.com
Cardiff Women's Safety Unit (CWSU)	CWSU provides a central point of access for women and their children experiencing domestic violence in the Cardiff area.	Tel: 029 20 825111
ChildLine	ChildLine is the free 24-hour helpline for children and young people in the UK about any problem, day or night.	Tel: 0800 1111
Devon Men's Advice Line and Enquiries, (M.A.L.E.)	A confidential service supported by a charity with over 12 years' experience specializing in domestic violence.	Men's Advice Line and Enquiries, PO Box 285, Exeter EX4 3ZT Tel: 0845 064 6800 Email: devonmale@ahimsa.org.uk www.ahimsa.org.uk

Organization	Role of organization	Contact Details
Elder Abuse	To prevent abuse in old age by raising awareness, education, promoting research and the collection and dissemination of information.	Astral House, 1268 London Road, London SW16 4ER. Tel: 020 8765 7000 Fax: 020 8679 4074 Email: enquiries@elderabuse.org.uk
Greater London Domestic Violence Project	Aims to increase safety for survivors of domestic violence, and to hold abusers accountable for their behaviour. The team works to ensure that good practice in domestic violence work is transferred across London, bringing together key agencies to develop London-wide policies, raise awareness about domestic violence, and increase the effectiveness of inter-agency work.	Joanne Creighton (Information Manager) Tel: 020 7983 4976 Email: joanne.creighton@london.gov.uk
HALT Domestic Violence	HALT Domestic Violence (help, advice, and law team) is a Leeds based charity providing practical legal help, support, and advocacy to women experiencing domestic violence, regarding their right and choices in both the civil and criminal justice systems.	HALT, PO Box 332, Leeds LS1 3RD Public Advice line: 0113 243 2632 Administration: 0113 244 2578 Email: halt@ukgateway.net www.halt.org.uk
IMKAAN	IMKAAN is a national policy training and research initiative, dedicated to providing support and advocacy to the specialist refuge sector, supporting Asian women and children experiencing violence.	76 Brewer Street, London W1F 9TX Tel: 020 7434 9945

Organization	Role of organization	Contact Details
National Child Protection Helpline	Helpline for people concerned about a child at risk of abuse, including children themselves. Offers counselling, information, and advice about the care of children, legal issues, sexual, physical or emotional abuse, neglect, etc.	42 Curtain Road, London EC24 3 NH Tel: 0800 800 500
National Association of Gypsy Women	Support group for Gypsy women and Travellers experiencing domestic violence.	National Association of Gypsy Women CVS Building, Church Row, Darlington DL1 5QD
Refuge	Refuge is the national charity for women and children who experience domestic violence. It is the UK's largest single provider of specialist accommodation and support to women and children escaping domestic violence.	Refuge, 2–8 Maltravers Street, London WC2R 3EE Tel: 020 7395 7700 Email: info@refuge.org.uk www.refuge.org.uk
Respect	Respect is a UK-wide membership organization for practitioners and organizations working with perpetrators of domestic violence and associated work with women partners and ex-partners. Respect's core aim is to increase the safety of women and children who have experienced domestic violence, by promoting best practice in work with perpetrators of domestic violence and associated work with women.	PO Box 34434, London W6 0YS Tel: 020 8563 8523 Email: info@respect.uk.net

Organization	Role of organization	Contact Details
Southall Black Sisters (SBS)	SBS provides a range of services to women and children who have experienced violence and abuse. They provide crisis/emergency intervention, counselling, support group activities, and educational and development work.	52 Norwood Road, Southall, UB2 4DW Tel: 020 8571 9595 Fax: 020 8574 6781 Email: sbs@leonet.co.uk Hours: Mon–Fri 10am–4pm Closed for lunch 12.30pm–1.30pm and all day Wednesday
Standing Together	Aims to: 1) promote for the public benefit the provision of services which are directed towards the prevention of domestic violence and meet the needs of survivors of domestic violence and their families; 2) advance the education of voluntary and statutory agencies and the public in all aspects of domestic violence.	Address: Room 44D, 4th Floor, The Polish Centre, 238–246 King St, London W6 0RF Tel: 020 8748 5717 Email: admin@standingtogether.org.uk
Victim Support	Victim Support is the national charity which helps people affected by crime. It provides free and confidential support.	Victim Support line— 0845 30 30 900 9am–9pm Mondays to Fridays 9am–7pm weekends 9am–5pm Bank Holidays For those with hearing difficulties—Tel: 020 7896 3776
Welsh Women's Aid	Welsh Women's Aid is the leading provider of services for vulnerable women and children experiencing domestic abuse in Wales.	Welsh Women's Aid, 38–48 Crwys Road, Cardiff CF24 4NN Tel: 029 2039 0874 Best time to telephone: 10am–3pm Monday–Friday www.welshwomensaid.org www.cymorthifenywod.org

Organization	Role of organization	Contact Details
Witness Service	Victim Support runs the witness service in every criminal court in England and Wales to give information and support to witnesses, victims, their families, and friends when they go to court.	National Office, Cranmer House, 39 Brixton Road, London SW9 Tel: 020 7735 9166 Fax: 020 7582 5712 Email: contact@victimsupport.org.uk
Women's Aid	Women's Aid agenda for action against domestic violence has three major strands: 1) work at a strategic level to promote the protection of women and children by representing their needs to policy and decision makers; 2) work towards the long-term prevention of domestic violence through public awareness and education programmes; 3) work which supports the provision of services to meet the needs of all abused women and children.	PO Box 391, Bristol BS99 7WS Tel: 0808 2000 247 Email: info@womensaid.org.uk www.womensaid.org.uk

ANNEX F: HOME OFFICE AND CPS LINKS TO NEW LEGISLATION

Female Genital Mutilation Act 2003

Home Office	CPS Intranet	Acts of Parliament
• Home Office—Female Genital Mutilation Act 2003 Search Results • Home Office Circular 10/2004		• Female Genital Mutilation Act 2003 • The Female Genital Mutilation Act 2003 (Commencement) Order 2004

Sexual Offences Act 2003

Home Office	CPS Intranet	Acts of Parliament
• Home Office—Sexual Offences Act 2003 Search Results • HO History of the Act • HO Guidance on the Sexual Offences Act 2003	• Sexual Offences and Child Abuse section on intranet Legal Guidance section • CPS Policy on Prosecuting Cases of Rape • Legal Update 28 June 2004 • POL 11/2004 • POL 32/2004	• Sexual Offences Act 2003

Youth Justice and Criminal Evidence Act 1999

Home Office	CPS Intranet	Acts of Parliament
• Home Office—Youth Justice and Criminal Evidence Act 1999 Search Results • Youth Justice and Criminal Evidence Act	• POL 54/2004	• Youth Justice and Criminal Evidence Act 1999

Powers of Criminal Courts (Sentencing) Act 2000

Home Office	CPS Intranet	Acts of Parliament
• Home Office—Powers of Criminal Courts (Sentencing) Act 2000 Search Results • Home Office Circular 31/00 Powers of Criminal Courts (Sentencing) Act 2000	• Legal Update 08 June 2004	• Powers of Criminal Courts (Sentencing) Act 2000

Criminal Justice Act 2003
Bad Character and Hearsay

Home Office	CPS Intranet	Acts of Parliament
• Home Office—Criminal Justice Act 2003 Search Results • Criminal Justice Act 2003 • Home Office—Bad Character Search Results • Press Releases • Home Office—Hearsay Search Results	POL 68/2004—Disclosure POL 76/2004—Bad Character POL 81 2004—Bad Character Legal News 17.12.2004	• Criminal Justice Act 2003

Domestic Violence Crime and Victims Act 2004

Home Office	CPS Intranet	Acts of Parliament
• Home Office—Domestic Violence Crime and Victims Act 2004 Search Results • Crime—Domestic Violence—Publications • Press Releases	POL 18/2004 POL 70/2004 POL 71/2004 Legal News 25.11.2004	• Domestic Violence Crime and Victims Act 2004

10

Policy for Prosecuting Cases of Rape

1 INTRODUCTION

This document explains the way we deal with cases in which an allegation of rape has been made.

Rape is one of the most serious offences, and our aim is to prosecute each case effectively.

There is a general perception that most rapes are committed by a single man against a woman unknown to him. In fact, the majority of rape victims know their rapist. Rape involves male victims too. This policy statement covers the handling of all types of rape case, including marital and relationship rape, acquaintance and stranger rape, against male and female victims. All are equally serious and traumatic for the victim. Rape also has a devastating effect on families of victims.

We realize that victims of rape have difficult decisions to make that will affect their lives and the lives of those close to them.

We acknowledge that barriers exist, which mean that some people are less likely to report offences.

Victims who are or have been in a relationship with their attacker may blame themselves or feel that agencies will blame them, as well as facing wider difficulties such as disruption to the lives of their children and extended families.

People from Black and minority ethnic communities may have experienced racism. They may fear that they will not be believed, or that they will not be treated properly. As a result they may be reluctant to report offences or support a prosecution. Cultural and religious beliefs may also prevent people from reporting offences or supporting a prosecution. In cases involving rape within same-sex relationships, victims may fear homophobic reactions from the CPS or the wider criminal justice system, as well as being 'outed' by the process. Disabled people may fear reporting rape if the offender is a carer, or fear the loss of residential care. Lack of transport may also be a barrier to disabled people reporting rape.

We currently work with a number of national and local organizations, for example the Witness Support Service, which offer support to victims throughout the proceedings. Special measures that can be used to help a victim or witness to give evidence are discussed below at paragraph 8. We will consider every case carefully and sensitively. Our decisions will be objective but made within a framework that promotes support for victims by keeping them informed.

2 WHAT IS THE DEFINITION OF RAPE?

The definition of rape has been substantially changed by the Sexual Offences Act 2003, which came into force on 1 May 2004.

Under the previous law as set out in the Sexual Offences Act 1956, the statutory definition of rape is any act of non-consensual intercourse by a man with a person; the victim can be either male or female. Intercourse can be vaginal or anal. It does not include non-consensual oral sex. Consent is given its ordinary meaning, and lack of consent can be inferred from the surrounding circumstances, such as submission through fear. It is a defence if the defendant believed that the victim was consenting, even if this belief was unreasonable, and this is a matter of fact for the jury. Offences committed before 1 May 2004 will be prosecuted under the 1956 Act.

Offences committed on or after 1 May 2004 will be prosecuted under the Sexual Offences Act 2003. The Act extends the definition of rape to include the penetration by a penis of the vagina, anus, or mouth of another person. The new Act changes the law about consent and belief in consent.

The meaning of consent was not defined in previous legislation. Instead, the meaning was established in case law, which meant that the legal meaning of consent was not always clearly understood.

The word 'consent' in the context of the offence of rape is now defined in the Sexual Offences Act 2003. A person consents if he or she agrees by choice, and has the freedom and capacity to make that choice. The essence of this definition is the agreement by choice. The law does not require the victim to have resisted physically. The question of whether the victim consented is a matter for the jury to decide, although we consider this issue very carefully when first reviewing the file. The prosecutor will take into account evidence of all the circumstances surrounding the offence.

We are aware that the meaning of consent can be of particular relevance in rapes where there has been, or is, a pre-existing relationship between the defendant and the victim, or where domestic violence has existed prior to the rape. As the 2003 Act makes it clearer what is meant by the term 'consent', it will help juries in deciding whether the victim was able to, and did in fact, give his or her consent at the time.

The defendant must now show that his belief in consent was reasonable. In deciding whether the belief of the defendant was reasonable, a jury must have regard to all the circumstances, including any steps he has taken to ascertain whether the victim consented. In certain circumstances, it is presumed that the victim did not consent to sexual activity and the defendant did not reasonably believe that the victim consented, unless he can show otherwise. Examples of circumstances where the presumption applies are where the victim was unconscious, drugged, abducted, or subject to threats or fear of serious harm.

3 THE ROLE OF THE CPS

The police are responsible for investigating allegations of rape and for gathering the evidence. Recent changes in the law mean that the CPS will take over responsibility for deciding the charge in all but the most minor offences. This change is gradually being introduced from May 2004. It will mean that prosecutors will become involved at an early stage in advising on all aspects of cases.

As we are committed to improving the way that allegations of rape are handled we have established a network of specialist prosecutors in each CPS Area. Specialist prosecutors will work closely with the police to ensure that all possible avenues of evidence are explored and that the correct charge is identified. A specialist prosecutor will be responsible for the case from advice stage to the end of the case.

This degree of continuity is important. It will allow us to ensure that the victim is provided with the best possible support throughout the progress of the case.

We will ensure that the prosecuting advocate has the right skills for rape prosecutions, and efforts will be made, wherever possible, for the same prosecuting advocate to deal with the case throughout.

Where we decide to drop or substantially reduce the charge, the specialist will refer the case to a second specialist rape prosecutor before the final decision is made. In all cases of rape where a decision is taken not to proceed after charge, or to reduce the charge, the victim will be informed in writing of the decision and the reasons for it. The letter will offer the victim a meeting with the prosecutor. If the victim wishes, a meeting with the prosecutor will then be arranged to provide a fuller explanation.

4 THE CODE FOR CROWN PROSECUTORS

The Code for Crown Prosecutors provides guidance on how Crown Prosecutors make decisions about whether or not to prosecute. The Code is a public document. We review the cases referred by the police to us in accordance with the two tests set out in the Code.

First Test—the Evidential Test

Crown Prosecutors must first be satisfied that there is enough evidence to provide a 'realistic prospect of conviction against each defendant on each charge'. This means that a jury, properly directed in accordance with the law, is more likely than not to convict the defendant of the charge alleged.

If a case does not pass the first test (the evidential test), it must not go ahead, no matter how important or serious it may be.

Second Test—the Public Interest Test

If a case does pass the evidential test, the Crown Prosecutor must decide if a prosecution is needed in the public interest. A prosecution will usually take place unless 'there are public interest factors tending against prosecution which clearly outweigh those tending in favour'.

When considering the public interest test, one of the factors Crown Prosecutors should always take into account is the consequences for the victim of the decision whether or not to prosecute and any views expressed by the victim.

If the evidential test is passed, we believe that rape is so serious that a prosecution is almost certainly required in the public interest.

The Burden and Standard of Proof

If a case passes the tests in the Code, and proceeds to trial, it is for the prosecution to prove the case so that the jury is sure that the defendant is guilty.

5 IS THERE ENOUGH EVIDENCE TO PROSECUTE?

Rape usually takes place in a private setting where the victim is the only witness. Unless the defendant pleads guilty, the victim will almost certainly have to give evidence in court. Where there is conflicting evidence, the prosecutor has a duty to assess the credibility and reliability of the victim's evidence. This will always be done in a careful and sensitive way, using all the information provided to the prosecutor. A case may not proceed, not because the prosecution does not believe the victim, but because the test in the Code for Crown Prosecutors indicates that there is not a realistic prospect of conviction.

There are rules about disclosing to the defence relevant material obtained during the investigation, which is not part of the prosecution case. The rules are complex, but broadly speaking, there is a duty to disclose to the defence any such material that might undermine the prosecution case or assist the defence.

The police will always look for corroboration or supporting evidence, particularly any medical or scientific evidence, but it is not essential and a prosecution can still go ahead without it. However, the prosecution must always prove the defendant's guilt. Cases may fail because a jury cannot decide between what the victim says and what the defendant says. This is why it is essential to obtain all possible forensic and scientific evidence as soon as possible. The earlier a rape is reported, the higher the chance of this being done, and the higher the chance of a realistic prospect of conviction.

We know that some victims will find it very difficult to give evidence and may need practical and emotional support. The prosecutor will also be aware that some complaints of rape are not made immediately and that any delay could be attributed to a fear of reprisals, intimidation, or a significant number of other factors. It is possible that the effect on rape victims may render them emotionally incapable of providing a written statement shortly after an attack, or even for days or weeks. Specialist agencies can provide support and advice.

Contact details for some support agencies are given at Annex A.

What Happens when the Victim Withdraws Support for the Prosecution or no Longer Wishes to give Evidence?

Sometimes a victim will ask the police not to proceed any further with the case, or will ask to withdraw the complaint. This does not necessarily mean that the case will be stopped—we will first consider what other evidence is available.

As a general rule we will prosecute all cases where there is sufficient evidence and there are no factors preventing us from doing so.

If the victim has decided to withdraw support we have to find out why. This may involve delaying a court hearing to investigate the facts and decide the best course of action.

We will take the following steps:

- if the information about the victim's decision to withdraw support has come from the defendant, we will ask the police to find out from the victim whether this information is true; if the victim confirms that the information is true, we will ask the police to take a written statement explaining the reasons for withdrawing support, saying whether the original complaint was true and whether the victim has been put under pressure to withdraw support;
- we will ask the police what they think about the case and, in particular, to carry out a full assessment of the risks to the victim and any other person's safety so that we can decide whether the case should proceed or not;
- we will also ask the police how they think the victim might react to being required to attend court.

If the victim's statement after withdrawing the complaint is not the same as the earlier statement, the police will ask the victim to explain why it has changed.

If we suspect that the victim has been pressured or frightened into withdrawing the complaint, we will ask the police to investigate further. If necessary, we will ask the court to delay any hearing so that a thorough investigation can take place before we decide about the future of the case.

If the victim confirms that the complaint is true but still wants to withdraw that complaint, we will consider first whether it is possible to continue with the prosecution without that evidence (the evidential test) and then, if it is possible, whether we should continue with the case against the victim's wishes (the public interest test).

We will explore all of these options fully before we decide whether or not to proceed with a prosecution. The safety of the victim will be a prime consideration in reaching our decision.

What Happens when a Decision is Taken to Continue with a Prosecution Against a Victim's Wishes?

Some cases may be so serious, for example where there is a real and continuing danger to the victim or others, that the public interest in going ahead with a prosecution has to outweigh the victim's wishes.

If we think that a case should continue and that it would be necessary to call the victim to prove the case, we have to decide:

- whether we should require the victim to give evidence in person in court; or
- whether we could apply to use the victim's statement as evidence without the victim having to give evidence in court.

The law allows us to use the victim's statement as evidence without calling the victim to court, but only in very limited circumstances. The court ultimately makes the decision whether to allow such a statement to be used in this manner and only if it is convinced that it is in the interests of justice to do so.

If the victim is the only witness to the offence it may be very difficult to satisfy the court that justice is being served when the defence cannot cross-examine the only witness against them.

In cases where it is necessary to call a victim against his or her wishes then the decision will only be taken by a specialist prosecutor after consultation with the police.

6 ACCEPTING PLEAS

In some cases we may consider accepting a guilty plea from the defendant to a different charge. This might arise, for example, if a defendant pleads guilty to some but not all of the charges, or because the victim may not wish to proceed, or because new evidence comes to light. Again, in these circumstances, we will write to the victim informing him or her of the decision and offering a meeting.

We are committed to keeping victims informed and to taking their interests and views into account when considering accepting a plea.

Guidelines on the Acceptance of Pleas issued by the Attorney General in December 2000 emphasize the importance of ensuring that save in the most exceptional circumstances, the acceptance of pleas should be conducted in public with the prosecution able to explain their reasons for accepting the pleas in open court. If a defendant offers to plead guilty to a different, and possibly less serious, charge, the prosecutor should only accept the plea if he or she thinks the court is able to pass a sentence that matches the seriousness of the offence, particularly where there may be aggravating features.

7 BAIL ISSUES

Once a suspect has been charged with rape, the police will take the decision as to whether it is appropriate to release the suspect on bail to attend a court hearing within a short period of time. However, because rape is such a serious offence, the decision may be taken to keep the suspect in custody so that he may appear at the next available court for a remand hearing.

At the bail hearing the magistrates decide whether bail is appropriate after they have heard representations from both the prosecution and the defence. A defendant has a right to bail. The court can only refuse bail if it is satisfied that the defendant would fail to surrender to custody, commit an offence while on bail, or would interfere with witnesses or otherwise obstruct the course of justice. Bail can also be refused if the offence was committed while the defendant was already on bail for another serious offence, or for the defendant's own protection. There is an exception to the right to bail for some serious repeat offenders including those previously convicted of rape. Then the court can only grant bail in exceptional circumstances.

At the hearing the police will provide sufficient information to prosecutors to enable a decision to be made on whether to oppose bail for the defendant. Where there has been a relationship between the victim and the defendant, the police will provide as much background information as possible. This might include such information as the number and ages of the children and the proximity of the addresses of the relations of the defendant to that of the victim. It will also include details of any civil orders in force and any other relevant information.

The prosecutor will take into account the Victim Personal Statement, if the victim has decided to make one, in making decisions as to whether or not to oppose bail, and what conditions could be agreed. In the Victim Personal Statement, the victim can choose to describe the effects of the rape and any concerns about the defendant being granted bail. Any decision during the case will take account of the Victim Personal Statement.

To protect the victim or witnesses from the risk of danger, threats, or pressure, which might obstruct the course of justice, we may ask that the defendant be kept in custody.

Magistrates are required to give reasons in open court if they grant bail to a defendant. If they do not give reasons, we will ask them to state their reasons.

If the prosecutor opposes bail, but the magistrates grant bail, the prosecutor will make a decision about whether or not to appeal that decision. If an appeal is made, the defendant will be kept in custody until a judge at the Crown Court hears the appeal.

We will work closely with the police to obtain the views of victims and witnesses about bail conditions and any proposed changes to them, before a decision is made to agree changes, or an application is made to the court if we do not agree. The police will also inform victims and witnesses of any changes.

8 HELPING VICTIMS AND WITNESSES TO GIVE EVIDENCE

Special Measures

Giving evidence can be a particularly traumatic experience for victims of rape offences. Some find it difficult to give evidence in the sight of the defendant. If this is so, we can apply for the victim to give evidence in another way so that he or she can give their best evidence. Examples of special measures include screening of the victim from the defendant, or giving evidence by live television link. Evidence can also be given in private by clearing the public gallery.

The court makes the decision about whether special measures will be allowed. A victim of rape is automatically presumed to be eligible for the help of special measures unless the court is informed that he or she does not require this.

We discuss with the police what special measures might assist the victim or witnesses to give evidence in court, and then make an application to the court to grant these. The views of the victim and witnesses are taken into account. Ideally, early decisions should be taken about special measures to assist victims and witnesses; however, circumstances might change and it is always possible to apply at any stage of the proceedings. If necessary a meeting can be arranged with the victim or witnesses to discuss what special measures would be appropriate. If the victim or witness is a child, their evidence is video-recorded and played in court unless the court considers that it is not in the interests of justice for this to be done.

We will ensure that victims and witnesses are made aware that they can change their minds about special measures. In some cases victims initially state that they do not require special measures and may subsequently realize that they do but are afraid to say so.

Further information about meetings with vulnerable or intimidated witnesses is contained in the Statement on the Treatment of Victims and Witnesses which we have published together with the police. Copies can be obtained from the CPS website (www.cps.gov.uk).

Other Decisions

Often, decisions about the progress of a case may be taken at court. Victims will be informed about those decisions when they are at court, either by us or by the prosecuting advocate we have instructed. If they are not at court, they will be informed as soon as possible afterwards, either by us or by the police.

We are committed to instructing advocates who have the right skills to prosecute rape cases, including their ability to deal sensitively with victims and witnesses. We will instruct them to speak to victims and witnesses before they give evidence and try to put nervous witnesses at ease.

In most trials the defence advocate will seek to challenge the victim's account of the allegations. This is normal and permissible. The defence have a duty to challenge the victim about his or her account.

However, there are rules about inappropriate cross-examination, and particularly questioning about a victim's previous sexual behaviour. This type of questioning can only take place with the permission of the judge. We will ensure that the prosecuting advocate is proactive in objecting to such questioning.

If the defence seek to introduce such evidence or questioning and the judge considers that its real purpose is to undermine the victim, then it should not be allowed. We will instruct prosecuting advocates to challenge defence applications in all appropriate cases.

We will also object to allegations about the character or demeanour of the victim which are irrelevant to the issues in the case.

When a decision to drop or substantially reduce the charge takes place, we will write to the victim to explain why. In cases involving allegations of rape, we will also offer a meeting to provide a full explanation.

This meeting will be arranged as early as possible at the convenience of the victim.

If the victim or witnesses agree, we will notify the Victim Support Witness Service of hearing dates so that they can offer court familiarization visits and other support to victims and witnesses. We will provide details of the victim or witnesses, any special measures that have been agreed, and the hearing dates.

If there are local groups providing specialist support to victims of rape, we will work with them to develop good practice guidelines.

9 SENTENCING

If the defendant is convicted of rape, the judge decides the sentence. There are guidelines for judges when sentencing defendants convicted of rape.

The prosecuting advocate has a duty actively to assist the judge with the law and guidelines on sentencing, including any ancillary orders that may be available to the court. He or she must also be alert to mitigation detracting from the character of a witness, and challenge anything which is misleading, untrue, or unfair.

The guidelines state that relationship and acquaintance rapes should be treated by the courts as equally serious as stranger rape. Male rapes are as serious as those between a man and a woman, and all types of rape are equally serious.

If the judge passes a sentence which the prosecution consider is unduly lenient in that it does not reflect the seriousness of the offence, the CPS will ask the Attorney General to review the sentence.

If the prosecution do not consider the sentence unduly lenient but the victim disagrees, he or she can ask in person for the Attorney General to consider it, but this has to be done within twenty-eight days of the sentencing decision. If the CPS decides not to submit the case for Law Officer consideration, it must notify the complainant without delay so that the complainant's option of complaining direct to the Law Officers is preserved, and the Law Officers will have sufficient time, if a complaint is made, to consider the case.

If the Attorney General thinks that the sentence is unduly lenient, he can refer it to the Court of Appeal.

The application to the Court of Appeal must be made within twenty-eight days of the sentence. The Court of Appeal decides whether or not the sentence is unduly lenient and, if it is, whether to increase the sentence.

We will, through the police, keep victims informed of any appeals by the defence against conviction and sentence. We will also inform victims if a defendant is granted bail following a successful application for leave to appeal, or where an appeal is granted.

10 CONCLUSION

We are committed to playing our part in improving the way that rape cases are dealt with in the criminal justice system. We want victims to have confidence in the way in which we review and progress cases.

We hope that this document will help victims of rape and their families to understand the work of the CPS, how we make our decisions, and the different stages of the prosecution process.

We will continue to work with our colleagues in the criminal justice system and the voluntary and community sector at national and local levels to help us develop best practice.

We will review this policy statement regularly so that it reflects current law and thinking. We welcome any comments and observations that help us to do this. Comments and suggestions can be made to the Policy Directorate, 6th Floor, CPS, 50 Ludgate Hill, London, EC4M 7EX.

ANNEX A

National 24-Hour Domestic Violence Freephone Helpline

Run in partnership between Women's Aid and Refuge. 0808 200 0247

Women's Aid Federation of England

A National Domestic Violence charity working with women and children.
PO Box 391
Bristol
BS99 7WS
Tel: 0117 944 4411
Web: www.womensaid.org.uk

Refuge

A National charity which provides emergency accommodation and emotional and practical support for women and children who experience domestic violence.
2–8 Maltravers Street
London
WC2R 3EE
Tel: 020 7395 7700
Web: www.refuge.org.uk

Southall Black Sisters

21 Avenue Road
Southall
Middlesex
UB1 3BL
Tel: 020 8571 9595 (Closed Wednesday)
E-mail: sbs@leonet.co.uk
Web: www.southallblacksisters.org.uk

Victim Support

Cranmer House
39 Brixton Road
London, SW9 6DZ
Tel: 020 7735 9166
Web: www.victimsupport.org.uk

Victim Supportline

Tel: 0845 30 30 90
9 am–9 pm weekdays

9 am–7 pm weekends
9 am–5 pm bank holidays

ChildLine

UK-wide free 24-hour telephone helpline for children and young people in danger or distress.
Tel: 0800 1111
Web: www.childline.org.uk

Women's Rape and Sexual Abuse Centre Cornwall

Free confidential support for women and teenage girls.
Helpline: 01208 77 099
Helpline Hours: Monday to Thursday, 10 am–1 pm
                Monday Evenings, 7.30 pm–10 pm
                Plus 24-hour answerphone

Survivors UK Helpline

Supports and provides resources for men who have experienced any form of sexual violence.
Tel: 0845 122 1201 (Helpline open Tuesday and Thursday 7 pm–10 pm)
Web: www.survivorsuk.co.uk

National Child Protection Helpline

Tel: 0808 800 500 (24 hr)

11

Guidance on Prosecuting Cases of Racist and Religious Crime

1 INTRODUCTION

We are publishing a Public Policy Statement on prosecuting racist and religious crime to make clear our commitment to dealing effectively with this type of offending and to let the community at large know what they can expect from us.

This guidance document is designed to give more detail about some of the key areas of the policy statement to assist prosecutors when they deal with this type of crime.

It is complementary to our existing guidance on the legislation (on the CPS Intranet—Legal Guidance) and to our training on diversity awareness and on prosecuting racially and religiously aggravated crime.

The need for a Public Policy Statement was based a number of factors, including:

- the target in the Criminal Justice System Public Service Agreement for 2003 and beyond to improve levels of public confidence in the criminal justice system, including increasing that of black and minority ethnic communities and increasing year on year the satisfaction of victims and witnesses, whilst respecting the rights of defendants;
- the recommendations made by Her Majesty's Crown Prosecution Service Inspectorate (HMCPSI) in the Thematic Report on Casework having a Minority Ethnic Dimension (April 2002), which are designed to improve the way that we deal with such cases; and
- to demonstrate our commitment to promoting race equality in accordance with our obligations as a public authority under the Race Relations (Amendment) Act 2000, as set out in the CPS Race Equality Scheme (May 2002).

This policy statement and the guidance also contribute to our efforts to raise awareness of issues relating to hate crime generally, as demonstrated already by our publishing statements and guidance on prosecuting domestic violence and prosecuting cases of homophobic crime.

Impact of Racist and Religious Crimes on Individuals and Communities

We have published our policy statement and guidance because we want victims and their families, as well as the general public, to be confident that the CPS understands the serious nature of this type of crime and the real and lasting effects it has on victims and their families, as well as on communities and society as a whole. By letting people know what they can expect from us when we prosecute racist or religious crime, we aim to improve confidence in the criminal justice system.

Publishing a policy statement and guidance also helps to raise awareness of the relevant issues for prosecutors to assist them when making decisions about prosecuting racist or religious crime.

We have consulted people from black and minority ethnic communities and faith communities, and taken their comments into account in writing our policy and guidance. By doing this we have gained a better understanding of the things that are important to them and that we need to know about.

Racist and religious crime is particularly hurtful to victims as they are being targeted solely because of their personal identity, their actual or perceived racial or ethnic origin, or their beliefs or faith. Black and minority ethnic victims can also be targeted because they belong to other minority groups, and may experience multiple discrimination.

These crimes can happen randomly, for example, at nightclubs, at takeaways or restaurants, on public transport, at football matches, or on shopping trips, or can be a part of a campaign of continued harassment and victimization by, for example, neighbours, customers, extremist groups, customers, or even family members. Crimes can sometimes be a combination of these things—harassment by neighbours, or attacks by organized gangs on a person and their home, or random attacks in public places. Activity by extremist groups in an area may also manifest itself on the terraces at football matches.

The impact on victims is different for each individual, but many experience similar problems. They can feel extremely isolated, or fearful of going out or even staying at home. They may become withdrawn, and suspicious of organizations and strangers. Their mental and physical health may suffer in a variety of ways. For young people in particular, the impact can be damaging to self-esteem and identity, and, without potential support, a form of self-hatred of their racial or religious identity can result, which may take the form of self-harm or even suicide.

The confusion, fear, and lack of safety felt by individuals has a ripple effect in the wider community of their racial or religious group. Communities can feel victimized and vulnerable to further attack.

2 RACIST AND RELIGIOUS CRIME—THE LEGISLATION

We can mean any one of a number of different types of offence when we use the term 'racist or religious crime'.

Parliament has passed a number of pieces of legislation aimed at outlawing crime where the offender is motivated by hostility or hatred towards the victim's race or religious beliefs (actual or perceived). A table setting out some of the more commonly used legislation is attached at Annex A.

Two of the most significant pieces of legislation are:

- Crime and Disorder Act 1998 (as amended by the Anti-terrorism, Crime and Security Act 2001);
- Public Order Act 1986, Part III.

There are other offences, such as racialist chanting at football matches and religious offences which can be committed at places of religious worship.

It is important that prosecutors are aware of the full range of available offences when deciding on the most appropriate charge to prosecute in a particular case.

Crime and Disorder Act 1998 (as amended)

This Act came into force on 30 September 1998 and created a number of specific offences of racially aggravated crime, based on offences of wounding, assault, damage, harassment, and threatening/abusive behaviour. Monitoring had indicated that these types of crime were those most commonly experienced by victims of racial violence or harassment.

The Act was amended by the Anti-terrorism, Crime and Security Act 2001, which came into effect on 14 December 2001. It extended the scope of the Crime and Disorder Act by creating new, specific, religiously aggravated offences and applying the same sentencing duty to all other offences where there is evidence of religious aggravation.

The legislation provides definitions of racial groups and religious groups in the following terms:

- A racial group means a group of persons defined by reference to race, colour, nationality (including citizenship), or ethnic or national origins. The definition is wide and victims may come within the definition under more than one of the references. Travellers, refugees, or asylum seekers, or others from less visible minorities, would be included within this definition. There has been a legal ruling that Jews and Sikhs are included in the definition of a racial group (*Mandla v Dowell-Lee* [1983] 2 AC 548).
- A religious group means a group of persons defined by reference to religious belief, or lack of religious belief. This would include Muslims, Hindus, and Christians, and different sects within a religion. It also includes people who hold no religious beliefs at all.

Hostility

To prove that an offence is racially or religiously aggravated, the prosecution have to prove the 'basic' offence followed by racial or religious aggravation, as defined by s. 28 of the Crime and Disorder Act 1998. An offence will be racially or religiously aggravated if:

(a) at the time of the offence (or shortly before or after) the offender demonstrates to the victim hostility based on the victim's membership (or presumed membership) of a racial or religious group; or

(b) the offence is motivated wholly or partly by hostility towards members of a racial or religious group based on their membership (or presumed membership) of that group.

'Demonstrating hostility' is not defined by the Act. The ordinary dictionary definition of hostile includes simply being 'unfriendly'. Proving this limb of the offence requires evidence of words or actions which show hostility toward the victim. However, this hostility may be totally unconnected with the 'basic' offence which may have been committed for other, non-racially or religiously motivated reasons. For example, an assault which takes place because of an argument over a parking place, but where the offender then utters racial abuse to the victim of the assault, would come within the scope of this part of s. 28.

'Motivated by hostility' may prove more difficult in practice. In the absence of a clear statement by the accused that his/her actions were motivated by his hostility to his victim based on his race or religious belief, for example, an admission under caution, how can motive be shown? In some cases, background evidence could well be important if relevant to establish motive, for example, evidence of membership of or association with a racist group, or evidence of expressed racist views in the past might, dependent on the facts, be admissible in evidence.

Two cases decided by the Administrative Court illustrate the approach that courts have adopted when interpreting the law:

- In *DPP v McFarlane* [2002] EWHC Admin 485, Rose LJ found that once the 'basic' offence was proved (in this case a public order offence) and that racist language was used that was hostile or threatening to the victim, it made no difference that the defendant may have had an additional reason for using the language; the test under s. 28(1)(a) was satisfied.
- In *DPP v Woods* [2002] EWHC Admin 85, the defendant used racially abusive language to a doorman at a nightclub when expressing anger and frustration over being refused admittance. It was held, as in *McFarlane*, that the primary reason for the offence was other than a racist motivation; nonetheless, the use of racist abuse during the commission of the basic offence made out the test for racial aggravation in s. 28(1)(a). The point was made that, ordinarily, the use of racially (or religiously) insulting remarks would in the normal course of events be enough to establish a demonstration of hostility.

Enhanced sentencing powers for racially or religiously aggravated offences

The new offences under the Crime and Disorder Act carry higher maximum penalties than the basic offence equivalents.

Some of them also become either way offences in the aggravated form.

Prosecutors need to be familiar with this aspect of the legislation for the following reasons:

- making decisions on mode of trial;
- deciding whether it is necessary to include alternative charges or counts on the indictment.

New statutory sentencing duty

In addition to the creation of specific offences, the law also provides a general duty on criminal courts when sentencing an offender to treat more seriously any offence which can be shown to be aggravated by a demonstration of hostility towards a person, or to be motivated by hostility based on a person's membership or presumed membership of a racial or religious group (s. 153 of the Powers of Criminal Court (Sentencing) Act 2000).

Part III of the Public Order Act 1986—Incitement to Racial Hatred

Article 10 of the European Convention on Human Rights (ECHR) allows the freedom of expression save in certain limited circumstances. These circumstances include the offences contained within Part III of the Public Order Act 1986 (ss. 18–23).

Additionally, Article 17 of the Convention states:

Nothing in this Convention may be interpreted as implying for any State, group or person any right to engage in any activity or perform any act aimed at the destruction of any of the rights and freedoms set forth herein or at their limitation to a greater extent than is provided for in the Convention.

Relevant case law includes *Glimmerveen and Hagenbeek v Netherlands* (1987) 18 DR 187 and *Kuhnen v Germany* (1988) 56 DR 205.

For an offence to be committed under any of these sections of the Public Order Act 1986, there has to be one of the acts described therein: it has to be 'threatening, abusive or insulting', and it has to be intended to, or likely in all the circumstances to, stir up racial hatred.

The words 'threatening, abusive or insulting' are to be given their ordinary meaning, and case law dealing with other provisions of the Public Order Act 1986 can assist with this.

Racial hatred is defined in s. 17 of the Act. It must be borne in mind that there is no specific offence of inciting religious hatred. However, the courts have yet to decide if behaviour that is aimed ostensibly at a *religious* group is capable of amounting to an incitement to *racial* hatred where the members of the group are also members of a racial group.

We have to prove that hatred was likely to be stirred up, not just that it was liable or possible.

All such allegations are by their very nature politically sensitive. For that reason, and to ensure a consistent approach, any allegation under this legislation, whether by way of an advice file or a charge, must be referred to the Casework Directorate. Referral means the submission of a report which is sufficient to enable the Casework Directorate and the Area to have an informed discussion as to where the responsibility for the case should lie.

Where an Area becomes aware of such a case, it should be referred to the Casework Directorate within seven days. If it is decided that the case should be prosecuted as an offence of incitement to racial hatred, the Casework Directorate will take over the conduct of the case from the Area. If the Casework Directorate considers that other offences are more appropriate and that the case is more suitable to be dealt with by the Area they should refer it to the Area within seven days thereafter.

If the Casework Directorate decides to deal with a case, the file is held and dealt with there. Thereafter cases can only proceed with the consent of the Attorney General.

Racialist Chanting at Football Matches

This offence is committed when a group of people, or one person acting alone, chants something of a racialist nature at a designated football match. 'Racialist' means the same as 'racist'.

To prove this offence we have to show that the chanting, which means the repeated uttering of words or sounds, was threatening, abusive, or insulting to another person because of that person's colour, race, nationality, or ethnic or national origin.

We do not have to prove that the chanting was directed at a particular individual or group, although it will often be directed from the terraces at a player or players from black and minority ethnic communities.

We do have to prove that the football match was being played between teams from the Premier League, the Football League, or the Conference League.

If convicted the accused person can be fined (level 3) and, in addition to any other penalty, banned from attending football matches both in this country and abroad.

Even when a person is not charged with an offence, a magistrates' court can issue a similar banning order against a person who has been involved in violent behaviour before, if the court is satisfied that this would help to prevent violence or disorder at football matches in the future. The police (and not the CPS) have the power to apply to the court for a banning order in these circumstances. Breach of a banning order is punishable by a maximum penalty of up to six months' imprisonment.

The crime does not apply to chanting which is of a religious nature, although other offences might be available to prosecute this type of behaviour.

This offence is aimed at specific behaviour within football grounds at designated matches and was introduced to combat the problem of mass racist chanting.

However, this offence should not be seen in isolation, and it is not the only legislative tool available to deal with racist or religious football-related crime.

In some situations, it might be more appropriate to charge other offences, such as specific racially or religiously aggravated public order offences. This may be the case, for example, where:

- the offence is committed outside the stadium at a designated football match;
- a public order offence where religious, as opposed to racist, hostility is demonstrated to the victim or victims;
- racial abuse and harassment of black and minority ethnic players takes place at a non-designated football match, such as at an amateur game.

Dependent on the facts of each case, we should consider carefully all the available information so that we prosecute an offence (or offences) that reflects most accurately the offender's behaviour and which allows the court to take account of any racist or religious hostility or motivation.

Other Religious Offences

In addition to the religiously aggravated offences, prosecutors should be aware that there are other religious offences that can be prosecuted:

- Blasphemy is an attack on the Christian religion, either verbal or written, made in terms that are likely to shock or outrage the feelings of most Christian believers. Society's attitudes have changed, however, and people are free to express anti-religious views providing they do so in a reasonable manner. As a result, there has been only one prosecution in the last eighty years. We would, however, consider carefully any future case referred to us for advice and make a decision based on the evidence available.
- There are several other statutory offences designed to protect acts of worship of various kinds, and although they are somewhat archaic, they are nonetheless useful offences for prosecutors to bear in mind when particular circumstances apply:
  - Section 2 of the Ecclesiastical Courts Jurisdiction Act 1860 creates an offence of violent or indecent behaviour in any place of worship that has been certified under the Places of Worship Registration Act 1855, and also affords protection for a person preaching or carrying out other religious duties. Mosques and synagogues are certified and are therefore covered by this legislation.
    The penalty on conviction is a level 1 fine or up to two months, imprisonment. This may account for the fact that other legislation, with a higher maximum penalty, is sometimes preferred to deal with the kind of criminal behaviour covered by s. 2 of the 1860 Act. There might, however, be circumstances in which a s. 2 offence is more appropriate simply to mark the anti-religious nature of the offence and where the available penalty is not the primary consideration.
  - Section 36 of the Offences Against the Person Act 1861 creates an offence of assaulting clergymen or other ministers, or preventing them from officiating at religious services. This is an either way offence that has a maximum penalty of two years' imprisonment on indictment.
- There are also specific offences under the Cemeteries Clauses Act 1847 and the Burial Laws Amendment Act 1880 of causing disturbances in cemeteries, or disrupting or obstructing burials respectively. These are old and rarely used offences, but they are still in force and prosecutors need to be aware of them.

3 HOW TO MAKE SURE WE TAKE FULL ACCOUNT OF A RACIAL OR RELIGIOUS ELEMENT WHEN WE PROSECUTE A CASE

It is essential that we make sure that we identify all those cases that might properly be prosecuted as specific racist or religious crimes, or where we can put that evidence before a court when it is deciding on sentence.

This begins right at the point where we receive a file from the police. We have an agreement with the Association of Chief Police Officers (ACPO) that the police will identify a file that meets the Stephen Lawrence Inquiry Report definition of a racist incident when they send it to the CPS to prosecute.

The CPS uses this common definition to identify these cases and monitor the decisions and outcomes.

The definition is:

A racist incident is any incident which is perceived to be racist by the victim or any other person

We use a similar definition for religious incidents.

Both definitions help in raising awareness of the racist or religious element in any offence right from the point of reporting, through investigation, up to and including any prosecution. By using these definitions, the intention was to raise levels of confidence and therefore reporting of racist incidents, and this has proved to be the case. Since we began to keep records in 1996, the number of cases we have prosecuted for racist crime has more than doubled, and there continues to be a steady increase every year.

Religiously aggravated offences were introduced in December 2001. To collect information about how this aspect of the law is working, we track these cases through the CPS Racist Incident Monitoring Scheme (RIMS) by asking CPS Areas to indicate on the Racist Incident Data Sheet (RIDS form) that the case was a religious rather than a racist incident. Currently, any religiously aggravated crimes are referred to the Director for him to express his view on the prosecution decision. This is so that the Director can report to the Attorney General on the effectiveness of the new offences.

There is a gap between the number of racist incidents reported and the number of cases that result in prosecution. It is too early to say yet whether the same is true in relation to religiously aggravated offences.

4 PROSECUTING CASES OF RACIST AND RELIGIOUS CRIME

Generally

The prosecutor has a key role to play in making sure that racist or religious crime is prosecuted fairly and robustly, and that the racial or religious element of an offence is taken into account appropriately at all stages of a case as it is prosecuted at court. It is important that these cases are handled in a timely manner and that steps are taken to ensure that cases are prosecuted at court without delay.

The stages that are identified in the following paragraphs are especially important.

The HMCPSI Thematic Inspection Report on Casework Having a Minority Ethnic Dimension (April 2002) recommended that CPS Areas put into place arrangements for such cases to be reviewed or supervised by particularly experienced or 'specialist' prosecutors, or to have lawyers fulfilling the role of a 'consultant' or 'lead'.

Training for CPS staff has been developed to familiarize and raise awareness of issues relating to racially and religiously aggravated crime, and all CPS Areas have nominated at least one member of staff to be lead trainers to deliver this training. We have also delivered diversity awareness training to all our staff.

CPS Areas should also have arrangements in place to collate and analyse information provided by the CPS Racist Incident Monitoring Scheme (see section 7, 'The Racist Incident Monitoring Scheme').

Counsel or solicitor agents instructed to prosecute on behalf of the CPS should have a clear understanding of our policy on prosecuting racist and religious crime. It is essential that arrangements are in place to ensure that they act in accordance with our policy and receive clear instructions to that effect.

A checklist summarizing some of the key issues that prosecutors should consider when prosecuting racist or religious crime is attached at Annex B. Prosecutors may find it useful to assist case management, or simply as an aide memoire.

Identification of Relevant Information

Flagging a case as a racist or religious crime puts the prosecutor on notice that someone at some stage—victim, witness, defendant, and/or investigator—has perceived that the incident that gave rise to the charge had a racist or religious element.

However, it is important that prosecutors do not become too reliant on the police making this initial identification. Although police identification has improved significantly, the police still do not identify all cases that we ultimately prosecute. Prosecutors need to be vigilant to make sure that at every review they consider the possibility of a case being a racist or religious case. When they do, we will track the case through our Racist Incident Monitoring Scheme.

Prosecutors must adopt a proactive approach to seeking further information from the police to help them decide if a case can properly be prosecuted as a racially or religiously aggravated offence, or as one of the offences with a racial or religious element, or if there is evidence that should be presented to the court at sentence.

This information may be already available (for example, in a Victim Personal Statement—see below) and may just need more detail, or be collected in a form that will allow it to be presented to the court as evidence.

In some cases, the CPS may advise the police to follow up other possible avenues of enquiry. This might include looking at previous reported incidents involving the same victim, or the same suspect. It may also involve seeking information or evidence from other agencies. For example, there may be current or previous eviction proceedings taken by a local authority or housing association involving the parties in the criminal proceedings. In all cases, prosecutors should liaise directly with the officer in the case to make sure all available evidence has been obtained and sent to the CPS to consider when reviewing the case. This may be especially important if the situation represents repeat victimization.

Some repeat victims may themselves be charged as a result of counter allegations made by those against whom they have complained. This situation is not uncommon, and such cases require a careful consideration by the prosecutor of all the facts of the present incident and any previous history when deciding who should be prosecuted.

Charge Selection

It is vital that prosecutors select charges that reflect the seriousness of the offence charged and which allow the court to sentence in accordance with the law. The charges must also help us to present the case clearly and simply. This is especially important in the light of the new arrangements for charging suspects, which mean greater CPS involvement in deciding the charges that a suspect will face from the outset.

The CPS and the police have agreed charging standards for certain types of offence, including assaults and public order offences. These are guidelines that help us to make consistent decisions about the right charges. We use them when considering some of the racially or religiously aggravated offences to decide what should be the correct 'basic' offence. Details of the relevant charging standards are available in the CPS Legal Guidance on the Intranet.

Prosecutors need to be conversant with recent changes in the law dealing with racist or religious crime that can have an impact on charge selection and decisions about mode of trial.

Alternative Charges

It is important that prosecutors are familiar with the circumstances in which courts can return alternative verdicts without the need for alternative charges being laid, or alternative counts on an indictment being preferred.

The Crime and Disorder Act 1998 makes provision for statutory alternatives in respect of certain of the racially or religiously aggravated offences.

Section 6(3) of the Criminal Law Act 1967 allows for alternative verdicts in trials on indictment where the allegations in the indictment amount to or include (expressly or by implication) an allegation of another offence falling within the jurisdiction of the court of trial.

Where the Criminal Law Act 1967 does not apply (e.g. in the magistrates' court), or where there are no statutory provisions for alternative verdicts, then consideration has to be given to including alternative counts on the indictment, or drafting charges in the alternative.

In summary cases, there is no power for the court of trial to return an alternative verdict to a lesser or alternative offence. Consideration should therefore be given in all cases to putting alternative charges to both the basic and the racially or religiously aggravated offences.

It must be made clear to the court, the defence, and the victim the reason why this is being done. It is not an admission of weakness of the case, nor is it an indication that a plea of guilty to the 'basic' and therefore less serious offence is acceptable.

Where the allegation involves evidence of both racial and religious aggravation, it will normally be necessary to include separate charges to reflect both aspects of the aggravation, as well as a basic offence.

Victim Personal Statements

A Victim Personal Statement (VPS) is a statement made by a victim of crime to a police officer explaining the effect that the crime has had on him or her. It is optional, and the victim will be asked whether or not s/he wishes to make such a statement.

This will generally happen at the same time as the police officer takes a statement from the victim about the circumstances of the crime. A VPS will normally follow on after this statement.

However, if a victim does not choose to make a VPS at this stage, s/he can tell the police later on that s/he now wishes to make such a statement.

If there is no VPS with the file, prosecutors should check with the police whether the victim has chosen not to make such a statement at this point in time.

A VPS will be used at various stages of the case, from the first review of the case by the CPS, to making decisions about bail, and up to giving the court the information to help it decide on the appropriate sentence.

Where there is a VPS setting out the effect of the crime on the victim, it is important that such information is brought to the attention of the court. It allows the court to determine the seriousness of the case and to sentence accordingly.

Leaflets explaining the use of VPS have been published by the Home Office and can be obtained from the Home Office Communications Directorate.

Bail

The police will make the initial decision to bail a defendant either to attend the next available court hearing, or to keep the defendant in custody to appear before the court the next day. Once a defendant appears before a court, the decision about bail is made by the court and is governed by the provisions of the Bail Act 1976. If a case is not dealt with on the first hearing, the court has to decide whether to grant bail to a defendant or to remand into custody.

It is important that prosecutors are satisfied that information to support an application to remand in custody or to impose conditions on bail are founded on fact and are justifiable under the Bail Act.

Victims of racist or religious crime may be afraid of what will happen to them once a defendant is charged. To protect victims and witnesses from the risk of danger or threats or repeat offences, the CPS may ask the court to impose conditions on the bail, or may ask for the defendant to be remanded in custody. The court can only agree if we can show that there are substantial grounds for not granting bail as set out in the Bail Act.

It is vital that the CPS gets as much information about the offence, the effect on the victim, and any fears or concerns that the victim may have about repeat offending or intimidation. Normally, the police will supply such information with the case file, but prosecutors need to be proactive to make sure that every effort is made to protect vulnerable victims or witnesses by seeking confirmation or further information about any views or concerns expressed by the victim or any witnesses.

A victim may have expressed concerns in a Victim Personal Statement (see above) about the effect the crime has had on them and may raise particular issues about bail in such a statement. These must be taken into account when making decisions about bail.

It is also important that any changes to the bail conditions or custody status of a defendant are communicated to victims, either by the police or by the CPS in accordance with local arrangements.

Witnesses who Withdraw Support for the Prosecution or Indicate that they are no Longer Willing to give Evidence

In cases with a racist or religious element—as in all cases—the reviewing prosecutor must apply the Code for Crown Prosecutors with regard to the determination of the public interest. The CPS prosecutes on behalf of the public at large and not just in the interest of any particular individual. However, when considering the public interest test, prosecutors should always take into account the consequences for the victim of the decision whether or not to prosecute, and any views expressed by the victim.

Many members of black and minority ethnic communities and faith communities make an immediate decision not to report racist or religious crime to the police due to lack of confidence in the criminal justice system. By building better links with these communities, we will raise their level of confidence in us, and reduce under-reporting of this type of crime. When offences are eventually reported, previous failures to report should not be seen as diminishing a witness's credibility.

We can have greater input in cases where the victim or witness has reported the incident to the police, and the defendant is charged, but the victim or witness decides that they no longer wish to give evidence. It is essential in these cases that we ask the police to make full enquiries into why support for the prosecution is being withdrawn.

Background information is vital to making the best possible public interest decision in these cases. Before taking a final decision, the prosecutor will want to know the reasons why the victim or witness no longer wishes to give evidence. In cases with racial or religious elements, this may be because the victim lives or works in a community in which they feel isolated or particularly vulnerable, and is fearful of the consequences of giving support to the prosecution.

In such cases, the prosecutor must have regard to any special measures available to the prosecution or the court that may help the victim or witness to overcome their concerns. It is also important to ensure that the case is prosecuted without undue delay (see Annex C for details of available special measures).

In cases where the victim or witness does wish to withdraw their support for the prosecution, an experienced prosecutor must oversee the case. The prosecutor should ask the police to take a formal statement from the victim or witness fully explaining their decision to withdraw their support. The prosecutor should also seek the views of the police about the reason for withdrawal and the way forward with the prosecution. The police should also be specifically asked to comment on the victim's or witness's likely reaction to being summoned to attend court.

If the reason for a victim's or witness's withdrawal is based on fear or intimidation, the prosecutor needs to have such evidence brought to their attention. This will allow appropriate decisions to be made about any applications under s. 23 of the Criminal Justice Act 1988. Such applications are only likely to succeed where there is other evidence to put before the court. Section 23 applications are often unsuccessful when the victim is the only witness to the offence, because in such cases it is very difficult to satisfy the court that justice is being served when the defence cannot cross-examine the only witness against them.

If there is insufficient evidence to continue without the evidence of the witness or victim, the reviewing prosecutor will need to weigh up whether the facts of the case are sufficiently serious to require the victim or witness to attend court under a witness summons. Factors that will help in determining the public interest in these cases are:

- the seriousness of the offence;
- the victim's injuries—whether physical or psychological;
- if the defendant used a weapon;
- if the defendant has made any threats before the attack;
- if the defendant planned the attack;
- the chances of the defendant offending again;
- the continuing threat to the health and safety of the victim or anyone else who is, or may become, involved;
- the victim's relationship to the defendant;
- the defendant's criminal history, particularly any previous offences based on race or religion;
- if the offence is widespread in the area where it is committed;
- repeat victimization by that defendant (reported or unreported).

The final decision is that of the prosecutor, but the decision to compel witnesses may be construed negatively by the communities affected by the decision, so every attempt should be made to regain the victim's or witness's support for the prosecution wherever possible.

If there remains sufficient evidence to satisfy the evidential test, without the evidence of the victim or witness, the reviewing lawyer must still consider whether it remains in the public interest to proceed against the wishes of the victim or witness.

Accepting Pleas

It is CPS policy not to accept pleas to lesser offences, or omit or minimize admissible evidence of racial or religious aggravation for the sake of expediency.

This commitment was repeated in response to recommendation 34 of the Stephen Lawrence Inquiry Report, always recognizing that there may be cases where an offence may no longer be capable of proof, e.g. because the evidence to prove the racial or religious aggravation was no longer available or was ruled inadmissible. The commitment is repeated and reinforced in the CPS Action Plan in response to the HMCPSI Thematic Inspection Report on Casework having a Minority Ethnic Dimension (April 2002).

Where it is thought appropriate to accept a plea, full regard should be had to the Attorney General's Guidelines on accepting pleas. This guidance was published in Casework Bulletin 34/2000 - 7/12/00, and is available on the CPS Intranet.

It follows from the above statement of policy that prosecutors must place evidence of racial aggravation before a court in a plea or a trial when it is proper to do so. Acceptance of a plea to a lesser offence will only be appropriate in circumstances such as those outlined above.

Full notes of the reasons for accepting pleas must be recorded, and such decisions should be referred to nominated senior or specialist prosecutors for ratification.

Explaining Decisions to Drop a Case or to Alter Charges

Under our Direct Communication with Victims (DCV) policy, we are committed to communicating our decisions to victims where a charge is dropped or is significantly altered. In such cases the victim will be written a letter that explains the decision and why it has been made. In cases of racist or religious crime, we will also offer the victim the opportunity to meet the prosecutor to get a more detailed explanation for the decision. Such a meeting is optional and the decision to take up the offer of such a meeting rests with the victim.

We now have in place well-established procedures for writing to victims and holding meetings to explain decisions, and staff have received training to help in explaining decisions both in writing and in person.

When holding a meeting with the victim, we should take into account as far as possible a victim's wishes as to who comes with them to the meeting, and the time and place of such a meeting. For example, there may be a need to take account of gender issues in some cases, which may have a bearing on who should be present at the meeting; or the timing of appointments should be made to take into account religious festivals or observances.

Prosecutors should be aware that even where evidence is insufficient for criminal proceedings, information could be admissible in civil proceedings.

5 VICTIMS AND WITNESSES

Past experiences of victims and witnesses or their communities, as well as a fear of reporting cases, may have led to a lack of faith, trust, and confidence in the system, and that they will be treated fairly and that their case will be considered to be important.

The views, interests, and concerns of victims and witnesses are important to the CPS, and we are committed to ensuring proper care and treatment of victims and witnesses.

The CPS will treat all people fairly and will review and prosecute cases in accordance with the Code for Crown Prosecutors. The CPS accepts that institutional racism and discrimination exist, and is working actively to remove this. CPS staff have received training on diversity and discrimination issues, and will apply this training to developing policies, procedures, and practices that do not discriminate in the way in which we provide a service to victims and witnesses from black and minority communities, or from faith groups/communities.

Under the Race Relations (Amendment) Act 2000, the CPS has a statutory obligation to look at its policies, procedures, and practices to ensure that they do not discriminate against people on the grounds of their race (see CPS Race Equality Scheme [May 2002]).

Understanding and Taking Account of Cultural Differences or Sensitivities

The CPS will actively try to ensure cultural and religious sensitivity in the prosecution process.

The CPS will make arrangements to collect as much information as possible about a witness before a case goes to court and a witness has to attend court to give evidence. For example, we would want to know which holy book would be appropriate for taking an oath, or whether the witness preferred to affirm.

We would want to take account of a witness's availability to attend court to make sure that factors such as religious festivals are taken into consideration when setting hearing dates.

We will also try and take account of sensitivities relating to gender, so that witnesses can feel as comfortable as possible when meeting CPS staff or when attending court.

Giving Evidence with the Assistance of Special Measures

As well as identifying whether the case is a racist or religious crime, prosecutors also need to consider whether the victim or any witness in the case might be 'vulnerable or intimidated' and thus eligible for assistance at court by means of a special measure under the Youth Justice and Criminal Evidence Act 1999.

Annex C sets out in more detail the definition of a vulnerable or intimidated witness provided by the Act and the range of special measures that may be available to qualifying witnesses.

The police have agreed to identify vulnerable/intimidated witness cases to us when they submit the file, but prosecutors must also be proactive and consider every case at review to assess whether the case may involve a potentially eligible witness. Where this is the case, the prosecutor should consider arranging a meeting with the police (an Early Special Measures Meeting) to discuss whether a victim or witness might be eligible for special measures and to consider what information or additional information might be needed to make such an application to the court.

It is also important at this stage to find out what views the witness has about special measures and whether they think they might be helped by the prosecutor asking the court to allow them to give evidence with the assistance of a special measure.

Even if the prosecutor asks for a special measure for a witness, the court has the final say and may not agree that the witness can have a special measure.

Applying to the Court for Anonymity for a Witness

Witnesses may be afraid that if details about where they live are made known, that they will be subjected to repeat victimization, or may suffer harassment or reprisals.

As a general rule, although a witness's address will be recorded on the back of the statement that is made to the police, details of that address are not given to the defendant. Obviously, in cases where the defendant knows the victim or witness personally, or if the offence takes place on the witness's home or business premises, that information is likely to be known to the offender.

The court can allow a witness to give evidence in court in the absence of the general public in certain circumstances. This is a special measure under the Youth Justice and Criminal Evidence Act 1999 that the prosecutor can ask for if a witness qualifies under the Act. In general terms, this includes victims of sexual offences, or any witness where the court has reason to believe that the witness has been, or might be, intimidated by someone other than the defendant in connection with giving evidence to the court.

In addition to this provision, s. 46 of the Youth Justice and Criminal Evidence Act also allows for a court to make a 'reporting direction' in the case of certain witnesses, which means that nothing will be published during a witness's lifetime that might lead to that person being identified. The circumstances in which this can be allowed are very closely defined, and the court has to take into account the general principle that justice should be open and public. More information about how s. 46 works is set out in Annex C.

Meetings between the CPS and Vulnerable or Intimidated Witnesses

The CPS is committed to meeting vulnerable or intimidated witnesses for whom special measures might be appropriate. The purpose of such meetings is:

- to establish a link between the CPS and the witness; and
- to provide reassurance that the needs of the witness will be taken into account.

Such a meeting can also be used to explain court procedure and the roles and responsibilities of the various parties at trial, if arrangements have not already been put in place for this to be done as part of any pre-court familiarization visit organized by the Witness Service.

The CPS has published guidance about meetings with vulnerable or intimidated witnesses in the booklet *Early Special Measures Meetings between the Police and the Crown Prosecution Service and Meetings between the Crown Prosecution Service and Vulnerable or Intimidated Witnesses—Practice Guidance.*

Copies of the booklet can be obtained from the CPS Communications Branch, or from the Home Office Communications Directorate, or by clicking on the CPS website, www.cps.gov.uk.

Interpreters

An interpreter will be made available by the police during the investigation stage of a case. Later, when a witness is giving evidence at court, the prosecution will make sure that an independent interpreter is provided to help the witness give evidence in his/her first language. Depending on the stage that the case has reached, the interpreter's fee will be paid by either the police or the CPS.

It is important that steps are taken from the very start of a case to find out if a witness needs to be helped by an interpreter, and to find out not only which language but whether the witness uses a particular dialect. Getting this information early in a case will reduce the risk that the wrong interpreter is selected, which might delay the case unnecessarily.

Interpreters must be independent of the witness's family and of the investigation.

Guidance on the use of interpreters in criminal proceedings is contained in Casework Bulletin 10/2002 (CPS intranet—Casework Bulletins).

Witnesses at Court

There are a number of things that can be done to try and remove as far as possible the worries a witness has about going to court.

These can include arranging with the Witness Service for a pre-trial familiarization visit to the court ahead of the trial, to let the witness see what the court looks like and how it is set out. Knowing where a witness is expected to wait, where the toilet facilities are, where to go in the courtroom, and where the various people will sit, can all help to reassure the witness.

Witnesses may want to meet the prosecutor before the trial starts. We should make sure that the prosecutor on the day of the trial introduces him/herself to the witness before the trial starts, wherever possible.

6 SENTENCING

Prosecutors have a duty to present all relevant material to allow the court to pass sentence in accordance with the law. Racial or religious aggravation makes an offence more serious, and the court has a duty to take this into account when it sentences a defendant.

Prosecutors will not minimize nor omit relevant and admissible evidence of racial or religious aggravation. To do so would be contrary to the CPS commitment made in response to the Home Secretary's Stephen Lawrence Inquiry Action Plan and commitments made to Parliament during consideration of the Crime and Disorder Bill.

Prosecutors should also make sure that they are aware of the guideline cases to assist the court in sentencing, in particular *R v Kelly & Donnelly* [2001] Crim LR, 411, which adopted the majority of recommendations made to the Court of Appeal by the Sentencing Advisory Panel Advice No. 4.

The Court of Appeal endorsed the following approach:

- the court should first decide on the appropriate sentence without the element of racial or religious aggravation, but including any other aggravating or mitigating features;
- the sentence should then be enhanced to take account of the racial or religious aggravation;
- if the offence itself merited custody, that sentence should be enhanced by an appropriate amount to reflect the degree of racial or religious aggravation;
- the judge should say publicly what the appropriate sentence would have been without the racial or religious aggravation;
- the court should take account of the factors identified by the Sentencing Advisory Panel as indicating either a high level of aggravation, or as being less serious;
- in a case of racially aggravated assault (like this case), the court should take into account that two years had been added to the maximum available penalty, but the correct increase depends on the facts of the individual case.

Although the original guidance applies to offences charged as specific racially aggravated offences and to all other offences where s. 145 of the Criminal Justice Act 2003 applies, it should also be taken as applying to religiously aggravated offences, following the amendment to the Crime and Disorder Act 1998.

Where there is a plea of guilty, the defence should be informed of the evidence in the case that the prosecution relies on to establish racial or religious aggravation, if this has not already been served on them. If the defence wish to dispute any of the facts that amount to the racial or religious aggravation, it may be appropriate for the court to conduct a 'Newton' hearing to resolve conflicting versions of the facts. This is of increased importance now that the court has a statutory duty under s. 145 to take account of racial or religious aggravation in assessing seriousness for the purpose of sentencing.

In the case of those offences which could be charged as specific racially or religiously aggravated offences, it would not be appropriate following conviction for a 'basic' offence to then seek to introduce evidence that the offence was racially or religiously aggravated under s. 145. To do so would amount to introducing evidence of a more serious offence than that for which the defendant had been convicted *R v Druce* 14 Cr App R (S) 691; *R v Davies* (1998) Cr App R (S) 380. It is important to bear this in mind at a number of key stages of the case, especially review and charge selection, and when considering any pleas offered by the defendant.

Where there is a Victim Personal Statement setting out the effect of the crime on the victim, it is important that such information is brought to the attention of the court. It allows the court to determine the seriousness of the case and to sentence accordingly.

Making Ancillary Orders at Sentence

Prosecutors should also be aware of courts' powers to make any ancillary orders when sentencing, and be in a position to provide the court with the information it requires to make such orders as necessary. Examples of ancillary orders the court might consider include:

- compensation;
- confiscation orders;
- restraining orders under Protection from Harassment Act 1997;
- football banning orders;
- Anti Social Behaviour Orders (ASBOs). Since 2 December 2002, ASBOs can be made following criminal conviction in addition to other penalties (s. 1C of the Crime and Disorder Act 1998, amended by s. 64 of the Police Reform Act 2002). Separate policy guidance is available on the role of the prosecutor in such cases.

Unduly Lenient Sentences

Sections 35 and 36 of the Criminal Justice Act 1988 (unduly lenient sentences) give the Attorney General power to refer cases to the Court of Appeal where it appears that the sentencing of the offender in the Crown Court was unduly lenient.

The range of offences to which this power applies is very limited—offences triable only on indictment, and offences specified by the Secretary of State in an Order. It does not currently apply to any of the specific racially or religiously aggravated offences under the Crime and Disorder Act 1998.

The procedures to adopt when considering whether to refer a case are contained in Legal Guidance (on CPS Intranet) and must be referred to Unit Head or equivalent. However, swift action is needed in any qualifying case to meet the stringent timescales.

7 THE RACIST INCIDENT MONITORING SCHEME (RIMS)

We have been gathering information on prosecution decisions and case outcomes in racist incident cases since 1995. We gave an undertaking to Parliament that we would monitor such cases, and from 1996 onwards we have published an annual report giving national and Area figures on all racist incidents sent to us by the police for prosecution.

We monitor cases to help us ensure that we handle cases in accordance with CPS policy.

A case is tracked by RIMS if it meets the Stephen Lawrence Inquiry Report definition of a racist incident, i.e. 'A racist incident is any incident which is perceived to be racist by the victim or any other person'. Information is recorded manually on the Racist Incident Data Sheet (RIDS), and completed RIDS are collated locally and sent to CPS HQ for inputting onto a national database.

Since religiously aggravated crime was introduced late in 2001 we have been tracking these cases through RIMS by asking CPS Areas to indicate on the RIDS that the case was a religious, rather than a racist, incident. Additionally, any religiously aggravated crimes are referred to the DPP for him to express his own view about the prosecution decision. The Director gave a commitment to the Attorney General that he would report on the effectiveness of the new offences as they formed an important part of the anti-terrorism legislation introduced in response to the events of 11 September 2001.

Operational guidance on how RIMS works is available on the CPS Intranet in the Legal Guidance section. This includes guidance on how to complete the Racist Incident Data Sheet. For the purposes of the monitoring scheme, the defendant is the unit of counting. One RIDS should be completed for each defendant charged with a racially or religiously aggravated offence. It follows that one case may generate more than one RIDS.

It is important that we track all cases. We have a national agreement with the police that they will mark the files they send us so as to draw our attention to racist incident cases. This will enable us immediately to begin to track the progress of the case through RIMS. If, for any reason, a case has not been identified by the police, it is important that the reviewing lawyer marks the file so that the case enters the tracking system.

We have also agreed with the police that they will supply a copy of their racist incident report form, or print-out of a computer record, with the case file. This may contain useful information about the case that could be of evidential value. If the police fail to supply their racist incident report, they should be asked to do so.

CPS Areas have appointed coordinators responsible for collecting and collating completed RIDS and submitting them to CPS Policy Directorate, who prepare an annual report. The RIMS annual report provides the following information: the number of defendants charged with offences to which the scheme applies; CPS decisions on the charges put by the police; the number and type of charges prosecuted; the number of charges discontinued and the reasons why; the results of prosecutions broken down by court type, including the sentences imposed.

The annual report provides national and Area figures. It therefore enables one Area to view its figures against the national profile and also to make comparisons with another Area with a similar profile to its own. It provides a baseline figure for the level of racist offending in each Area that can be checked against police figures to ensure accuracy and parity.

The information from the RIMS report can be used to help improve performance in a number of ways. Wide differences in the total numbers of recorded cases between Areas of similar size raise questions about case identification and form completion that need to be examined. Disproportionate numbers of acquittals or discontinuances might suggest problems with CPS decision-making or police file quality. A high proportion of CPS changes to police charges might suggest a need for police training. An unusually high percentage of racist incident cases failing as a result of witness difficulties might justify a joint police/CPS effort to identify specific causes and determine appropriate action.

The information available from RIMS is only as good as we make it. Accuracy of data collection is vitally important. We will be assisted in due course by the implementation of COMPASS and the ability to monitor the ethnicity of offenders and victims. We can only achieve accuracy and consistency by building management checks into the data collection process and then going on to validate the data by sharing it with other agencies. The police and the courts are obvious candidates, but equally important are multi-agency or local community groups with an interest in tackling racist attacks and harassment. They often have a different perspective to bring, and may have helpful advice and guidance to offer on how to make the best use of the information we are gathering.

The annual report is published widely and is available on the CPS website. Hard copies are provided to all CPS Areas and additional copies can be obtained from Policy Directorate. A copy is lodged in the House of Commons library as evidence of our continuing commitment to monitor prosecutions for racist crime.

The HMCPSI Review of Casework Having a Minority Ethnic Dimension (April 2002) made a number of recommendations, some of which are aimed at improving understanding of the monitoring scheme and making the best use of the information gathered. Staff awareness of the scheme and participation in the monitoring process are important. Those expected to operate any monitoring scheme must understand its purpose as well as the process itself. They also need to see the results of the monitoring and the use to which the information is put.

The Review recommends the appointment of a Racially Aggravated Crime Consultant to assume a 'quality assurance' role in the handling of racist crime. The consultant will also have a key responsibility, working with the Area RIMS Coordinator, to ensure that staff are fully trained on the operation and purpose of RIMS, and that mechanisms are in place to capture and record data in all racist incident cases.

The Review emphasizes the importance of reconciling CPS and police data, and taking action to remedy any failures in recording identified by the reconciliation process.

Gathering information is meaningless unless a proper analysis takes place in order to identify strengths and weaknesses, examine the reasons behind the figures, and learn lessons where appropriate. The information and the analysis must then be shared and discussed with regional representatives of other agencies and organizations as part of the drive to achieve an effective partnership approach to dealing with racist incidents. Regional Equality and Diversity Officers can offer valuable advice and guidance in this regard.

In response to the HMCPSI recommendations, we have produced a comprehensive action plan containing detailed practical suggestions on how we aim to implement the recommendations, together with a timetable within which we shall complete the work. All Areas need to familiarize themselves with the action plan and to nominate individuals tasked with responsibility for implementation.

8 COMMUNITY ENGAGEMENT

The Race Relations (Amendment) Act 2000 places a general duty on public authorities (which includes the CPS) to promote race equality. Community engagement and consultation is essential to help us meet this duty.

Working with Criminal Justice Partners

We have a responsibility to work with criminal justice partners to promote the confidence of black and minority ethnic communities and faith communities in the criminal justice system. The Local Criminal Justice Boards (LCJBs) have a pivotal role in raising levels of public confidence in the criminal justice system, and are an ideal vehicle for promoting and sharing the CPS policy.

As well as working with our partners through the LCJBs, we can work with them in other ways. For example, it is important that we discuss with the police at a senior level the way in which we can work together to ensure that cases with a religious and racial element receive the appropriate level of care and consideration in accordance with our public statement.

Chief Crown Prosecutors will want to ensure that our policy is made known to the Chief Officers of their other partner agencies, such as the Justices' Chief Executive; the Group Manager in the Crown Court; Chief Officers of Probation, Prison Service, YOT. They will also want to explain the policy and its rationale to local Resident Judges and magistrates within the Area, victim and witness agencies such as Victim Support and the Witness Service, as well as the Bar and the local Law Society.

Working with the Wider Community

Community engagement helps to build positive relationships between marginalized groups and public bodies or organizations. It enables organizations to combat social exclusion that can affect black and minority ethnic communities and faith communities, and informs the development of policies aimed at eliminating discrimination.

Effective community engagement has to take place at a local level if individual members of black and minority ethnic communities and faith communities can start to put their trust in us, in the work that we do, and in the decisions that we take.

We will work locally to identify and establish links with communities and representative groups in our Areas. We will use these opportunities to explain our policy and how we expect it to operate. It is important that we do not create false expectations about what the criminal justice system can offer people, but we should explain how the criminal justice system actually works to members of the public. Effective community engagement will give people the chance to ask questions about the relative roles of the CPS and the other agencies within the criminal justice system, and this can help to promote the CPS in a more positive light.

Community engagement is an ongoing and dynamic process, and there is never a time when it can be said that it has been completed. We need to be satisfied that we are in contact with all the appropriate groups in our local Area, and should keep the situation under review.

Statutory agencies such as the local authorities (specifically equalities units, housing, education, and social services departments), the Probation Service, and the police may have useful sources of information about local community groups, with whom they already have links or with whom they have developed working arrangements.

There are local groups such as Crime and Disorder Partnerships and Multi-agency Partnerships which work on issues relating to racist and religious crime. These groups can include local authority departments, police, Race Equality Councils, and Monitoring Projects. They will have their own links with black and minority ethnic communities and with faith communities, and can further help us to identify links to promote engagement with the wider community. We should discover whether such partnerships exist and what the remit and protocols are in terms of casework support for members of the black and minority ethnic community and the faith communities. By doing this we can find out how we can support and get involved with groups and initiatives.

Contacting community and voluntary groups directly is the ideal way of creating links and developing meaningful relationships. However, it is easy to fall into the trap of engaging with groups which will not be challenging and which do not represent their community. It is important to consult with as many groups as possible, particularly those which may be critical of the CPS. We can demonstrate our commitment by spending time with these groups, understanding the issues that they have, sharing information with them, and working to resolve any issues or concerns.

We have already started working to establish links, and to assist our staff in doing this in the best way possible we will provide further support, guidance, and training. Regional Equality and Diversity Officers are in place to advise and guide Areas on community engagement.

ANNEX A: LEGISLATION USED TO PROSECUTE RACIST AND RELIGIOUS CRIME

1 Racially or Religiously Aggravated Offences—Crime and Disorder Act 1998 (amended by Anti-terrorism, Crime and Security Act 2001)

Offence	Maximum Penalty—aggravated form	Maximum Penalty—basic form	Notes
Racially/religiously aggravated wounding (s. 29(1)(a) CDA)	Crown Court—7 years imp. Magistrates' court—6 months	Crown Court—5 years imp. Magistrates' court—6 months	
Racially/religiously aggravated assault (actual bodily harm) (s. 29(1)(b) CDA)	Crown Court—7 years imp. Magistrates' court—6 months	Crown Court—5 years imp. Magistrates' court—6 months	
Racially/religiously aggravated common assault (s. 29(1)(c) CDA)	Crown Court—2 years imp. Magistrates' court—6 months	Magistrates' court—6 months	Can only be tried in magistrates' court in basic form.
Racially/religiously aggravated damage (s. 30(1)(c) CDA)	Crown Court—14 years imp. Magistrates' court—6 months	Crown Court—10 years imp. Magistrates' court—3 months	Where value is less than £5,000 basic offence can only be tried in magistrates' court.
Racially/religiously aggravated fear/provocation of violence (s. 31(1)(a) CDA)	Crown Court—2 years imp. Magistrates' court—6 months	Magistrates' court—6 months	Can only be tried in magistrates' court in basic form.

Offence	Maximum Penalty—aggravated form	Maximum Penalty—basic form	Notes
Racially/religiously aggravated intentional harassment/alarm/distress (s. 31(1)(b) CDA)	Crown Court—2 years imp. Magistrates' court—6 months	Magistrates' court—6 months	Can only be tried in magistrates' court in basic form.
Racially/religiously aggravated harassment/alarm/distress (s. 31(1)(c) CDA)	Magistrates' court—fine up to level 4	Magistrates' court—fine up to level 3	Can only be tried in magistrates' court in either aggravated or basic form. Need to put charges for both aggravated and basic offence.
Racially/religiously aggravated harassment/stalking without violence (s. 32(1)(a) CDA)	Crown Court—2 years imp. Magistrates' court—6 months	Magistrates' court—6 months	Can only be tried in magistrates' court in basic form. Court can impose restraining order on conviction of either aggravated or basic offence.
Racially/religiously aggravated harassment/stalking with fear of violence (s. 32(1)(b) CDA)	Crown Court—7 years imp. Magistrates' court—6 months	Crown Court—5 years imp. Magistrates' court—6 months	Court can impose restraining order on conviction of either aggravated or basic offence.

2 Incitement to Racial Hatred—ss. 17–29 of the Public Order Act 1986

Offence	Maximum Penalty	Notes
s. 18—using threatening/abusive/insulting words or behaviour or displaying written material with intent/likely to stir up racial hatred	Crown Court—7 years' imprisonment Magistrates' Court—6 months	Can only be prosecuted with consent of Attorney General. Referred to CPS Casework Directorate to be dealt with by specialist prosecutor.
s. 19—publishing/distributing written material which is threatening/abusive/insulting with intent/likely to stir up racial hatred	Crown Court—7 years' imprisonment Magistrates' Court—6 months	Can only be prosecuted with consent of Attorney General. Referred to CPS Casework Directorate to be dealt with by specialist prosecutor.
s. 20—public performance of a play involving threatening/abusive/insulting words/behaviour with intent/likely to stir up racial hatred	Crown Court—7 years' imprisonment Magistrates' Court—6 months	Can only be prosecuted with consent of Attorney General. Referred to CPS Casework Directorate to be dealt with by specialist prosecutor.
s. 21—distributing/showing/playing a recording of visual images or sounds that are threatening/abusive/insulting with intent/likely to stir up racial hatred	Crown Court—7 years' imprisonment Magistrates' Court—6 months	Can only be prosecuted with consent of Attorney General. Referred to CPS Casework Directorate to be dealt with by specialist prosecutor.
s. 22—broadcasting or including programme in cable programme service involving threatening/abusive/insulting visual images or sounds with intent/likely to stir up racial hatred	Crown Court—7 years' imprisonment Magistrates' Court—6 months	Can only be prosecuted with consent of Attorney General. Referred to CPS Casework Directorate to be dealt with by specialist prosecutor.
s. 23—possessing racially inflammatory material/material for display/publication distribution with intent/likely to stir up racial hatred	Crown Court—7 years' imprisonment Magistrates' Court—6 months	Can only be prosecuted with consent of Attorney General. Referred to CPS Casework Directorate to be dealt with by specialist prosecutor.

3 Football Offences—s. 3 of the Football Offences Act (amended by s. 9 of the Football (Offences and Disorder) Act 1999)

Offence	Maximum Penalty	Notes
Engaging in or taking part in indecent/racialist chanting at a designated football match	Fine up to level 3	Court can impose a football banning order in addition to any other penalty. Breach of banning order carries up to 6 months' imprisonment. Does not apply to religious chanting—BUT NB. Other offences (such as racially/religiously aggravated public order offences or assaults) may be more appropriate.

ANNEX B: CHECKLIST—PROSECUTING RACIST OR RELIGIOUS CRIME

This list is not exhaustive, but prosecutors dealing with racist or religious crime may find it useful as both a checklist and a record of decision-making and an aid to file endorsement.

Areas may wish to adapt the checklist to meet their own requirements.

Issue to be considered	Decision/comment	Information date
1. INFORMATION NEEDED FROM THE POLICE		
Previous incidents against this victim —reported? —crime report? —prosecution action?		
Previous incidents involving this defendant —reported? —crime report? —action taken?		
Ability/willingness of victim to give evidence		
Effect on wider community		
Likelihood of recurrence		
Views on safety of victim/family		
Information from other agencies, e.g. Social Services, Housing Department, Health, Education.		
Information from other organizations, e.g. monitoring groups.		
Any current civil proceedings?		
Any other orders in existence, e.g. ASBOs, civil injunctions?		

Issue to be considered	Decision/comment	Information date
Is current incident in breach of any order?		
Any other information?		
2. BAIL		
Police view on victim and family safety		
Victim's view on own and family safety		
Method for informing victim promptly of bail decision		
Victim Personal Statement		
3. CHARGES		
Specific racially/religiously aggravated charge?		
Alternative verdict available?		
Need for alternative charge/count on indictment?		
4. RETRACTION		
Statement from victim giving full reasons		
Original complaint—does victim confirm if it was true or false?		
Duress/intimidation/ harassment?		
Other relevant information?		
Police Officer		
View of reasons given		
View on how case should be dealt with		

Issue to be considered	Decision/comment	Information date
View on how victim would react to being compelled		
View on safety of victim/family and future risk		
View on impact on wider community		
Victim		
Views on case proceeding		
Injuries (including psychological)		
Subsequent threats?		
Planned attack?		
Incident witnessed by others? Details?		
Risk of recurrence		
Defendant's criminal history towards victim		
Information from other agencies		
Where victim's evidence is vital		
Witness summons?		
Arrest warrant?		
Section 23, CJA 1988?		
Special measures?		
Witness protection measures?		
Where victim's evidence is not vital		
Sufficient other evidence?		
In public interest to proceed?		

Issue to be considered	Decision/comment	Information date
5. OTHER EVIDENCE		
Photographs of scene		
Medical evidence		
Admissions		
Res gestae		
999 records		
Independent evidence		
Similar fact evidence: Previous incidents? Previous convictions?		
6. TRIAL		
Victim vulnerable/intimated?		
Witness Service/other support agency involved?		
Waiting arrangements?		
Pagers?		
Eligibility for special measures YJ & CEA 1999?		
Early special measures meeting with police?		
Special measures meeting with victim/witness?		
Measures		
Screens		
Live TV link		
Video evidence		
Clear public gallery		
Restrictions on media reporting		

Issue to be considered	Decision/comment	Information date
Prohibition on cross-examination by accused in person		
Interpreter		
Required?		
Language/dialect?		
7. PLEA AND SENTENCE		
Reasons if accepting plea to lesser offence (specify in terms as set out in the Code for Crown Prosecutors)		
Consultation with line manager/specialist?		
Views of victim?		
DCV		
DCV letter sent to victim where charge dropped/altered?		
Meeting with victim offered?		
Meeting arranged? People to attend?		
Sentencing		
Evidence of racial/religious aggravation presented to court?		
Court indication that offence treated more seriously?		
Effect on victim—Victim Personal Statement?		

Issue to be considered	Decision/comment	Information date
8. MONITORING AND SHARING GOOD PRACTICE		
RIDS form completed? Sent to Area RIDS coordinator? Good practice to be shared with team/unit/Area/ EDO/Policy? Issues identified to raise with other cjs agencies (e.g. police/court) Share positive outcomes with the wider community through local initiatives/groups		

ANNEX C: SPEAKING UP FOR JUSTICE AND THE YOUTH JUSTICE AND CRIMINAL EVIDENCE ACT 1999

Speaking Up for Justice, the report of the interdepartmental working group on the treatment of vulnerable or intimidated witnesses in the criminal justice system, was published in 1997. It made seventy-eight recommendations for improvements to the criminal justice system, including the reporting of crime, identification of vulnerable or intimidated witnesses, and measures to assist witnesses before, during, and after the trial.

Many of the recommendations of Speaking Up for Justice required legislation to bring them into effect. This legislation is contained in Part II of the Youth Justice and Criminal Evidence Act 1999.

The Act received Royal Assent in July 1999, but is being brought into effect by way of a phased programme of implementation.

The Act provides:

- a definition of a vulnerable or intimidated witness;
- a test to determine eligibility;
- a range of special measures to assist eligible witnesses to give evidence;
- special provisions for child witnesses;
- a new definition of competence;
- a mandatory prohibition on cross-examination by defendants in person of complainants in sexual cases and of certain child witnesses, and a discretionary prohibition in the case of other witnesses;
- restrictions on cross-examination of a complainant in a sexual case about previous sexual behaviour;
- restrictions on media reporting.

Vulnerable or Intimidated Witness?—s. 16 and s. 17

A vulnerable witness is a witness defined by s. 16 of the Youth Justice and Criminal Evidence Act as being:

- under 17; or
- a person in respect of whom the quality of evidence is likely to be diminished due to any of the following circumstances:
  - he or she suffers from a mental disorder,
  - he or she has a significant impairment of intelligence and social functioning,
  - he or she has a physical disability or suffering from a physical disorder.

An intimidated witness is a witness defined by s. 17 of the Youth Justice and Criminal Evidence Act as being a witness in respect of whom:

- the court is satisfied that the quality of evidence given by the witness is likely to be diminished by reason of fear or distress on the part of the witness in connection with testifying in the proceedings.

A vulnerable witness or an intimidated witness will be eligible for assistance if any of the criteria in ss. 16 or 17 are satisfied.

Special Measures Available to Eligible Witnesses

The Youth Justice and Criminal Evidence Act provides a range of 'special measures' which are intended to assist vulnerable or intimidated witnesses to give evidence.
The measures are:

- Screens (s. 23).
- Evidence by live link (s. 24).
- Evidence in private (clearing the court in sexual cases or where there has been or may be intimidation) (s. 25).
- Removal of wigs and gowns (s. 26).
- Video-recorded evidence in chief (s. 27).
- Video-recorded cross-examination or re-examination (s. 28).
- Examination of witness through an intermediary (s. 29).
- Aids to communication (s. 30).

The court will make a special measures direction on the application of the party calling the witness, or of its own motion where it considers that a special measure or measures would be likely to improve the quality of the evidence given by the witness (s. 19).

NB. Intermediaries and communication aids are only available for vulnerable witnesses. But this does not affect the current arrangements for the provision of foreign language interpreters, or interpreters or signers for the deaf.

Special Provisions for Child Witnesses (s. 21)

The Youth Justice and Criminal Evidence Act makes special provisions for child witnesses.

It creates three categories of child witness:

(a) children giving evidence in a sexual offence case;
(b) children giving evidence in a case involving an offence of violence: abduction or neglect;
(c) children giving evidence in all other cases.

Children in categories (a) and (b) are 'in need of special protection' and benefit from strong presumptions about how they will give evidence.

Children 'in need of special protection' will have a video-recorded statement admitted as their evidence in chief (if there is one).

Children in sexual cases will be cross-examined on video (when available), unless they say they do not want to be.

Children in sexual cases who are not cross-examined on video and children in violence/abduction/neglect cases will be cross-examined via a live TV link.

Children in need of special protection are deemed eligible for the above measures without having to satisfy the test of 'maximizing quality of evidence'.

Children in category (c)—all other children—will have a video-recorded statement admitted as their evidence in chief (if there is one) and will give further evidence or be cross-examined via a live TV link, unless the court considers such measures will not maximize the quality of the child's evidence.

Implementation

At the time of publication, not all special measures were in effect in all courts. A phased programme of implementation began on 24 July 2002 and, thereafter, further implementation will be phased in following an evaluation of the first stage of implementation.

Crown court

All measures available in the Crown Court from 24 July 2002 (with the exception of video-recorded pre-trial cross-examination and intermediaries) are available for vulnerable (s. 16) witnesses. Measures are available in the Crown Court from 24 July 2002 for intimidated (s. 17) witnesses, with the above exceptions and with the additional exception of video-recorded evidence in chief.

Magistrates' and youth courts

From 24 July 2002 the measures of TV links and video-recorded evidence in chief are available for child witnesses in cases involving sexual offences, violence (including threats), abduction, and cruelty (see below).

NB. Pilot studies will be carried out before the measures of pre-trial video cross-examination and intermediaries are brought into effect.

Other provisions which came into effect on 24 July 2002

Other related provisions came into effect on 24 July 2002. These include:

- Discretionary prohibition on cross-examination by a defendant in person of any witness where it appears to the court that the quality of evidence given by the witness on cross-examination would be likely to be diminished if the cross-examination were to be conducted by the defendant in person *and* would be likely to be improved if a direction were given preventing it (s. 36).
- Restriction on media reporting of any matter relating to proceedings relating to an application for a special measures direction, or the fact of a special measures direction (s. 47).
- Competence of witnesses and the capacity to be sworn (ss. 53–57).

Other provisions

Some provisions came into force in 2000. These were:

- Prohibition on cross-examination by a defendant in person of a complainant in a case involving a sexual offence (s. 34)—implemented 4 September 2000.
- Prohibition on cross-examination by a defendant in person of a child witness (as defined by the Act) (s. 35)—implemented 4 September 2000.

- Restriction on the questioning of a complainant in a case involving a sexual offence about previous sexual behaviour (ss. 41–43)—implemented 4 December 2000.

Other provisions not yet in force

At the date of publication, some provisions were not in force. These include:

- Video-recorded pre-trial cross-examination (s. 28).
- Intermediaries (s. 29).
- Discretionary power to restrict media reporting about adult witnesses in criminal proceedings where the witness is considered to be eligible for protection from media reporting on the grounds that the quality of evidence that they give, or the level of cooperation by the witness, is likely to be diminished by reason of fear or distress about testifying, *and* that making a direction is likely to improve quality of evidence or level of cooperation of the witness. This is still subject to a further interest of justice test and consideration of the wider public interest in avoiding substantial and unreasonable restrictions on reporting (s. 46).

Section 46 came into effect on 7 October 2004, whilst ss. 28 and 29 will be the subject of pilot studies before implementation.

USEFUL INFORMATION AND CONTACTS FOR PRACTITIONERS IN THE CRIMINAL JUSTICE SYSTEM

Generic Organizations

Black Racial Attacks Independent Network (BRAIN)

BRAIN is a national network of community-based organizations engaged in activities working towards racial justice and the elimination of racism. BRAIN provides a forum for such organizations, often isolated within their own localities to exchange information, develop policy initiatives and provide mutual support.

63 The Broadway • Stratford • London • E15 4BQ • 020 8221 2930 • www.brain-network.co.uk • brain@nmp.org.uk Available all hours.

Campaign against Racism and Fascism (CARF)

CARF campaigns actively against racism and provides information, support, and speakers on race issues.

BM Box 8784 • London • WC1N 3XX • 020 7837 1450 • www.carf.demon.co.uk • info@carf.demon.co.uk

Commission for Racial Equality (CRE) London

The CRE was set up under the Race Relations Act in 1976 to tackle racial discrimination and promote racial equality. The CRE provides information and advice to people who feel they have experienced racial discrimination.

St Dunstan's House • 201–211 Borough High Street • London • SE1 1GZ • 020 7939 0000 • www.cre.gov.uk

Commission for Racial Equality (CRE) Wales

3rd Floor • Capital Tower • Greyfriars Road • Cardiff • CF10 3AG • 029 2072 9200 • www.cre.gov.uk

Chalkface Project

The Chalkface Project publishes educational resources on a range of topics including anti-racism.

84A High Street • Stony Stratford • Milton Keynes • MK11 1 AH • 0800 781 8858 • www.chalkface.com

Federation of Black Housing Organizations (FBHO)

FHBO is the umbrella body for the black-led housing sector. FBHO works to eliminate racism in housing. It provides information, advice, support, research, and training services. It represents the interests of its membership to housing policymakers, the government, and other controllers of housing resources.

1 King Edwards Road • London • E9 7SF • 020 8533 7053 • www.fbho.org.uk

IMKAAN

IMKAAN is a national policy training and research initiative, dedicated to providing support and advocacy to the specialist refuge sector, supporting Asian women and children experiencing violence.

76 Brewer Street • London • W1F 9TX • 020 7434 9945

Institute of Race Relations (IRR)

The Institute of Race Relations was established to carry out research, publish and collect resources on race relations. Today, the IRR is at the cutting edge of the research and analysis that informs the struggle for racial justice in Britain and internationally. It seeks to reflect the experience of those who suffer racial oppression and draws its perspectives from the most vulnerable in society. IRR also provides an independent race and refugee electronic news service.

Institute of Race Relations • 2–6 Leeke Street • London • WC1X 9HS • 020 7837 0041 • www.irr.org.uk

The Racial and Violent Crimes Task Force

Specialist unit set up within New Scotland Yard to review investigations of cases of racist and religious crime.

Metropolitan Police • Room 934 • New Scotland Yard • Broadway • London • SW1H 0BG • 020 7230 4374

RaceActionNet

This online service brings together expertise and experience in tackling racial harassment and racist attacks in the home and neighbourhood.

www.raceactionnet.co.uk

The Runnymede Trust

Runnymede is a leading independent think tank on ethnicity and cultural diversity. The Trust works to challenge racial discrimination, to influence related legislation, and to promote a successful multi-ethnic Britain.

The Runnymede Trust • Suite 106 • The London Fruit & Wool Exchange • Brushfield Street • London • E1 6EP • 020 7377 9222 • www.runnymedetrust.org • info@runnymedetrust.org

Racial Harassment Organization Website

This is an online service providing information to victims, individuals, and organizations tackling racial harassment. It offers advice and assistance to victims, and also to officers who support victims.

www.racialharassment.org.uk

Southall Black Sisters

Advice, emotional support, and help for Asian and black women.

52 Norwood Road • Southall • Middlesex • UB2 4DW • 020 8571 9595 • sbs@leonet.co.uk

The 1990 Trust

A national black organization which protects and pioneers the interests of Britain's black and minority ethnic communities. The Trust works in partnership with other organizations to engage in policy development and to articulate the perspective of black communities.

Suite 12 • Winchester House • 9 Cranmer House • London • SW9 6EJ • 020 7582 1990 • www.blink.org.uk

Faith Based Organizations

Board of Deputies of British Jews

The Board is an elected, national representative body of the British Jewish community. It works to support and promote the British Jewish community.

The Board of Deputies • 6 Bloomsbury Square • London • WC1A 2LP • 020 7543 5400 • www.bod.org.uk

Inter Faith Network

The Inter Faith Network for the UK works to build good relations between the communities of all the major faiths in Britain: Baha'i; Buddhist; Christian; Hindu; Jain; Jewish; Muslim; Sikh; and Zoroastrian. The Network provides an information service about faith communities and inter-faith issues, links national and local initiatives, shares good practice, and focuses on particular aspects of life in multi-faith Britain.

8 Grosvenor Place • London • SW1W 0EN • 020 7931 7766 • www.interfaith.org.uk

Muslim Council of Britain

The Muslim Council of Britain (MCB) works to eradicate disadvantage and discrimination faced by Muslims in the UK, and to promote good community relations.

Suite 5 • Boardman House • 64 Broadway • Stratford • London • E15 1NT • 020 8432 0585 • www.mcb.org.uk • admin@mcb.org.uk

Asylum Seeker and Refugee Organizations

Joint Council for the Welfare of Immigrants (JCWI)

JCWI is an independent and national voluntary organization campaigning for justice and combating racism in immigration, nationality, and asylum law and policy. JCWI provides free advice and casework, training courses, and publications.

115 Old Street • London • EC1V 9RT • 020 7251 8708 • www.jcwi.org.uk

National Asylum Support Service (NASS) Racial Harassment Unit

This unit processes cases of racial harassment against asylum seekers who are being supported by NASS.

Frank Corrigan • 27 Old Gloucester Street • Bloomsbury • London • WC1N 3XX • www.asylumsupport.info • info@asylumsupport.info

Refugee Action

Refugee Action is an independent national charity that enables refugees to build new lives in the UK. They provide practical advice and assistance for newly arrived asylum seekers, and long-term commitment to their settlement through community development work.

Head Office • The Old Fire Station • 150 Waterloo Road • London • SE1 8SB • 020 7654 7700 • www.refugee-action.org.uk

Refugee Council

The Refugee Council works across the UK with asylum seekers and refugees.

3–9 Bondway • Bondway • London • SW8 1SJ • 020 7820 3000 • www. refugeecouncil.org.uk

One stop service advice line offers advice and information to individuals and organizations on a range of issues operated by advisers with experience in asylum and immigration matters.
020 7346 6700—Information Line • 020 7820 3085 • Available Mon/Tue/Thur/Fri 10.00 am–4.00 pm and Wed 2.00 pm–4.00 pm

Football Based Organizations

Kick it Out
Kick it Out is football's anti-racism campaign. The campaign was initiated by the Commission for Racial Equality (CRE) and the Professional Footballers Association. It is supported by all the game's governing bodies, supporters organizations, and local authorities, and works to challenge racism at all levels of the game.
PO Box 29544 • London • EC2A 4WR • 020 7684 4884 • www.kickitout.org

Show Racism the Red Card
The campaign aims to combat racism through anti-racist education, and professional footballers show the way by making a stand and fighting racism. The campaign has involved hundreds of top footballers and managers, and has harnessed the high profile of these role models to combat racism.
Show Racism the Red Card • PO Box 141 • Whitley Bay • NE26 3YH • 0191 291 0160 • www.srtrc.org

Practitioner Networks

Association of Black Probation Officers
Grace Powell • The Probation Office • The Courthouse • London Road • Basingstoke • RG21 4AA • 012 5646 4272

Association of Muslim Police (AMP)
AMP aims to assist Muslims in the police service to observe their faith, to provide a forum for Muslims in the police, and to assist in the recruitment and retention of Muslim staff.
Mohammad Mahroof • Metropolitan Police • Room 910 • New Scotland Yard • Broadway • London • SW1H 0BG www.met.police.uk/associations/muslim_police. htm • amp@met.police.uk • muslimpolice@hotmail.com

National Black Crown Prosecution Service Association (NBCPA)
The NBCPA works to challenge racism within the CPS and wider Criminal Justice System, educate on issues of racism, and change the culture in the CPS and the wider CJS for the benefit of the communities that they serve.
The Cooperage • 8 Gainsford Street • London • SE1 2NE • 020 7378 4300 • www. nbcpa.co.uk

CPS Networking Group for Minority Ethnic Women
This is a support network for women.
Eunice Shang-Simpson • 50 Ludgate Hill • London • EC4M 7EX • 020 7710 6039

National Black Police Association (NBPA)

The objectives of the National Black Police Association are to promote good race relations and equality of opportunity within the police services of the United Kingdom and the wider community.

Room G04 • Allington Towers • 19 Allington Street • London • SW1E 5EB • 020 7035 5153 • www.nationalbpa.com • nbpa@nationalbpa.com

Index

Index

Index

Index

Index

Index

Learning Resources
Centre